PRINT AND THE POETICS
OF MODERN DRAMA

What does it matter what we read? The question of the materiality of the book has surprising consequences when applied to dramatic writing, where the bookish qualities of dramatic literature, qualities emphasized by the dominion of print culture, have always seemed antagonistic to plays' other life on the stage. In *Print and the Poetics of Modern Drama*, W. B. Worthen asks how the print form of drama bears on how we understand its dual identity – as play texts and in performance. Beginning with the most salient modern critique of printed drama – arising in the field of Shakespeare editing – Worthen then looks at the ways playwrights and performance artists from George Bernard Shaw and Gertrude Stein to Harold Pinter, Samuel Beckett, Anna Deavere Smith, and Sarah Kane stage the poetics of modern drama in the poetics of the page.

W. B. WORTHEN is the author of *The Idea of the Actor* (1984), *Modern Drama and the Rhetoric of Theater* (1992), *Shakespeare and the Authority of Performance* (Cambridge, 1997), and *Shakespeare and the Force of Modern Performance* (Cambridge, 2003). He has served as the editor of *Theatre Journal* and as the coeditor of *Modern Drama*, and has published widely in professional journals. He is also the editor of the widely used *Wadsworth Anthology of Drama* and of *Modern Drama: Plays/Criticism/Theory*, which won the 1995 Association for Theatre in Higher Education Research Award.

PRINT AND THE POETICS OF MODERN DRAMA

W. B. WORTHEN

CAMBRIDGE
UNIVERSITY PRESS

CAMBRIDGE UNIVERSITY PRESS
Cambridge, New York, Melbourne, Madrid, Cape Town, Singapore, São Paulo, Delhi

Cambridge University Press
The Edinburgh Building, Cambridge CB2 8RU, UK

Published in the United States of America by Cambridge University Press, New York

www.cambridge.org
Information on this title: www.cambridge.org/9780521841849

© W. B. Worthen 2005

First published 2005

A catalogue record for this publication is available from the British Library

ISBN 978-0-521-84184-9 hardback

Transferred to digital printing 2008

Contents

Illustrations

Acknowledgments

It's a privilege to have the chance to thank the many friends and colleagues who helped me to think through this project. I'm particularly grateful to Barbara Hodgdon for several informal seminars on the subject of writing and performance, to Peter Holland and the participants in the Redefining British Theatre History seminar at the Henry E. Huntington Library for their shrewd suggestions about my first explorations of print and performance, to the faculty and students of the International Centre for Advanced Theatre Studies, University of Helsinki, who energetically commented on several chapters of this book; and to Katarzyna Kwapisz and Shannon Jackson for their comments on early drafts of two chapters. I would also like to thank Jennifer Johung both for permission to cite an unpublished essay on Suzan-Lori Parks, and for her assistance in preparing the final manuscript. I'm also grateful to members of the Department of Theatre, Film, and Dance at Cornell University, to Peggy Phelan and the Stanford University Mellon Seminar in Performance and Politics, to James Loehlin and the English Department of the University of Texas at Austin, and to the Department of English at the University of California, Los Angeles, for their hospitality and challenging responses to earlier versions of various chapters of this book, and to audiences at the American Society for Theatre Research, the Comparative Drama Association, the Folger Shakespeare Library, the Group for Early Modern Cultural Studies, the Shakespeare Association of America, and the University of Industrial Art and Design Helsinki for their attention, commentary, and patience. It was a pure pleasure to meet Lyn Hejinian at the start of my work on the final chapter, and her work led me to several other beginnings. Sarah Stanton of Cambridge University Press provided much-needed encouragement when I hit the doldrums on this project, and Victoria Cooper saved the day in a crisis that can only be described as Pinteresque; I would also like to thank Mary Leighton and Annie Lovett of the Press, and Margaret Berrill, for their superb attention to the typescript as it made its way into print. Finally, I would not have been able to complete this project without the wisdom, advice, and support of my wife, Hana Worthen; this book is deeply dedicated to her.

My sincere thanks to Dean Ralph Hexter of the College of Letters and Science, and the Humanities Research Fellowship committee for awarding the sabbatical that made the writing possible, and to my colleague Mark Griffith for helping me to arrange to take it. I am also grateful to the British Museum for facilitating my access to the Pinter papers, to Linda Ashton of the Harry Ransom Humanities Research Center at the University of Texas at Austin, and to Julian Garforth of the University of Reading Samuel Beckett collection, for their indispensable help with Beckett's papers. The staff at the Bancroft Library of the University of California, Berkeley, have been unfailingly helpful and resourceful with both materials and images, and Jerry Kapler has provided superb assistance, often on very short notice, with photographic and digital reproduction. Martha Swope graciously provided the cover photograph, and I'm especially thankful to Naomi Tummons, Michael Fellmeth, and Kathy Sova for helping to resolve some permissions issues.

Finally, my thanks to Palgrave Macmillan for permission to reprint, in very different form, remarks originally published in: "The Imprint of Performance." *Theorizing Practice: Redefining Theatre History. Redefining British Theatre History: Vol. 1.* Ed. W. B. Worthen, Peter Holland. Houndmills: Palgrave, 2001. 217–34. I am also grateful to Emma Bennett, and Blackwell, Ltd. for permission to reprint, in a significantly altered form, my discussion of Shakespeare editing, which originally appeared in *The Blackwell Companion to Shakespeare and Performance.* Ed. Barbara Hodgdon and W. B. Worthen. Oxford: Blackwell, 2005. Although I have quoted published material frequently under the fair use provisions, I am grateful to several publishers who have granted permission for me to reprint passages to illustrate the page design of published drama, as follows:

Cover photograph: David Warrilow as the Reader and Rand Mitchell as the Listener in *Ohio Impromptu*, directed by Alan Schneider at the Harold Clurman Theater, New York, 1983. Photo: Martha Swope.

From "is this the right place?" by David Antin, from *talking at the boundaries*, copyright © 1974, 1975, 1976 by David Antin, used by permission of New Directions Publishing Corporation.

From *The Complete Dramatic Works of Samuel Beckett*, used by permission of Faber and Faber Ltd., publishers.

From *A Poetics* © 1992 Charles Bernstein, published by Harvard University Press, and from *My Way: Speeches and Poems* © 1999 Charles Bernstein, published by University of Chicago Press, both used by permission of Charles Bernstein.

From *The Beginner*, by Lyn Hejinian, copyright © 2002 Lyn Hejinian, published by Tuumba Press, used by permission of Lyn Hejinian.

From *Happily*, by Lyn Hejinian, copyright © 2000 Lyn Hejinian, published by Post-Apollo Press. Used by permission of Lyn Hejinian.

From *Victoria*, by David Greig, copyright © 2000 by David Greig, used by permission of Methuen Publishing, Ltd.

From *4.48 Psychosis* © 2000 by Sarah Kane, from *Blasted* © 1995 by Sarah Kane, from *Cleansed* © 1998 by Sarah Kane; texts as published in *Complete Plays*, 2001, used by permission of Methuen Publishing Ltd.

From the trade edition of *The Laramie Project*, by Moisés Kaufman and the Members of Tectonic Theater Project, copyright © 2001 by Moisés Kaufman, used by permission of Vintage Books, a division of Random House, Inc.

From the acting edition (including the Special Note) of *The Laramie Project*, by Moisés Kaufman and the Members of Tectonic Theater Project, copyright © 2001, by Moisés Kaufman, used by permission of Dramatists Play Service. CAUTION: The excerpts from *The Laramie Project* included in this volume are reprinted by permission of Dramatists Play Service, Inc. The English language stock and amateur stage performance rights in this Play are controlled exclusively by Dramatists Play Service, Inc., 440 Park Avenue South, New York NY 10016. No professional or nonprofessional performance of the Play may be given without obtaining, in advance, the written permission of Dramatists Play Service, Inc., and paying the requisite fee. Inquiries concerning all other rights should be addressed to Joyce Ketay Agency, 1501 Broadway, Suite 1908, New York NY 10036, Attn: Joyce Ketay.

From *Plays 1*, by Doug Lucie, copyright © 1998 by Doug Lucie, used by permission of Methuen Publishing, Ltd.

From *Plays 1*, by Anthony Nielson, copyright © 1998 by Anthony Nielson, used by permission of Methuen Publishing, Ltd.

From *Venus*, by Suzan-Lori Parks, copyright © 1997 by Suzan-Lori Parks, used by permission of Theatre Communications Group.

From *The Marginalization of Poetry*, by Bob Perelman © 1996 Princeton University Press, used by permission of Princeton University Press.

From *The Collection* © 1960 and 1962, as published in *Harold Pinter: Plays Two* © 1996, used by permission of Faber and Faber Ltd.

From the acting edition of *The Collection: A Play in One Act*, copyright © 1963 by Harold Pinter, used by permission of Samuel French Ltd.

From *The Homecoming* © 1965, as published in *Harold Pinter: Plays Three* ©1997, used by permission of Faber and Faber Ltd.

From *The Homecoming* © 1965 by Harold Pinter, and from *The Collection* in *Three Plays* © 1963 by Harold Pinter, used by permission of Grove/Atlantic.

From *Mrs Warren's Profession*, copyright © 1898, by Bernard Shaw, used by permission of the Society of Authors, on behalf of the Estate of Bernard Shaw.

From "Afterword," to *In the American Tree*, copyright © 2002 by Ron Silliman, published by National Poetry Foundation, used by permission of Ron Silliman.

From *Fires in the Mirror* by Anna Deavere Smith, copyright © 1993 by Anna Deavere Smith, used by permission of Doubleday, a division of Random House, Inc.

From *Twilight: Los Angeles, 1992*, by Anna Deavere Smith, copyright © 1994 by Anna Deavere Smith. Used by permission of Doubleday, a division of Random House, Inc.

From *Last Operas and Plays*. Ed. Carl Van Vechten. Introd. Bonnie Marranca. Baltimore: Johns Hopkins University Press, 1995, used by permission of the Estate of Gertrude Stein, through its Literary Executor, Mr. Stanford Gann, Jr., of Levin & Gann, P. A.

"The Red Wheelbarrow," by William Carlos Williams, from *Collected Poems: 1909–1939, Volume 1*, © 1938 by New Directions Publishing Corporation, used by permission of New Directions Publishing Corporation.

Introduction: booking the play

I want to recall one of the most concentrated scenes of modern drama, the hushed reading of the "sad tale a last time told" that occupies the brief action of Samuel Beckett's *Ohio Impromptu*. The play has all the elements of late Beckett: two nearly immobile figures, seated in a precise geometry (one in profile, one facing forward) at the end of a long table, each with "*Left hand on table. Long black coat. Long white hair.*"[1] The character in profile, audience right, called the Reader in the script, reads aloud from a book, while the character facing us, called the Listener, seems to listen. When the Listener knocks on the table, the Reader either repeats the passage he has just read, or resumes his recitation from the point of interruption.

The Reader is nearing the end of a long story, told in the third person, climaxing in what we take to be the Listener's violation of the final "unspoken words" of a lover, "Stay where we were so long alone together, my shade will comfort you." As in other plays – *Krapp's Last Tape* ("Farewell to love" read the notes on box three, spool five [217]) or *Not I* ("so no love . . . spared that" [376]) – the avoidance of love impels a mournful, even purgatorial retelling of the past. It seems to have been a long story. When the Listener hears "the fearful symptoms described at length page forty paragraph four," he restrains the Reader from turning back to check the citation. Having repeated the story, having again reached its end, they seem finally to have reached *the* end. The Reader reads:

So the sad tale a last time told they sat on as though
turned to stone. Through the single window dawn shed no
light. From the street no sound of reawakening. Or was it
that buried in who knows what thoughts they paid no
heed? To light of day. To sound of reawakening. What
thoughts who knows. Thoughts, no, not thoughts.
Profounds of mind. Buried in who knows what profounds
of mind. Of mindlessness. Whither no light can reach. No
sound. So sat on as though turned to stone. The sad tale

a last time told.
[*Pause.*]
Nothing is left to tell.
[*Pause.* R *makes to close book.*
Knock. Book is half closed.]
Nothing is left to tell.
[*Pause.* R *closes book.*
Knock.
Silence. Five seconds.
Simultaneously they lower their right hands to table,
raise their heads and look at each other. Unblinking.
Expressionless.
Ten seconds.
Fade out.]

Like the iconic heroes of Yeats's plays – in *At the Hawk's Well*, Cuchulain "receded but to inhabit as it were the deeps of the mind" ("Certain Noble Plays" 224) – Beckett's characters recede from speaking into silence, from narrative into image, frozen in an unblinking tableau that recalls Beckett's persistent interest in such final moments, Didi and Gogo's "Yes, let's go. [*They do not move.*]," Hamm reassuming his veil, Willie turning the gun on Winnie, Krapp motionless in the cone of white light listening to the spooling tape.

In play after play, Beckett's drama reflects on the condition of theatre, a series that comes to an ironic climax in the authoritarian, Beckett-like director's obsession with the interplay between language and gesture in *Catastrophe*, another play that ends in an eloquent image, as the Protagonist "*raises his head, fixes the audience*" while the applause falters, and the light fades out on his face (461). From Pozzo warming up with his atomizer to the torturing of Bam, Bem, Bim, and Bom to "say it" (472), Beckett's drama theatricalizes narrative, *staging* speech as the figure of human agency, human consciousness. *Ohio Impromptu* shares in this lineage, but the play is unique in Beckett's work for materializing that narrative onstage as a text, a book. Indeed, *Ohio Impromptu* is a rarity in the history of theatre in staging the book as the source of dramatic action. Yes, there are a number of famous "reading" scenes in classical (Malvolio's letter) and in modern drama (Ellie Dunn falling asleep over her copy of *Othello*), but these brief acts of reading are usually incidental means of advancing the plot. In *Ohio Impromptu* the action visibly arises from the book: as Jonathan Kalb noted in his 1983 review, "It's as if the characters cleverly steal brief moments of human contact while constrained to a physical situation which prohibits such exchange" (*Beckett in Performance* 50). The action of

Ohio Impromptu is the act of reading and listening. Insofar as the action emerges from the book, staging its complicity with writing, *Ohio Impromptu* allegorizes the situation of modern drama itself, the interdependence of the arts of writing and performance in the age of print.[2]

The material challenges that Beckett's writing pose to acting have been familiar for some time, but the challenge to our understanding of drama posed by the plays as printed objects, as books, is just coming into view. Is the identity of the drama held in the author's inert inscription or its betrayal into living performance? Beckett's writing, especially his elaborate stage directions, frames a rarefied aesthetic problem, one that has been engaged by several controversial stage productions, notably by JoAnne Akalaitis's *Endgame* at the American Repertory Theatre in 1984, and by Deborah Warner's 1994 environmental *Footfalls* at the Garrick Theatre in London, to name only the two most familiar cases. *Ohio Impromptu* captures the duplicitous impact of print on modern drama and on modern theatre. On the one hand, the Reader seems to control the action, modeling stage performance as a kind of reading, as though performance were governed, exhausted, even executed by the book. On the other hand, the Listener's act, knocking on the table, controls the pace and delivery of the text's incarnation in and as performance. His gestures determine the *repetition* (recalling the French), the quite literal *rehearsal* of the written text as spoken, acted dialogue, as stage action. As the Reader and the Listener merge into a single, divided image of the theatre's resistance and captivity to the text, they stage the friction between writing and enactment that defines modern drama.

Staging the book, *Ohio Impromptu* stages the constitutive questions of drama in the age of print: What is the work of "literature," or, to use a less contested term, "writing" in the theatre? What is the status or being or force of dramatic writing relative to the drama's existence as performance? Is the printed book an adequate delivery system for plays? Is it a delivery system at all?

Needless to say, to ask such questions means bracketing a number of crucial issues. Theatrical performance has everything to do with everything that's beyond the text: the practices and ideologies of directing and design, of acting and dance, of architecture and economics, the unscripted materiality of stage production. This may sound, for the moment, as though I'm bracketing *all* of theatre, and in one respect I am. To the extent that we consider bodies, spaces, and how we use them the stuff of dramatic performance, then writing (in those forms of theatre that use writing at all) is merely one among many such materials, not the abstract cause or governing logos of the stage, but another kind of raw material – like lumber and canvas, or the theatre space, or even the actors' bodies – that is refashioned and resignified in the rigorously pragmatic working-out of the creative business of the playing. The rise of a "literary," print-inflected understanding of drama has tended to overplay the role of writing in the work of theatre. For while we might think that it's the function of the stage to flesh out, fill out, even fulfill the playwright's design, this conventional understanding of the relationship between dramatic writing and its theatrical performance in Western theatre has little footing in the history of dramatic performance. As the changing forms of stage Chekhov in the past century or of stage Beckett in half that time imply, the rhetoric of embodiment and the panoply of practices deployed with, around, and beyond the text to create a meaningful dramatic event are remarkably volatile. Classical drama is even more instructive in this regard. In the past four centuries of playing Shakespeare, characters have dropped into and out of performance (Lear's fool, Rosencrantz and Guildenstern), have been entirely rewritten (Cordelia in Nahum Tate's *King Lear*) or invented (Miranda's brother in Dryden's *Tempest*), and various essentials of performance (the witches' *corps de ballet* in eighteenth-century *Macbeth*, Shylock's red wig, Beerbohm Tree's bunnies, the spare "epic" platform of the Royal Shakespeare Company in the 1960s) have come and gone. But the shifting designs of Shakespeare in performance are not merely a record of changing taste; they record a changing understanding of the ratio between writing and performance, of what the writing can and should be made to *do*. Even in the shorter span of the past century, the variety of "authentic" or "faithful" performances – Stanislavsky's tragic Chekhov, Andrei Serban's experimental Chekhov, André Gregory's ironic Chekhov – point to an important fact about writing in the theatre. The impression of a production's relation to the script, its fidelity to or betrayal of an "authorial" design, is not the cause of a performance's meaning but its consequence, the aftereffect of the work that the production has done to the text, with the text, through the text, against the text, and, *necessarily*, beyond the text. For performance does not so much interpret the text as rewrite it in the incommensurable idiom of the stage. Much as is the case when we read other forms of writing – aspects of T. S. Eliot's poems, or of W. B. Yeats's, that were quite literally invisible twenty or thirty years ago seem now to be massively, unavoidably *there*, to constitute the poems' central meanings – so the stage practices that seem most fully and essentially to express the drama's force in the physicality of theatre will appear and disappear as our ways of reading plays, performing ourselves, and acting in the theatre change.

Chekhov's claustral delicacy no longer seems to demand three standing walls and practical doors to take the stage; Didi and Gogo don't always wear bowlers.

Of course, bracketing theatre in this way only serves to underscore what we are bracketing it from: the massively literary understanding of dramatic performance that has arisen with and through the age of print. Print – the printing process, the forms and shapes of printed books – has long troped our understanding of the lush variety of cultural production. And while print is no longer the master metaphor of literate culture, as its shadow recedes we can gain a clearer sense of print's pervasive conceptual and ideological embrace of our understanding of stage performance. Historians (Elizabeth Eisenstein) and iconoclasts (Marshall McLuhan) of print have ably, if controversially, demonstrated the impact of print on most aspects of human culture, and on our understanding of what it means to be human, even as the models and metaphors of humanity derived from print are inexorably giving way to those drawn from digital technologies.[3] Print has also decisively fashioned our understanding of literature and the literary, both by making texts (including some, like Chaucer's, not originally printed, or like Homer's, not originally written) widely available, and – perhaps more fundamentally – by helping to frame our sense of the intrinsic values of writing itself. If theatre companies were among the earliest capitalist enterprises as joint stockholding corporations, printing houses helped to define the assembly-line: printing books requires a significant degree of rationalization, the organization of complex tasks in a sequence of production, assembly, and distribution. For this among other reasons the rise of print has tended to articulate certain values – standardization (of letterforms), regularization (of spelling and punctuation), formalization (of distinct genres, each with its own conventions of layout, design, marketing), repeatability and reiteration (of new editions) – which have become intrinsic to modern notions of literature and the literary, sustaining a canon of stable texts, promoting the "author" as a determining element of literary identity, and embodying "literary identity" as the closure of the qualities attributed to print. These are also the values ascribed to writing by the academic study of modern vernacular literatures, born at the moment – the late nineteenth century – when print culture might be said to have reached its zenith, still unrivalled by other means of mass communication (film, radio, television) or by digital means of creating and disseminating writing.

From the beginning, though, drama has been an anomaly in print culture. Print production cannot fully determine the identity of dramatic writing because drama also takes shape elsewhere, in the incommensurable practices of the stage. Through the first three hundred years of dramatic publishing, this duality was more or less unremarkable, however frequently it was remarked. True, Ben Jonson was lampooned for publishing *plays* in his *Works*, William Prynne inveighed against the printing of Shakespeare's plays on finer paper than was used in many Bibles, and William Congreve worked closely with his printer Jacob Tonson to regularize the look of his plays on the page, going so far as to purchase special type fonts from the Netherlands.[4] But while these chestnuts locate a series of efforts to inscribe printed drama with the signs of literature, a "literary" understanding of the integrity of the author's writing had relatively little impact on the stage — which enthusiastically rewrote, adapted, cut-and-pasted play texts — or, apparently, on the pleasure of audiences.

In the English-speaking world, the absorption of drama to literature and of the ontology of theatre to the iterative logic of print develops slowly and inconsistently, and as we might expect, Shakespeare's plays stand at the center of this history. The editing and reediting of Shakespearean drama in the eighteenth century, culminating in Edmond Malone's 1790 edition, marks a crucial sea-change not only in Shakespeare's fortunes but in the relationship between drama, literature, and the stage. As Margreta de Grazia has shown in *Shakespeare Verbatim*, Malone's edition did more than ride the wave of Shakespeare's increasing popularity and celebrity as the national poet and playwright. Malone's edition gave a bookish shape to Shakespeare as an "author," anachronistically mapping a modern, print-derived, sense of the organic stability of "literary" creation onto the fluid and pragmatic terms of Shakespeare's working life as a writer for the stage.[5] The consequences of understanding dramatic writing as print literature in this way, as both prior to and finally beyond the signifying limits of theatre, are refracted in complex ways throughout the nineteenth century: in the poets' dogged imitation of a "Shakespearean" verse drama that is (unlike Shakespeare's) often explicitly inimical to the stage; in Charles Lamb's notions of the intrinsic antipathy between Shakespeare's writing and live performance; in the developing practice of publishing reading editions of plays alongside stage productions, as books whose designs distinguish them from "acting editions" (which become popular at this time, too). This dialectic was part of Shakespeare's theatre, as Jonson's (to say nothing of Hamlet's) many complaints about the improvisations of actors imply. But the cultural identity of drama in the sixteenth and seventeenth centuries was still very much in flux, as the occasional efforts by playwrights (Jonson, Congreve) or "publishers" (Heminge and Condell for Shakespeare, Moseley for

Beaumont and Fletcher) to shape the drama's identity on the page were fully offset by the practices of successive eras of theatre, which clearly subject what we now take to be the prescriptive order of "the text" to forms of production that assiduously multiply, diversify, and disintegrate any sense of the page's priority to the stage. By the late nineteenth century, when Shaw and Ibsen not only attended to the formal design of their plays on the page but also to their appearance as books, this print-driven sense of the identity and proper transmission of writing came to sustain the common-sense view of dramatic performance, what it means to attend to the performance of a play.

As print becomes the dominant means of asserting and representing the literary identity of writing, it gradually assimilates the understanding of drama and dramatic performance to the rhetoric of print. Throughout the seventeenth and eighteenth centuries, and well into the nineteenth century, the notion that the staging of a play should reflect its bookish or literary form was belied by the practices of the theatre, which have only gradually approximated to the reiterative ideologies of print culture. Print inflects writing with certain properties, and with certain values as property, urging the singular, authorial and authorized identity of the work across its many reproductions, and so claiming the work's stability across time and space, and across matter, too, as it is materialized in new and different shapes, sizes, formats, and (in many cases) even in different words on the page. The insistence that these palpably distinct objects are *the same thing*, or – to use the rather theological jargon of editing – that they transmit the same *substantial* work, clothed in the merely *accidental* differences of punctuation, capitalization, type style, layout, words on the page, marks the deeply ideological working of print in print culture. Traditionally, print culture located print as the site of the work's identity, while also taking the individual printed object, the book, as a kind of surrogate. In this view, the work of art (*Hamlet*, *The Ambassadors*, "Easter 1916") can be reproduced in better or worse editions, more or less "faithfully," even with one set of words or another, but the *work itself* is finally unaltered by the material conditions of its emergence in history, its materialization in a specific printform. From the insistence that print merely reproduces or reiterates the *same* work across a range of editions (the notion that *Hamlet* is the same thing in all the quite different versions of it you might have on your shelf), it's a small step to the sense that the work can *and should* be understood as *the same thing* across different modes of production, in different media, the sense that performance is merely a reiteration of the text by other means, means that aspire to conditions of mechanical reproducibility that seem to guarantee the persistence of the work's ghostly substance across a varied range of incarnations.[6]

Theatre is particularly inimical to print, as print culture tends to derogate both manuscript and oral forms of transmission as lapses from the ideal, transparent, neutrality of mechanical reproduction. Despite the fact that the theatre remains dependent on residual means of production (treating even printed scripts as manuscript, marking them up, rewriting them, transforming them into speech and behavior that leaves the text behind), dramatic performance has increasingly come to be understood on the model of print transmission, as a reproduction or reiteration of *writing*, as though performance were merely a new edition of the substantial identity of the script. Our understanding of all of these terms – drama and theatre, dramatic literature, text and performance – takes place in the historical condition of print and print culture, a condition that inflects our common-sense understanding of dramatic performance as least as powerfully as the most trenchant and pervasive theory.

This is our inheritance today in what Michael Joyce calls "the late age of print" (*Othermindedness* 3). Although the relationship between writing and performance is always changing, for the past century or so the common understanding of dramatic performance has been "reiterative" in this way, as though theatre belatedly and incompletely reproduces a version of "the play," whose identity is held fully and completely within the text. This zombie-theory of drama, in which performance is only partly and provisionally inhabited by the transcendent work-of-art, which then moves on to seize other bodies, is particularly strong in literary studies, where performances are commonly characterized as incomplete "interpretations" of the text, an understanding of texts and performances transparently dependent on the ideology of print. In this view, the multiplex ambiguity of the drama is most richly and immediately experienced through the kind of performance native to print, *reading*. Stage production is modeled on "reading," in this view (as an interpretation of the *work itself*), and is understood as a kind of simplification as well: since directors have to make choices (readers don't?), a stage production realizes only one interpretation of a text, while the process of reading generates at every moment a multitude of alternatives which can be held simultaneously in the profounds of the mind.[7] Yet if we were to regard the performance as *the work itself*, we might well understand each moment of a stage production to be replete with alternative meanings, each nuance of voice and movement resonant with provocative possibilities, the playing not as an etiolated interpretation of something else but as a full and complex *event* to which our attention must strive to be adequate. The printed text would seem merely a sketch, an abstract, a cartoon, and reading merely a belated attempt to recall the full complexity of theatrical participation. Although we have come to understand and occasionally to repudiate these hierarchies of value, their persistence is palpable even as the terms – words, texts, and bodies – have been transformed by new theories, models, and technologies of modern culture.

Plays began to be printed in the sixteenth century, and modern drama arose at the moment of print's final achievement; both the printforms of modern plays and many aspects of modern performance reciprocate the rhetoric of print culture. The rise of the director, for example, can be seen as a way to implement the book on the stage, channeling the emergent, sometimes inchoate work of performance through a single authoritative, sometimes authoritarian agent, an agent who can claim to make the performance speak in the voice of the author. Yet we need only remember Chekhov's dismay with Stanislavsky's careful (and very successful) stagings of his plays, or the many changes to his play texts that Beckett made when he came to direct them, to see that the rhetoric of "fidelity" is only one of the stage's many strategies for striking an accommodation with the printed page. In a number of ways, modern drama stands in a distinctive relation to print. While print represented at best a deferred form of the drama's identity in Shakespeare's era, by Shaw's day print is the condition of drama. Much as the reiterative logic of print shaped a sense of the drama's relation to the stage, so too playwrights came to see print as a means at once to refine and reshape theatre practice, while also marking the page as an alternative and authentic site of the play's identity as a play. This is not to say that a printed text is used in every stage production, or that the status of print isn't thoroughly complicated and compromised by the habits of copying, interleaving, highlighting, and cutting essential to stage production. Rather than merely obeying the singular printed word, modern theatre characteristically requires an expansive multiplication of texts, one of the sure signs of its uneasy assimilation to the rhetoric of print. Nonetheless, to the extent that dramatic writing is understood in terms of the properties and proprieties of print, performance in the twentieth century engages the poetics of drama through the practices of print.

The work of theatre is always beyond the text. At the same time, performance is not the only way in which the drama is materialized in print culture. And while the theatre always develops its own ways of reading and producing writing as action and behavior, the forms, moods, and shapes of print have also worked to stage an understanding of drama and the dramatic. In *Print and the Poetics of Modern Drama*, I want to reflect on the drama's ways of occupying the page. Rather than seeing performances as failed editions, we might understand books also to materialize a certain kind of *performance* of the work. If books are like performances, it is not because they are individual interpretations of the metaphysical work of art; it is because they materialize the work as a unique event in time and space. Each *Hamlet* on the stage uses Shakespeare's words, and much else, to fashion a new and distinctive performance; each *Hamlet* on your shelf uses Shakespeare's words, and much else, to fashion a new and distinctive performance. A specific performance can't be extrapolated from the raw material of the text alone, much as a table can't be extrapolated from a tree (though if you've ever made or used a table, you know that oak is more durable than pine, and much harder to work with). To make a table, you need to know a hawk from a handsaw, and how to use them. It makes some difference whether a production of *Hamlet* takes Richard Burbage or Ethan Hawke as its physical prince. It also matters whether it uses a hand-copied playhouse side, an "acting version" of the play, or an edited modern text, the embodiment of four centuries of the developing ideology of print.

Printed texts are surprisingly effervescent in the ways they materialize writing in history, perform writing, so to speak. Like the revival of a play, a new edition can't be simply extrapolated from a previous one: its size, shape, design, typeface, paper, ink, binding materials, distribution all have to be decided and enacted, even if the "new" edition is only a facsimile or reprint of an old one. Moreover, we don't read a "work of art" when we are reading a play: we read a book, an object that organizes the play in specific ways, and so organizes an understanding of what a play – as literature, drama, theatre – *is*. The materiality of the text is the thing that gets read. How much does it matter *what* we read? In the rich literature of contemporary textual studies (where the theoretical and practical problems of editing Shakespeare's plays stand alongside the comparable challenges of editing Joyce or Yeats or Byron), the material appearance of writing is seen both as a record and as an instigation of a work's historical and social identity. Much as the theatrical identity of a given production of *Hamlet* depends on whether it took place in London or the provinces, with a professional or an amateur cast, on the opening or on a benefit night, whether it included Rosencrantz and Guildenstern, and so on, in the sphere of textual criticism, whether one is reading Yeats's "September 1913" in the Dublin newspaper in which it initially appeared, in a volume published by a nationalist press, or in the more impersonal and imperial volume of a British-published collected edition, makes a difference in how the words on the page perform, what meanings they materialized for readers in history, and what meanings they materialize today.[8]

As will already be clear to some readers, I am evoking here the complex critique of the traditional ideology of print that informs contemporary textual theory, in part derived from D. F. McKenzie's and Roger Chartier's landmark work on the sociology of books, and from Jerome McGann's brilliant and influential critique of the formal consequences of "the textual condition."[9] In this view, the materials and design of the book (size, binding, covers, paper, typeface) and even the "accidentals" of the printed page (spacing, punctuation, capitalization, orthography) – matter once taken as external to the authorial work's perdurable identity – don't merely mark the work's material passage through history: they are the condition of the work's meaning as literature. The book's "bibliographic codes" are not merely the bodily dross of the work's meaning; they materialize, locate, and so define the possibilities of the book's meaning (McGann, *Textual Condition* 10). The printing of plays resembles the printing of other forms of literary writing, but plays are notable in the history of print precisely because so much of the writing that appears on the page seems at best ambiguously related to a sense of the work's identity, its inherent, even authorized, *meaning*. Stage directions, speech prefixes, and the like are at once conventional means of framing the play on the page and, especially as print comes to be an authoritative means of the drama's embodiment, a means to shape the priority of page to stage. Sometimes – Beckett is notable here, as are a number of playwrights in the modern era – writers deploy these elements of the play's bookish form with the purpose of framing a specific sense of the play on the page, but such textual events need not be regarded in the register of authorial intention to have a significant bearing on the work of drama. For while punctuation, capitalization, exits and entrances, the placement and variation of speech prefixes are surely not the stuff of drama, by representing a relationship between writing and performance, the material properties of printed plays inevitably represent the identity of drama in the age of print: they frame the mise-en-page as a site of performance. Can we consider the materiality of writing not in opposition to performance (or, much the same thing, as governing or determining performance), but as a more dynamic index to the shifting equilibrium between writing and performance in the conception of the drama? If, like Jerome McGann, we take any writing as "a laced network of linguistic and bibliographic codes," then a fuller account of the cultural work of writing should respond to "the thickness of the textual condition," the layers of signification that materialize writing, and relate it to other practices of embodiment (*Textual Condition* 13–14).

Even those of us interested in a more reciprocal sense of the relationship between writing and performance, drama and theatre, would have to admit the limitations in how we account for the multiform meanings and identities of dramatic texts and performances. In this brief book, I want to ask a simple question: does the material form of dramatic writing matter, matter as matter, to the imagining of drama in the modern era? How might our assumptions about the work of performance, of interpretation, and of dramatic literature be altered by paying some attention to the scene of the play's performance on the page? I pursue this line of thinking by touching on a series of controversies, leaning heavily on contemporary writing and performance. I begin with a controversy involving printed drama that has shaped modern literature, the modern theatre, and the practice of editing: how should we interpret the printform of Shakespeare's plays? The past century has witnessed two revolutions in how we realize the plays that Shakespeare and his fellows had printed in late sixteenth- and early seventeenth-century London in the pages of modern books. What is striking about these two moments in the history of Shakespeare editing is the way they articulate changing views of the relationship between dramatic writing, print, and performance, conceptions of drama that often hinge not on the words of dialogue that Shakespeare wrote, but on the *accessories* – speech prefixes, stage directions, act and scene divisions – that stage the play on the page. The editing of Shakespeare's plays, and – at least as important – the extensive body of theoretical and critical literature interrogating the principles of Shakespeare editing, represents the most cogent, meticulous, and often brilliant effort in English to conceive of the practices of print relative to the (perhaps putative) poetics of performance. In this chapter, then, my interest in Shakespeare editing has less to do with the fascinating nitty-gritty of Shakespeare's early modern plays than with what textual critique might tell us more generally about our ways of implicating plays and print in the late modern era. We might imagine that the ways of making Shakespeare's mise-en-page legible for modern readers, whatever their power of historical explanation, have considerable explanatory potential for the printforms of the plays with which they are contemporary; contemporary editions of Shakespeare, after all, share both the stage and the shelf with Shaw, and Stoppard, and Smith. The ways that modern scholarship imagines the printform of Shakespeare's plays speaks directly to the emerging printforms of modern drama.

Using contemporary Shakespeare editing to derive some of the principles for reading the working of print in the work of modern drama, I then turn to two general questions: how do the *accessories* of the page dramatize modern drama's ongoing engagement with print, and what might the design of the page tell us about the design of the drama? In the second chapter, "Accessory Acts," I consider how various aspects of page design, typography, act and scene numbering, speech prefixes, and stage directions articulate a shifting sense of the drama's printform materiality. Opening from R. B. McKerrow's fascinating distinction in the editing of Shakespeare's plays "between the actual text of the plays, in the sense of the matter which is intended to be spoken by the characters, and such accessories as act and scene headings, the speakers' names, and to some extent also stage directions," I consider the impact of such accessories on the conception of drama in the late age of print, and their persistence today (*Prolegomena* 19). Bernard Shaw's idiosyncratic notions about (well, about everything, but particularly about) how his plays should be done into print mark a decisive moment in the booking of modern drama, the effort to render the book a distinctive platform for the play's realization. Shaw's designs stage insistently bookish plays on the page, using elements of typography and layout generally ignored by later playwrights. But they nonetheless mark an effort to redefine the authority of the page in ways anticipating the project of modernist writing more generally, and particularly forecasting more "experimental" dramatic writing from Gertrude Stein to Beckett and beyond. Shaw's blackened pages reflect what we might take to be the hallmark of later playwrights, the effort to make the white space of the page part of the play's semantic field of play. While Shaw's comedies of political manners have little to do with the thematics of *Doctor Faustus Lights the Lights* or *Footfalls*, the sense that the *accessories* of printed drama can be made a significant feature of the identity of drama links Shaw with the major innovations of modernist playwriting. Tracing the conquest of the page through Stein's determinedly antitheatrical drama, I then turn to the ways that Pinter's plays – with their famous gaps, ellipses, *Pauses* and *Silences* – not only use the mise-en-page as a stage of dramatic meaning, but have shaped the page in ways that have had considerable impact in the theatre. But as the well-worn term "Pinteresque" perhaps suggests, Pinter may be a special case: to conclude this chapter, I turn to a more recent, and apparently more innovative stage work, *The Laramie Project*, by Moisés Kaufman and members of Tectonic Theater Project. Although *The Laramie Project* has its roots in the de-authorizing practices of contemporary performance – notably in the rise of performance ethnography – the book form of the play is revealing of our contemporary concern for the proprieties of print, its ability to stabilize and transmit not merely the work of art but a certain understanding of *authorized* writing, even at the moment that print seems to be on the wane as the defining means of creating and transmitting writing. Much as the *accessories* of *Plays: Pleasant and Unpleasant* framed the effort to define the drama at the climax of print culture, so *The Laramie Project* is one of many works marking the troubled interface between writing and performance today.

In the final chapter, "Something like Poetry," I explore the materiality of printed drama from a reciprocal perspective, now looking less at the accidentals that frame dramatic speech on the page but at the words themselves, as the design of the page signals the ethics of enactment. As print has become part of the definition of conventional drama and theatre, resistance both to the forms of theatre – character, plot, mimesis – and to written drama has driven one of the characteristic forms of contemporary dramatic innovation: performance art. Of course, much performance art has little to do with writing, and rarely finds its way into print. But the vogue of "performative writing," and the desire to record, preserve, and transmit the scripts of a wide range of performances has resulted in a surprising phenomenon: the appearance of performance art works in print. What do these books do? Do these plays point – as their resistance to print might suggest – toward new, nonprint forms of recording and representing performance? Or do they look back, nostalgically enough, to the "permanence" promised by print, as might be suggested by their suppressed complicity with developments in contemporary poetry, a field similarly concerned in the 1980s and beyond with the relationship between language, writing, and performance? In this chapter, then, I track how the words of performance art texts occupy the page, often assuming the likeness of free-verse poems, and so materialize the drama's engagement with its performers – characters, actors, readers, spectators – through the rhetoric of poetry. I open this chapter with a consideration of how Anna Deavere Smith's plays participate in several now-familiar controversies (and conventions) of solo performance and print. While the innovative cast of Smith's performances is well known, relatively little has been said about how her plays appear on the page, and how their appearance bears on Smith's conception of the drama. To gain access to this problem, I set Smith's writing in the context of contemporary poetics, which at once explores the material "performance" of language on the page, and remains urgently, if rather anxiously, committed to a cognate performance genre: the poetry reading. I conclude this chapter by turning from the implication of solo performance in the terrain of poetry to Sarah Kane's *4.48 Psychosis*. Kane's play is striking in several respects, not least for its ways of implicating language and performance by refusing many of the *accessories* of drama – speech prefixes, scenes – that typically serve to objectify the play on the page. Instead, it uses the visual design of contemporary poetry as the principal vehicle of the drama. Like Smith's plays, Kane's *4.48 Psychosis* invites us to consider the implication of the "bibliographic code" in fashioning the ethics of dramatic performance.

Beginning with Beckett, I also conclude with Beckett. Beckett's plays are an essential part of the modern drama's seizure of the page. Yet while Beckett's plays are surely among the most original, innovative, and powerful documents of modern dramatic writing and stage performance, they are also strikingly evocative as books, not least for the ways in which Beckett's familiar accessories – the texture of production notes and stage directions – trouble the distinction between the authorial "work," the conventional apparatus that stages it on the page, and the conventions (many of them legal) that transfer the play from page to stage. I want to conclude this consideration of the booking of modern drama by thinking through what has become one of the defining controversies of the modern theatre: the insistence of the author, his press representatives, and now his estate that these *accessories* have an authorial force not only in objectifying the play on the page, but in realizing it on the stage. Such controversies are usually cast merely as a contest of authority between author and director, page and stage, but they are considerably more complex. For Beckett's plays participate in the effort to render the page of modern drama significant, and so frame the warrant of authorial propriety in specific ways. Can the author claim control over the theatrical accessories with which his play shares the page? Do these accessories have a proper, and proprietary role in stage performance? Finally, it's striking that these controversies – particularly the debate surrounding Deborah Warner's *Footfalls* in 1994, which subjected Beckett's play to a thorough retheatricalizing of its unspoken verbal *accessories* – arise at a moment of considerable anxiety about the cultural authority of print, as writing finds its way into new technologies of performance. *Footfalls* stages the desire to bring the book to the stage at just the moment that the story of writing seems to be changing, morphing like the print-emulating letterforms of the screen into new and unanticipated shapes. The story of writing is an old one, a story of persistence amid constant technological change. How the transformation of print by digital technologies will change the interface of drama, the interface between writing and performance, is hard to say. But one thing is clear: the dominion of print on the poetics of modern performance may now be a story a last time told.

CHAPTER 1

Prefixing the author; or, As it was Plaide: Shakespeare, editing, and the design of modern drama

> [. . .] writing is a form of fossilized talking   which gets put
> inside of a can   called a book   and i respect that can   its a
>   means of preservation   or maybe we should say in a frozen food
>   container called a book   but on the other hand if you dont know
>   how to handle that frozen food container that icy block will never
>   turn back into talking   and if it will never turn back into talking
> it will never be of any use to you again
>   David Antin, "is this the right place?" (45–46)

We might take our bearings on print and the poetics of modern performance by thinking for a moment about David Antin's "talk poems." Antin improvises his poems in performance, and when the poems are published in print, they register those origins on the page: Antin's talk poems typically use almost no punctuation, keep both the left and right margins unjustified, and insert gaps of five or six spaces between phrases. While these features of Antin's poetry insist on the poem's grounding in orality, the page makes complex claims about the poem's identity as writing and performance. As it turns out, the page is not really a memorial record of an actual performance, for Antin closely edits the appearance of the page when he decides to print the poem, long after its initial performance. Nor is it exactly a score for future performances, because Antin rejects the notion that this kind of poetry can be pre-scribed (Antin gave up "reading" already-written poems because it felt too much like "acting"). In print, Antin's scripts dramatize an ambivalent regard for the implication of print and performance, an anxiety that sustains modern dramatic writing as well. Is the printed page the origin of the play or merely a side-effect? Does it record and/or instigate performance? The page always enacts and represents performance: can the book teach us to thaw that frozen event?

Such questions may seem purely academic. Surely in the rough-and-ready ways we use plays, reading them as books-in-dialogue, or exercising them in the problem-solving work of the stage, questions like these have already been sorted out in practice. Yet Antin's poems touch the pulse of a largely unacknowledged problem. Our behavior as readers – whether in the armchair or in the rehearsal room – often relies on unexamined assumptions that have less to do with plays per se than with what books can tell us about them, how books encode and represent the drama. How does printed drama contain, express, represent the play, and (in some cases, at least) represent its potential playing?

In at least one sphere of contemporary scholarship, such concerns are far from recondite: the question of how to represent plays in print is the everyday business of the editing of Shakespeare's plays. Shakespeare wrote plays at the inception of two modern enterprises, the professional repertory theatre and professional print publishing. These institutions were at once new and rapidly changing. Their values, with regard to the proprieties of writing and performing and the practices that enacted them, were both in flux and considerably different from those that developed over the next four centuries. The printed books that bear the plays of Shakespeare and of his contemporaries are at once deceptively familiar and decidedly foreign things. Following recognizable ways of booking the drama (dividing the play into scenes, identifying speeches with a prefixed name, indicating the dramatic setting and some stage business, and deploying print conventions to distinguish these indications from the dialogue), the plays are nonetheless replete with errors, inconsistencies, incoherencies, and mysteries, complexities further complicated when a given play was published in more than one version. Shakespeare's plays have, arguably, been "edited" from the outset; many of the plays appearing in the 1623 Folio differ substantially from the texts published in Shakespeare's lifetime, often in ways that suggest systematic rewriting, whether by Shakespeare or by his company. And since the late seventeenth century, Shakespeare's plays have been corrected, altered, revised, and repackaged for the delight and instruction of readers, and/or for the use of scholars and performers. Moreover, editors have necessarily confronted the infelicities of Shakespeare's plays in print and have attempted, often brilliantly, to resolve them. In some cases, Shakespeare's or his printer's lapses were corrected through an appeal to contemporary taste; in others, arising for instance from modern research into the habits of early modern printshops, apparent errors in Shakespeare's printed plays can be corrected through a sensible and informed appeal to the ways printers – and even individual compositors – worked. Needless to say, contemporary editors of Shakespeare's plays base their judgments on how best to render the plays as modern books on a wide range of research into stage practice, the casting and personnel of the Lord Chamberlain's/King's Men, the book trade, political legislation, censorship, available notions of literary genre, the sources and analogues in Shakespeare's apparent reading, and much more. Shakespeare's editors continually reenact the defining problem of plays in print, a problem Shakespeare's plays helped to inaugurate: the play's dual status as writing and performance, in literature and in the theatre.

Rebooking Shakespeare's plays for modern readers, Shakespeare's editors and textual critics must address the pragmatic and theoretical implications of how print stages the play on the page. Rather than offering a history or critique of Shakespeare editing, then, in this chapter I turn to editing with somewhat tangential questions in mind. How do some of the challenges and controversies of the past century of Shakespeare editing provide a lens for assessing the printforms of modern plays? And what might the kinds of problems – and (ir)resolutions – seized by Shakespeare's editors tell us about the ongoing bearing of print on the drama, about our ways of understanding modern plays in print and performance?

In the past century, Shakespeare studies has seen two revolutions in editorial practice and textual theory, revolutions in how we understand the relationship between writing, print, and performance in Shakespeare's era, and in how best to perform that relationship in an edition of the plays for modern readers (editions, in other words, that encode the identity of the "drama" in ways recognizable to us). The intensive, even "scientific" study of Shakespeare's printed drama in the first half of the twentieth century – the New Bibliography associated with W. W. Greg, A. W. Pollard, R. B. McKerrow, Fredson Bowers and others – integrated a Romantic, basically literary concern for the authentic transmission of Shakespeare's writing from the (now lost) manuscripts to print with an inevitable attention to the subordinate function of his writing in the theatre. Foundational though they are, many of the practices and judgments of the New Bibliography have been reinterpreted, revised, or rejected in the New-New wave of textual scholarship begun in the 1970s, epitomized by the 1986 Oxford Shakespeare, and expanded in other editions and in a brilliant efflorescence of textual criticism and theory. These two moments in the history of Shakespearean editing represent a pragmatic encounter with the conceptualization of drama in print and its production for modern readers and audiences. More important, we can also understand this engagement with the printform of Shakespeare's plays as the index of a typically modern desire to render the anomalies of drama coherent within the regime of a dominant print culture. Changes in editorial practice enact a changing valuation of dramatic writing. The outline of the shift from the

New to the New-New Bibliography in Shakespeare studies is generally familiar – the multiplication of texts, decentering of the author, revaluation of the "theatrical" elements in the textual transmission process. But this shift also articulates with a changing valuation of the nature and purposes of writing and performance in the contemporary theatre. Far from being mere eccentricities thankfully resolved by print's growing sophistication, the challenges posed by dramatic writing in the first days of print point to ongoing instabilities in the working of printed drama and its changing relationship to the institutions of performance. And our ways of understanding those eccentricities point to the ways the mise-en-page of contemporary plays continues to represent the drama at the axis between writing and performance.

In his influential study, *On Editing Shakespeare and the Elizabethan Dramatists* (1955), Fredson Bowers frames a series of questions that all editors of Shakespeare's plays must face as they work, in his now infamous phrase, to "strip the veil of print" (*On Editing Shakespeare* 87) from the early books that construct and conceal Shakespeare's plays: "What was the nature of the lost manuscript which served as printer's copy," "What was the nature of the printing process itself, and what can be gathered from this to shed light on the transmission of the text from the lost manuscript to the derived printed document with which the editor must work," and "What is the relation between all preserved examples of the text, in printed or in manuscript form, and what are the degrees of authority, both specific and general, in these examples" (8). Print is intricate, not to say seductive, in the ways it veils the author's hand, but Bowers works to lay out the various possible states of copy text, "of every conceivable variety," which nonetheless fall "into the following major classes, some of them speculative":

(1) author's foul papers; (2) authorial or scribal fair copies not intended for direct theatrical use; (3) foul papers or fair copies partially marked by the prompter as a preliminary for transcription into prompt; (4) scribal transcripts made for private individuals and not for theatrical purposes, the source being foul papers, fair copy, or theatrical promptbook; (5) a manuscript prompt book itself; (6) a scribal transcript of a prompt book; (7) an unrevised copy of an earlier printed edition; (8) an unauthoritatively revised copy of an earlier printed edition, the revisions presumably originating with the publisher or his agent; (9) an authoritatively revised copy of an earlier edition marked by the author; (10) a copy of an earlier printed edition annotated by comparison with some manuscript, usually assumed to be authorial or prompt, preserved in the theatre's archives; (11) a subdivision of the above, consisting of an earlier printed edition marked and used by the theatre company as a prompt book, or another copy of an edition marked for the printer to conform to such a printed prompt book; (12) another possible subdivision of

the above, a new and as yet untested theory, which conjectures a scribal transcript made for the printer of such a marked printed promptbook, or else a manuscript made up for the printer by an independent act of conflating a printed edition with a manuscript preserved in the theatre; (13) the "foul papers," fair copy, prompt book, or transcript of a promptbook of a memorial reconstruction of the text without direct transcriptional link with any manuscript derived from author's autograph, in other words, the copy for a so-called "bad quarto." (11–12)

None of the actual copy texts used in the printing, and none of the manuscripts, fair or foul, of Shakespeare's plays have survived (*Sir Thomas More* may be partly an exception), though manuscript plays by other playwrights do remain. Perhaps not surprisingly, then, the veils multiply: "Many of these classes may be mixed by introducing additional manuscript material, as a new scene, of different textual history from that of the main copy; or, in reverse, of introducing leaves from a printed edition to fill out gaps in a manuscript or to obviate transcription in part; or the patching of printed copy by leaves from a different edition."

For many early modern plays the genetic record is very shallow (one, occasionally two relevant print editions) and often confused. Providing an authoritative modern edition, the editor typically tracks the ghostly hand of the author through the scattering of signs on the surface of a single printed page. These signs may stem from a number of agents – the writer, various playhouse copyists, the compositors setting the type – and the ideological character of the editor's work is perhaps most readily visible in the ways those signs are made to register changing conceptions of authorship, and of what the author creates, the drama. Bowers admits the "speculative" character of some of his thinking, and the main lines of contemporary textual critique begin precisely from that point of speculation, by noting how the assumptions guiding the New Bibliography's understanding of authorship determine the evidentiary status of the print record, and of the various texts hypothesized behind it. Even when it recognized (as Greg, Bowers, and others often did) the challenges posed by the collaborative character of early modern theatre practice to a Romantic sense of individual authorship, the New Bibliography tended to see the impact of theatre, as it remains in the signs and signals of the page, as a distraction from, and corruption of, the proper transmission of the author's writing, the properly *scripted* authorial work. Greg, for instance, was well aware of the bearing of theatre practice on Shakespeare's writing: in Shakespeare's theatre, "the author may never have produced a definitive text for us to recover" ("Preface to the First Edition," *Editorial Problem in Shakespeare* ix). Greg understands Shakespeare as a literary author, a writer of books, even if this anachronistic model of authorship remained only implicit in practice and was apparently unacknowledged by the author throughout his working life as a playwright. In Shakespeare's "earlier days particularly it is the conditions of the theatre" that "appear to have determined the manner of his composition," leading to a "carelessness" in managing the details of "action and of language [that] were apt to be left standing with the knowledge that they could be trusted to straighten themselves out in rehearsal," an insouciance that nonetheless "remained generally unaltered so long as he continued to be actively connected with the stage." Despite Shakespeare's absolute identification with the professional theatre, for Greg the value of Shakespearean writing, and the practice of editorially recovering it for modern readers, arises from the symmetry between playwriting and more individualized modes of composition: "I do not think that Shakespeare, in his later days at least, wrote for the stage only: the length of some of his pieces, which must always have rendered their complete performance difficult, suggest that he had some sort of publication in mind" (viii).

Greg's sense of the essentially literary or poetic character of Shakespeare's practice as a writer, and of the plays he wrote, was (and remains) commonplace. What is arresting is the role of print in determining the literary identity of the drama. Despite his unrivalled familiarity with early modern dramatic manuscripts – which clearly violate many of the claims made for the hypothesized relationship between the "foul papers," "fair copy," and "prompt copy" of Shakespeare's plays – Greg represents an author writing for posterity in print, producing an ideal and complete dramatic script that he knew could not be fully realized onstage, transmitting that manuscript (with the errors and omissions typical of a writer working with colleagues in a standing company) to the theatre where it would necessarily be altered by performance, and (through even more indirect and uncertain channels) finally make its way into print, embodied in a sense by its final cause, its motivating material form: the book. Print at once creates the possibility of a dramatic *author* in the modern sense (a writer whose designs transcend their merely momentary and functional use on the stage) and also guarantees this literary notion of playwriting, provided we can read through the seductive veils of the printed page to see the signs of the evanescent authorial writing embodied there. This playwright sounds a bit more like Jonson than like Shakespeare, but if we are thinking of the proportion of nontheatrical, "literary" matter to stageable dialogue and business as an index to the ways print can establish a pretension to authorship, the playwright who comes most to mind is Greg's (1875–1959) older contemporary Bernard Shaw (1856–1950), whose prefaces rival the length of some of his plays and fulfill Greg's sense of the modern play-wright as a writer of *books*.[1]

Contemporary textual theory stands on the shoulders of the New Bibliography, while occasionally trying to cut it off at the knees. Greg was unsurpassed in his understanding of Shakespeare's theatre, but resolutely subordinated the collaborative work of the stage to the implicit design of Shakespeare's hypothesized writing as the determining principle of his editorial work, and so as the determining principle of the bookish identity of the play. In an important sense, to the New Bibliography nearly all forms of materiality – the slipshod work of the printshop, the tawdry work of the stage – degrade the author's creation. And it is precisely this sense of the materiality of the work of art that has been resisted and redefined in the wave of Shakespeare editing associated with the 1986 Oxford Shakespeare, and by cognate work in the sociology of print and in the theory of textuality across the humanities. Taking Shakespeare's writing not to transcend its enabling conditions but to be defined by them, this "materialist" view also trans-forms the New Bibliography's conception of how writing and performance relate to print. This New-New Shakespeare was neither unconcerned by nor obsessed by print, nor was his writing essentially corrupted by its han-dling in the theatre and in the printshop. Instead, Shakespearean writing is understood as fully collaborative with the process of stage production, a process that undermines (or at least alters) the presumptive authority of "foul papers," that may place a new and higher value on transcripts made for various (legal, theatrical, patronage) purposes, and that often requires revision and so tends to produce multiple copies of the same play text with different claims to authority. The multiple agency of theatrical writing may well also remain visible in the printed play, traced in the "acciden-tal" or "inconsistent" features of the mise-en-page that nonetheless speak to the play's use value. Habits of punctuation, varying speech prefixes, the use of actors' names in place of characters', and so on, may not so much witness carelessness as the consequences of writing for and within a business that insistently subjects writing to the pressure of orality: the theatre. And much as drama is a creature of the collaborative interplay of the stage, the plays are also creatures of the early modern printshop, where compositors worked to produce plays as printed books, struggling with unfamiliar and irregular conventions for printing drama, with their own education and work routines, with the technological limits of the press and the practices of printing and proofing, and inevitably with the legibility of the copy texts they were supplied. The kerning of letterforms, the distribution of type, the casting off of the text and laying out of the formes, even the composition of the ink itself all bear on the process that brought Shakespeare's plays to book. The New Bibliography – epitomized in this case by Charlton Hinman's magisterial edition of and commentary on the First Folio – refined the study of printshop practice and its bearing on the process and product of Shakespeare's plays in print, and regarded the printshop – much as it regarded the theatre – as throwing a veil of corruption between the author and the modern reader.[2] Yet while early modern printshop practice hardly accords with late modern notions of iterative consistency as the hallmark of print (a value that had yet fully to emerge), the ways the plays were done into print may well register considerably more than error. The plays as printed not only record the difficult circumstances in which the drama gained a bookish shape, but also register the printers' agency in bringing the plays into this crucial form and moment of their historical being.

The tension between a Romantic and a materialist Shakespeare has been enacted in visible form by the Oxford Shakespeare and its Norton successor, and by several more newly edited Shakespeares for students, teachers, and scholars. The new Shakespeare edition is unmistakable. It typically contains both a quarto- and a Folio-based version of *King Lear* (sometimes with a third, conflated text); alters familiar names (no "Falstaff" in the Oxford *1 Henry IV*, and no "Puck" either) and renames plays, too (the Oxford editors believe *Henry VIII* was popularly known as *All Is True*, so that's the title they use); it may even include some plays (*Edward III* in the Riverside second edition) or parts of plays (*Sir Thomas More*) in which Shakespeare may have had a hand. The consequences of this new attitude toward "The Materiality of the Shakespearean Text," to recall the provocative essay by Margreta de Grazia and Peter Stallybrass, have become increasingly prominent: the "old typefaces and spellings, irregular line and scene divisions, title pages and other paratextual matter," the irregularities of stage directions, and speech prefixes and other "character" designations, "remain obstinately on the pages of the early texts, insisting upon being looked *at*, not seen *through*," and recent editions have worked to retain elements of this complexity for scholars, teachers, and students (de Grazia and Stallybrass, "Materiality" 256–57). To the extent that modern editions also insist on "being looked *at* rather than seen *through*" they draw our attention back to the conceptual problems posed by printed drama today. How do we read a play in print? Textual multiplicity and materiality draw attention away from the notion of the perdurable work, identical in all its manifestations, and toward a sense of writing changing and being changed by the circumstances of its use, a sense, in other words, of the fungibility of dramatic writing that's intrinsic to the history of early and late modern drama.

Neither the New nor the New-New Bibliography resolves the dual identity of plays in print. Editorial work has always attended carefully to the printed text's ways of signaling the identity of the drama, the ways the text assumes, absorbs, or deflects the forms of authorship characteristic of print, and the interdependence of the drama's two modes of textuality, the literary (the dialogue) and the theatrical (the *didascalia*). Editing is pragmatic, and not surprisingly editors tend to have instrumental ways of answering ontological questions: what the printed play *is* emerges from what we might be asking it to *do*. The complex ways that Shakespeare's editors figure the working of print, its conceptual categories and its licensed uses, extend well beyond the precincts of early modern drama.

Modern plays, for instance, are nearly universally authorized. A play in print today is usually "by" someone, and the sign of the author assimilates the play to the legal structure of copyright, to the literarizing conventions of contemporary print publishing, and so to modern notions of drama as a species of literature. In the sixteenth and seventeenth centuries the reciprocal identities of printed and performed drama were weighted differently than they are today, after the dominion of print. With a very few, notable exceptions, print played little role in Shakespeare's theatre, as plays were submitted, copied, distributed into parts, and learned from manuscript. It's perhaps not surprising, then, that the theatrical identity of drama is persistently registered in the printform of early modern plays. If we regard the naming of the "author" as one sign of the emerging character of dramatic writing as print *literature*, then many early modern printed plays seem to represent *performance* as defining the drama's identity, and the printed book as a kind of by-product, a memorial record of that event. The title pages of many quarto editions of plays either locate the author as an afterthought to the play's performed identity – "The Tragedy of Othello | The Moor of Venice | As it hath been diverse times acted at the | Globe, and at the Black-Friars, by | his Majesty's Servants | Written by William Shakespeare" – or are just unconcerned or uninterested in the category of authorship as a way to mark the play or its marketability. For many printed plays, such as the first quarto of Shakespeare's *Titus Andronicus* (which neglects to mention the author's name), the identity of drama seems to lie in how "it was Plaide."[3]

As Jonson and Middleton make clear (to say nothing of Heminge and Condell), some writers (and actors) not only saw the written text as independent from production, but also put considerable effort into making fair-copy manuscripts for presentation, and overseeing the details of print (Jonson revised plays for inclusion in his 1616 *Works*). Arguing that Shakespeare may have understood himself both as a writer of scripts for theatrical use and as a "literary dramatist," Lukas Erne reminds us that Heminge and Condell advertised the 1623 Folio of Shakespeare's plays as "cur'd, and perfect of their limbes; and all the rest, absolute in their numbers, as he conceived them," distinguishing their edition from the "diuerse stolne, and surreptitious copies" previously in circulation. This convention was echoed in the 1647 Folio edition of Beaumont and Fletcher's *Comedies and Tragedies*, which notes that "When these *Comedies* and *Tragedies* were presented on the Stage, the *Actours* omitted some *Scenes* and Passages (with the *Authour's* consent) as occasion led them; and when private friends desir'd a Copy, they then (and justly too) transcribed what they *Acted*. But now you have both All that was *Acted*, and all that was not; even the perfect full Originalls without the least mutilation" (Erne, *Shakespeare as Literary Dramatist* 149). These claims at once witness a "literary" desire to register the entire, original, authorial composition in print as "the work of drama," and the emerging marketability of this notion of the play's identity.

Moreover, Erne has recently developed Greg's sense of Shakespeare writing for print posterity to argue that the unplayable length of many of Shakespeare's printed plays records the drama's dual identity. While plays were necessarily cut and reshaped for performance, the length of many of Shakespeare's plays suggests that they were not "meant for performance before undergoing abridgement and adaptation for the stage" (219). That is, rather than seeing – as many editors, including those of the Oxford edition have done – the longer and shorter versions of some of Shakespeare's plays to represent a literary original and a subsequent theatrical version of "the play," Erne argues that Shakespeare, as the Lord Chamberlain's/King's Men house playwright, did not have to churn out plays to spec. As a sharer in the company, he was not under the economic pressure felt by other playwrights to write only as much as could and would be performed, in order to get another play written for sale to a company, and he was unusually intimate with how, by whom, and perhaps even when his plays would be remade for and in performance. For this and other reasons (the pretensions to a "literary" career registered throughout the sonnets, and documented in the widespread appropriation of Shakespeare's writing in popular miscellanies), Shakespeare may well have supplied his company with "much material that was never, nor was ever intended to be, performed" (136). Whether or not the excessive "material" of Shakespeare's too-long plays signals the rise of the "literary dramatist," or perhaps witnesses other alternatives is not at issue here. (Is it at all plausible that as house playwright, Shakespeare might well have had the incentive and the freedom to write extra material not for a literary posterity but to provide a wider range of options and opportunities for his company to think through the play's performance potentialities? Did Shakespeare provide not a full and organic text to be cut down for performance, but a kind of dramatic miscellany to be shaped, selectively, into performance?) What is important is that Erne's challenging and sophisticated reading of the state of Shakespeare's printed plays enacts the ongoing problem of plays in print, the ways that writing in and for the theatre regularly troubles the notions of authorial agency inherent in print culture. Print invites us to locate the possibility of writing as a "literary dramatist" at the origin of print publishing, at precisely the moment that the "literary" drama is represented on the page by the theatrical activity in which it first took shape, *As it was Plaide*.

Whether or not we take Shakespeare to have written his plays with print in mind, the possibility of a "literary" drama is cognate with the rise of print, enacted not only by the Jonson, Shakespeare, and Beaumont and Fletcher Folios, but also by Molière's close supervision of the printing of his plays (apparently insisting on a rhetorical pattern of punctuation that would be undone by later editors) and by Congreve's attention both to layout and design elements (sending his publisher Jacob Tonson to the Netherlands to purchase special type fonts, so that he could differentiate between *i* and *j* and between *u* and *v*).[4] The rise of standard, literary editions of Shakespeare in the eighteenth and nineteenth centuries also opened the possibility of rival theatrical editions, a genre that has persisted not only in the "acting editions" of plays addressed specifically to the purpose of professional stage production, but that is also embodied in the screenplays of Shakespeare films (the Craig Pearce and Baz Luhrmann script for *William Shakespeare's Romeo + Juliet* comes to mind).[5] To say nothing of performance practice, the history of drama in print points to the difficulty of essentializing the relationship between the literary and the theatrical identities of the drama in the figure of the author. And while it's commonplace today to take this relationship as fixed by its late nineteenth-century form, typified by the novelization of printed drama characteristic of Ibsen's and Shaw's plays, the "author" remains a significant pressure point in contemporary printed drama, a place where we can continue to see the drama's resistance to the order of the book.

Attention to Shakespeare's texts has enabled a rethinking of the purpose and function not only of writing in print culture generally, but of the slippery relationship between dramatic writing, print culture, and the pervasively oral culture of the theatre as well.[6] This strikes me as the burden of the most surprising element of the current revolution in editorial practice: the changing value of theatrical orality. From the outset, orality was linked to "badness," largely through Greg's sense that the badness of the "bad quartos" conceived by A. W. Pollard in 1909 could be explained as the result of the "memorial reconstruction" of Shakespeare's plays, whether by actors, by other playhouse personnel, or even by scribes in the audience (we might remember that compositors, too, need to remember what they've seen long enough to set the words in type).[7] Despite the fact that in oral culture oral means may well be valued as more complete, more accurate than written means of recording communications, the New Bibliography evoked its modernity by relying on writing as the guarantor of authenticity (remember Bowers's dance of the thirteen veils?), asserting a homology between the function of writing in Shakespeare's theatre and on the print-oriented modern stage. Greg observes, "that it is safer to base the selection of the folio in preference to the quarto text of *Richard II* and *King Lear* upon a recognition of the fact that in both the quarto shows evidence of reporting, whereas the folio seems to derive its general character from manuscript tradition, rather than upon any literary judgment of textual probability, will hardly be questioned" (*Editorial Problem* xxiii).[8]

Yet "memorial reconstruction" – or, more fairly, the transmission of texts by nontextual means – is not only intrinsic to a culture on the border between orality and literacy, but remains essential to an institution (theatre) fundamentally reliant on oral means of production.[9] While recent scholarship has rehabilitated the "bad" quartos, and has revalued the bearing of orality on textual transmission, what this debate most recalls is the problematic of Antin's talk poems: whether as memorial record or motivating score, print can only (mis)represent performance in the terms of print. And despite the pervasive consequences of the rise of print on the practice of theatre, and on our understanding of theatre relative to literature, the stage remains a venue where texts are written and rewritten on the basis of what makes sense as speech and action; where writing is transformed into and communicated by behavior, not as writing; where skills are taught and transmitted not through reading and writing but through personal training; and where the vagaries of memory – vagaries, it should be noted, only from the perspective of print – are essential to the practices of live performance. To conceive of oral transmission as the sign of the "badness" of the "bad quartos" is to see the stage as inimical to dramatic literature, to the identity that drama assumes when veiled in the glamor of print. (In an effort to recalibrate the "badness" of the "bad" quartos, Laurie Maguire memorably compared the published texts of *The BBC-TV Shakespeare Plays* with the licensed video performances; perhaps surprisingly, she found most

of the purported solecisms of "bad" memorial transmission to be committed by the "good" performers of the series. Interested readers – or those
who want to get a jump on the last chapter of this book – might compare
the spoken text of Anna Deavere Smith's video performances of *Fires in
the Mirror: Crown Heights, Brooklyn and Other Identities* or of *Twilight: Los
Angeles, 1992* with the print versions of those plays, in which the author-
as-performer seems to indulge in many of the "bad" practices attributed to
Shakespeare's alleged pirates. As an actor, was Shakespeare word-perfect?
given to extemporization? to rewriting in performance?)[10]

The problems posed by early texts are distinctive, but they also point
to longer-term slippages between print, performance, and the identity of
drama. Stage directions and speech prefixes are important because they
are where the authorial meets the theatrical, where the writing meets the
performer, where the poetics of the drama meet the conventions of the
stage. Editors of Shakespeare's plays are faced with a baffling set of textual events, at least from a modern point of view. In many of the plays,
a given role will be indicated by several different speech prefixes, sometimes in the same scene (as when the character "Lady Capulet" is variously indicated by "Wife" or "Lady," among other labels); sometimes the
name of an actor will replace the prefix or the character's name in a stage
direction (as when "WIll Kemp" enters, rather than "Peter" in Q2 *Romeo
and Juliet*, or "Kemp" and "Cowley" replace "Dogberry" and "Verges" in
Much Ado About Nothing). Since the prefixes are abbreviated in the early
texts, it's even occasionally difficult to know which role the abbreviated
prefix may be for: Coriolanus or Cominius in *Coriolanus*, for instance.
Characters are frequently listed as entering a scene in which they have no
lines; in some cases, characters having no lines in the entire play haunt the
stage directions, and sometimes characters are told to *exit* the page when
they still have matter to speak onstage. Granted, these problems arose in
the first era of dramatic publishing, when the textual status of the play's
agents – actors or characters – had yet to be decided (if it has been decided)
or fully regularized, and the copy texts sent to the printshop no doubt
often posed their own challenges of interpretation. Is it possible, though,
that these inconsistencies point to a tension in the relationship between
print and performance still vital in contemporary drama?

All editions are acts of interpretation, but they interpret considerably
more than the words on the page. Particularly in the case of drama, an
interpretation of the purpose of the text tends to guide how editors understand what the text is, or, perhaps better phrased, what *is* the text and what
is not. This sense that the play's theatrical use can be distinguished from

its literary identity, and that these two registers can be distinguished on the page, informs the editorial treatment of the "accidentals" of design, typography, orthography, and punctuation, what R. B. McKerrow called the drama's "accessories" – distinguishing "between the actual text of the plays, in the sense of the matter which is intended to be spoken by the characters, and such accessories as act and scene headings, the speakers' names, and to some extent also the stage directions" (*Prolegomena* 19). McKerrow's distinction between the authorial (the characters' speech) and the conventional (everything else) not only reflects the typical critical understanding of the authorial warrant of dramatic writing (it's about the *characters* created by an *author*, not *roles* created for an *actor*) but the conventions of modern publishing and theatre practice as well, which tend to regard everything outside the dialogue as nondramatic and nonauthorial, having different properties and propriety, and different status as property (the Beckett controversies again come to mind). The play depends on the sign of the Author: yet authority is variably registered in different zones of the book, even in different zones of a given page. The widespread practice of lifting stage design and even some actors' business from the premiere production and silently incorporating them as stage directions in the printed play merely substantiates the notion that while the author's creation may end with the dialogue, his property may extend considerably farther on the page. As recent litigation suggests, this appropriation absorbs the designers' and the stage manager's work into the apparently "authorial" text, work which receives no credit or payment, despite the fact that it can now be copied in subsequent productions licensed by the author and his or her agents, and is generally understood to be part of the author's writing.[11]

Oddly enough, then, dealing with speech prefixes becomes a way of tracking one element of the conception of printed drama: how the print-form of the play represents the interface between authorial writing and stage practice. It's perhaps not surprising that McKerrow withholds the authorial from the taint of the theatrical, but this distinction persists in more recent editorial work. Involved in the most radical revision of Shakespeare editing in recent memory, the Oxford Shakespeare, Stanley Wells provides a useful summary of the ways some of the inconsistencies of early modern printed plays may reflect the business of the stage: "Shakespeare wrote, not as a dramatist whose work would be completed at the moment that he delivered his script to the company for which it was written, but as one who knew that he would be involved in the production process," with the result that "there is frequently little attempt in the [printed] scripts that survive to objectify many aspects of the imagined performance which would nevertheless have had to be communicated to the performers before the play could exist on the stage" – in this case, failing to "objectify" the fictional characters of the drama by naming them consistently in the theatrical speech prefixes (*Re-Editing Shakespeare* 57). The various inconsistencies in the attribution of roles and the direction of stage business can be smoothed over (and so smoothed away) only by regarding them as at once ancillary to the author's work – the dialogue – and as so fully overdetermined by the authorial dialogue as to be fully derivable from it. Shakespeare was, in this view, "so overridingly preoccupied by thoughts of what the characters should say that he could content himself with the sketchiest of stage directions, sometimes even omitting to indicate that a character should be present, frequently omitting to indicate when he should leave, sometimes not even bothering too much about who should speak particular lines or about providing dialogue to cover necessary action" (58). Shakespeare was providing dialogue to be copied into parts. The various headings – Kemp or Dogberry, Cowley or Verges, in *Much Ado* – would be clear enough to allow the distribution of sides to the actors. While the sides would not have contained prefixes, it's just conceivable that the alternation of "name" and dramatic function (as in the slippage between "Armado" and "Braggart" in *Love's Labour's Lost*), or of "name" and social function in the drama ("Lady," "Capulet Wife," "Mother," or "Old Lady" in *Romeo and Juliet*) might have had a purpose in casting, rehearsing, or otherwise conceptualizing the play for performance.[12] It is, finally, the principle that what dramatic authors create is *character* that enables us to regularize these theatrical expediencies to dramatic, literary form, as though the purpose of the script is to "objectify" the play's performance for consumption by readers, rather than to provide the performers with the raw material for their performance.

Even the more assertively "theatrical" conception of Shakespeare rightfully claimed by the innovative Oxford edition's text nonetheless extends Greg's sense of Shakespeare writing for print posterity, a posterity requiring Kemp's exit from the page of a fully "objectified" drama.[13] Although the Oxford Shakespeare no longer transcends the evanescent business of the stage through print, he is a fabricator of characters whose literary identity (their words *as* characters) is hedged off from contamination by the merely theatrical accessories that surround them, the speech prefixes and the actors who use them. Given the modern relationship between conventions of printed drama and conventions of "character," and the edition's scrupulous attention to the needs of modern readers, it's hard to imagine a different, more workable compromise than the one the Oxford edition achieves. Thinking of "characters" rather than "roles" leads to the choice of "Dogberry" over "Kemp." When the edition departs from tradition and allows prefixes to change – often to indicate a change in social and political status – it regularizes this variability to an objective view of the dramatic action. The Oxford edition's "Princess" becomes "Queen" at the appropriate moment in the last act of *Love's Labour's Lost* (though the editors note that the first quarto alternates these prefixes throughout the play); in *Richard II*, "Bolingbroke" becomes "King Henry" after his accession to the throne (again noting and regularizing the first quarto practice, which changes the prefix later in the play).[14] This kind of prefix problem suggests that the plays' use in the theatre may conflict with an "objectified" scripted drama. It also implies that the notion that writing should "objectify" the play for readers is perhaps more Shavian than Shakespearean in flavor.

McKerrow arrestingly refers to these elements – speech prefixes, speech headings, or speech attributions, take your pick – as *names*, "the names by which the characters are indicated" ("Suggestion" 2).[15] For McKerrow, Shakespeare's irregular names may well register important authorial commitments: "I believe that, although Shakespeare generally fixed upon a name for each of his characters at his or her first introduction, in the heat of composition their qualities or the part which they played in the action were often more strongly present to his imagination than their personal names, and that he therefore came instinctively to substitute descriptive titles for their original designations, *Braggart* for *Armado, Father* for *Capulet*, and so on, while in other cases he may simply have forgotten whether he had, for example, previously referred to a character as *Princess* or *Queen*" (*Prolegomena* 57). Yet such accessories are, finally, just that, standing alongside the dramatic writing that the book should deliver to the reader: "To follow the original texts in this irregularity would, however, be unnecessarily confusing to a reader, and as, after all, these speech-prefixes are merely labels intended to show to whom the various speeches are to be attributed, it seems to me an editor's clear duty to treat them as labels and to make the labels uniform."

How we understand Shakespeare's variable names depends on the warrant of the drama on the page. Are such accessories merely (merely!) a record of the author's writing process, or a legitimate part of the finished play? Are they innate to the literary drama, or only part of the accessory business of the stage? Do these accessories register in the fictive plane of dramatic representation (as names, in other words) or on the functional plane of theatrical presentation, as directions? The Oxford edition's invented prefix "King Claudius" marks this tension, a desire to have it both ways – the prefix as name (*Claudius*, which does not occur as a prefix in Q1, Q2, or F *Hamlet*) and as social, dramatic, and even theatrical function (play the King). This tension cannot be resolved because the rise of print ensures that texts can be, and will be, read in both ways by different readers with different purposes, and sometimes by the same reader with different purposes, and sometimes by the same reader with different purposes at the same time. One way to understand the materiality of early modern texts is to take this fact of their (dis)organization seriously, as opening onto an ongoing problem in the identities of printed drama, rather than as a simple failure yet to understand or imagine how plays must and should be represented on the page, in print. De Grazia and Stallybrass, for instance, suggest that the variability of prefixes in printed drama implies the possibility that "character is posterior to speech," rather than a coherent entity that dictates a consistent label ("Materiality" 268). And Randall McLeod notes that the erasure of these differences – which are also mainly erased from editions like the Oxford, which choose different prefixes (Oxford uses "Robin" in place of the conventional "Puck," but uses it consistently throughout; the Folio uses these prefixes interchangeably) – actually makes it rather difficult to know what impact they might have on our reading or performing practices, and so on our sense of the drama itself: the plays "abound in these polynomials, but as the editors have hidden all trace of them, the Newton of their calculation has yet to appear" ("UN *Editing*" 83). We are all, in this sense, still in the Bradleyan orbit of "character" criticism, not so much because we want to know the number of Lady Macbeth's children as because our understanding of the materiality of the text, of its signifying features, continues to locate the trace of the author in discriminate places in the text, here in logic of "character" which should be represented with a singular, individualized *name*, rather than by a changing set of prefixes (A. C. Bradley – 1851–1935 – was almost Shaw's exact contemporary, and was already an eminence in the early decades of Greg's work; R. B. McKerrow 1872–1940). As McLeod suggests, concealing the inconsistencies of the text, foisting "single names on characters to whom Shakespeare responded, while creating them, with many names, is to impose retrospective understanding on the text, to seek artofficial [*sic*] rather than real creating," a tradition he terms "obliterature" ("UN *Editing*" 84). This reading of prefixes goes considerably beyond the fact that early modern texts tend to be irregular in announcing the entrance or exit of characters in the proper locations in the text. The text provides ambiguous information about who the characters are, who is speaking, precisely by refusing to name the roles *as* characters in the modern sense.[16]

Prefixes may, now, be so fully laminated to modern notions of character – as *names* – as to be impossible to leverage away, even despite the Oxford edition's considerable effort in this direction. And yet there's an important sense in which early modern prefixes register a reality of theatre: onstage, "character" isn't something you are, it's something you do. After all, actors don't really need a "name" for the character, and in Shakespeare's theatre may well not have received a "name" with the side on which the lines were written. Thinking about speech prefixes as "names" is a markedly literary notion, as though "character" is something prior to its enactment. It is also, in theatrical terms, a markedly modern notion. Given the composition of Shakespeare's and of other early modern companies, and what we know of the distribution of parts, the pace of the repertory, and what we can hypothesize about rehearsal, it seems more than apparent that a given actor would deploy a given line of business as his performance métier. Playing a part like Bottom or Hamlet involves not so much finding the character's original "name," but in creatively assimilating the language and action given in the text to the paradigmatic theatrical business that is the actor's particular professional competence – what audiences come to see, what he has to sell, his *stuff*. Bottom's "lover or a tyrant" parodies this notion of theatre, but the success of *A Midsummer Night's Dream* depends on it. The play requires a good physical comic, an irascible old man, winsome and winning lovers, and perhaps just a touch of melancholy, unpredictable violence in Theseus and Oberon. In Shakespeare's theatre, the actor's line precedes the role and the role precedes its name. There *is* something in a name, of course. "Volpone" and "Mosca" and "Shallow" and "Silence" are hardly irrelevant labels for the characters they name (or the performances they instigate), some of Othello's magic surely arises from those open, exotic vowels, and young Will Shakespeare was no doubt right to prefer "Romeo and Juliet" to "Romeo and Ethel" in the film *Shakespeare in Love*. The "name" individuates and specifies the role, and can deepen and expand its significance, but it does not give local habitation to an entirely airy nothing. In the early modern theatre, the names of the drama often name something that's already there – *Enter Will Kemp*.

The notion that the text's primary work is to objectify the fictive world of the play to readers, and only secondarily to signal aspects of the practical working of the play to performers, again evokes a rather Shavian Shakespeare. The multiple designation "Armado"/"Braggart" (or "Dogberry"/ "Kemp") implies an attitude toward the script distinct from the "novelized" writing of Ibsen or Shaw or O'Neill, and perhaps also points to the sense in which thinking of speech prefixes as "names" is distinctive of a certain, historically bound sense of drama and the dramatic: the "objectiv-ity" of modern realism. It may even be possible to argue, as Lukas Erne has done, that those accessories that most seem indices of the play text's theatri-cal provenance might instead be marks of an originally literary conception. Claiming that the excessive length of some of Shakespeare's plays implies a literary purpose, Erne also suggests that stage directions are part of the playwright's conversation not with his fellow actors, but with an audience of readers, objectifying the play in the theatre of the mind. For instance, in the second quarto *Romeo and Juliet*, when Juliet is told by her father that she will marry Paris the following Thursday, she says "Good Father, I beseech you on my knees"; in the first quarto version, we find the line, "Good father, heare me speake?" followed by the stage direction "*She kneeles downe*" (*Shakespeare as Literary Dramatist* 223). Here, and elsewhere, Erne argues that stage directions speak not to the text as an instigation to act, nor as a record of performance, but instead to a desire to use the text to "allow a reader to imagine a point of stage business that could otherwise only be conveyed in performance" (222). Alternatively, the famous Chorus speeches of *Henry V* may not have been performed onstage, creating the possibility that "Writing longer plays for readers than his company needed for the theatre, Shake-speare encourages and enables his readers to use their 'imaginary forces' to construct in their mind's eye the 'wooden O'": the text, in this sense, records the "literary dramatist's" efforts to enable readers to imagine not the fictive scene of the drama, but the theatrical immediacy of performance (225). Taking stage directions as the sign of the "literary dramatist's" effort to objectify the play is reminiscent of McKerrow's distinction between the literary and the theatrical, but in Erne's view the playwright's author-ity extends across the page, absorbing the signifiers of the stage into the narrative structure of the literary drama. Shakespeare, meet Beckett.

Whether Greg and Erne or di Grazia and Stallybrass have it right is less at issue here than the ways they locate enduring problems in the printform of plays. Modern Shakespeare editing faces challenges that seem not to afflict readers of modern drama. Modern plays are printed more accurately, tend to use the conventions of print more consistently, and generally seem more comfortable with their bookish form as the price of a robust and durable literary identity. And yet many of the slippages worrying the printforms of Shakespeare's plays remain with us: the nature of dramatic authorship and authority and their representation in print; the extent of the author's trace across the printed page; the ways the printed play appears to reject, absent, repudiate, direct, or rival the play's performance on the stage. Written at the emergence of print and of professional theatre, Shakespeare's plays might be expected to evoke a complex duplicity. Modern drama, written in the era of print's dominion over the word, seems to prolong, even to thematize some of these instabilities as its condition of creation. We're not Shakespeare's inheritors exactly, nor do we share exactly the same problems in booking the play. Nonetheless print remains troubling for us as a delivery system for the drama, troubling in ways that Shakespeare might have recognized.

Dogberry's capricious morphing into Kemp may seem both to evoke an elusive theatrical world where writers and actors shared in the bustling creation of the play, and the dusty libraries where tweedy scholars labor to correct such trivialities. Yet, the desire of contemporary editors to retain a "polynomial" conception of the drama's agents also resonates in another sphere: in the ways print materializes a relation between character and actor, the written and performed identities of the drama, in contemporary play-writing and performance. If Greg's Shakespeare sometimes looks like Shaw, we might wonder whether the materialist Shakespeare resembles Samuel Beckett or even Suzan-Lori Parks. Will Kemp may be exiled from contemporary Shakespeare, but the plays with which contemporary Shakespeare shares the stage – and the shelf – often use the design of the speech prefix (critical on the page, irrelevant in performance) to trouble an easy assimilation of the role to the standing conventions of literary character and theatrical performance. I'm thinking here not only of the published texts of performance art where the slippage between writer/performer/character may be in part what the work is about, but also of some of the most challenging roles of recent drama: BLACK MAN WITH WATERMELON, LOTS OF GREASE AND LOTS OF PORK, SHE WHO IS CLARA PASSMORE WHO IS THE VIRGIN MARY WHO IS THE BAS-TARD WHO IS THE OWL, MOUTH, AUDITOR, W2, to name only a few of the more interesting designations of the past forty years or so (and to set aside plays, such as Heiner Müller's *Hamletmachine* or Sarah Kane's *4.48 Psychosis* which dispense with prefixes altogether).[17] One of the most widely staged American plays of recent years, *The Laramie Project*, is notable here, too. In print, the name "Moisés Kaufman" shares the authorial by-line of *The Laramie Project* ("by Moisés Kaufman and members of Tectonic Theater Project"), holds the copyright accreditation, stands as the sole author of the volume's Introduction, is listed among the play's Characters, and appears as a speech prefix for a role in the play (though in both the Denver and New York openings, the role was played by John McAdams, a member of Tectonic Theater Project listed on the title page as a dramaturg). Several of the play's "Associate Writers" – Stephen Belber and Greg Pierotti – are also listed as "Characters," and also appear as speech prefixes; these two "Characters" were also played in Denver and New York by actors named Stephen Belber and Greg Pierotti (who played several other "Characters" too), though – like all the roles in the play – they have been played by many other actors since (the HBO film of *The Laramie Project* features many of the Tectonic Theater Project actors, but they don't play themselves, nor do they generally play the other "Characters" they played onstage).[18] I will return to these issues later, but for now suffice it to say that while performer and character, role and name, theatrical writer and dramatic author are earnestly rationalized on the page, the tensions marked in different ways by the irruption of Kemp and Cowley into the drama, by Puck's inability to keep his name straight, or by the complexities of literary ("Written by William Shakespeare") and theatrical ("As it was Plaide") attribution played out on the pages of early modern plays have not been entirely resolved by modern dramatic publishing.

How do books represent plays? Surely much of the inconsistency of printed drama in Shakespeare's era has to do with the absence of strict conventions of dramatic publishing, conventions that would emerge fitfully over the next four hundred years, becoming at once much more uniform and yet remaining considerably more volatile than the conditions of, say, published fiction or poetry. Not only are the problems posed by the multiple texts of Shakespeare's plays reenacted in the contemporary practice of publishing both trade and acting editions of many plays, but the problems of the play's materialization on the page, and what that performance might or might not say about the play's materialization on that other stage, also remain very much with us. We have, of course, become considerably more habituated to the "radiant textuality" of the print-emulating computer screen, and of digital writing's ways of multiplying and distributing texts and textual authority.[19] Oddly, even collaboratively authorized, openly bearing the traces of many different kinds of compositional agency, printed drama had at one time seemed a special case of print literature, but in the revolution of textual theory it seems the representative case. Where once plays were seen as tangential and troublesome elements in the history of print, texts whose collaborative or communal character intrudes a sense of accidental and irregular inconsistency into the reiterative mode privileged as print's proper history, it's now the case that insofar as "playtexts [. . .] are designed to change as the conditions of performance change" they are exemplary of the condition of print, in which (recalling the influence of D. F. McKenzie, Jerome McGann, Peter Shillingsburg and others), texts cannot be seen as "independent of [their] material embodiment," an embodiment which is at once the record of their individual and cultural fashioning, a semantically rich context of signification, the moment and mode of their irruption into history (Stephen Orgel, "What is an Editor?" 117, 118). The language of "embodiment" suffuses editorial theory today, perhaps best summarized by Peter L. Shillingsburg: "one could say that every new embodiment of a literary work of art is a new, additional, and altered embodiment of it. That is important because a reader approaching a new text, particularly a reader alert to what is being read, cannot help being influenced in certain ways by the object that 'contains' the literary work" ("Polymorphic" 33). If dramatic writing in its collaborative dimension troubles the category of print authorship, dramatic production – the multiplication of different texts for a single stage production *and* the sense of difference that emerges between different stage productions – troubles the "reiterative" rhetoric of print, in ways that are coming, now, both to be appreciated and to be absorbed into the ways plays take the page.

What would it mean to an understanding of modern dramatic performance to attend to the printed form of plays (remembering that Shakespeare is the most often performed *and printed* of modern playwrights)? Perhaps, as Margreta de Grazia suggests, it's not only the historicity of Shakespeare's texts but the historicity of the interface between writing and performance that "eludes the binary logic of the One and the Many, as well as the two reproductive technologies of staticizing print and generative images" ("Question" 251). In this sense, the movement to a more materialist textual theory and editorial practice in Shakespeare studies can also be seen not only as a symptom of a shifting understanding of print and performance, but also of changing ways of *making* performance and of *using* writing in the theatre. These changes are immediately visible in performance art, in the emphasis on "performance" in certain aspects of contemporary poetry and poetics, even perhaps in the rise of the resolutely antiliterary field of "performance studies." If Shakespearean editing takes place less in the world of Okes and Jaggard than of Michael Best and (inevitably) of Steve Jobs and Bill Gates, so too it also takes place less in the world of the Burbages, Heminge and Condell, and Marlowe and Jonson than the world of Beckett and Parks and Churchill, the world of Declan Donnellan and Anne Bogart, of Baz Luhrmann and Michael Almereyda.[20] Contemporary performance culture – a term I mean here to embrace writing, publishing, and performing practices across a range of media, including the theatre – isn't what it was in 1600 or in 1900.

Shakespeare editing has taught us to read the semantic properties of the book's material design, but our own performance culture is also part of the context of modern Shakespeare on the stage and on the page. While the interrogation of early texts enacts a principally historical concern, a concern actively to represent the pastness of the plays in modern books, editions enact this concern on the horizon of contemporary writing, contemporary publishing, and contemporary performance. Like a performance on the stage, print materializes the play in specific ways, inevitably assimilating it to notions of print literature and representing its implication – however distant, marginal, or rebarbative – in performance. Of course, the differences between O'Neill's Emperor Jones and Parks's Black Man With Watermelon can't be attributed solely to the traces of ink on the page, even to the traces recognized as "dialogue." Yet the events of the page record the changing interface between writing and performance, a history that took a new shape in Shakespeare's day with the rise of print, and is undergoing a second transformation today under the impact of digital textualities. Alert to the meanings of print, we can now ask how the accessories of modern drama's apparition on the page perform, what kind of work they do in materializing the play on the page, and how modern drama's strategies for occupying the page also work to represent an understanding of the drama, and of its work in that other scene, the scene of its lively enactment on the stage. The printed page may point to a shifting relation between writing and enactment in the conception of modernism's unwanted orphan: modern drama.

CHAPTER 2

Accessory acts

[. . .] the public does not read plays, or at least did not a very few years
ago. Have you any reason to suppose that it has changed its habits?
Bernard Shaw to Grant Richards, 8 November 1896
(*Collected Letters* 698)

The booking of modern drama in English arguably begins, as does much
else in modern drama in English, with Bernard Shaw. Shaw was obsessed
by the stage, and wrote his plays for performance, even when he knew
they could not be licensed under English censorship law. He also strove
assiduously to use the accessories of the page to articulate a place for modern
dramatic writing in the age of print. In his superb book on the literarization
of modern drama, Martin Puchner has argued that the "emergence within
modern drama of elaborately descriptive and narrative stage directions is
an instance of a more general reliance on the part of modern drama on
language that mediates, describes, prescribes, and interrupts the mimetic
space of the theater," and Shaw's effort at once to incorporate a literary
drama and to strike a visible accommodation with the stage positions Shaw
at the outset of modern drama's inquiry into the uses of the mise-en-page
(*Stage Fright* 21). Many of Shaw's ways of figuring the drama on the page –
his use of spacing to indicate e m p h a s i s, so as to reserve italics for *stage
directions* – are familiar, but while his overall effort to reframe the written
drama as a (loquacious) dialogue with the reader has been influential (think
of Eugene O'Neill's stage directions, or Tom Stoppard's), many of Shaw's
distinctive ways of doing plays into print have been more or less ignored.
Nonetheless, Shaw saw the accessories of the page as a means to frame
the distinctive identity of dramatic writing. His ways of conceiving and
representing his plays define the problem of the identity of drama in the
late age of print.

MRS WARREN'S PROFESSION

ACT I

Summer afternoon in a cottage garden on the eastern slope of a hill a little south of Haslemere in Surrey. Looking up the hill, the cottage is seen in the left hand corner of the garden, with its thatched roof and porch, and a large latticed window to the left of the porch. Farther back a little wing is built out, making an angle with the right side wall. From the end of this wing a paling curves across and forward, completely shutting in the garden, except for a gate on the right. The common rises uphill beyond the paling to the sky line. Some folded canvas garden chairs are leaning against the side bench in the porch. A lady's bicycle is propped against the wall, under the window. A little to the right of the porch a hammock is slung from two posts. A big canvas umbrella, stuck in the ground, keeps the sun off the hammock, in which a young lady lies reading and making notes, her head towards the cottage and her feet towards the gate. In front of the hammock, and within reach of her hand, is a common kitchen chair, with a pile of serious-looking books and a supply of writing paper upon it.

A gentleman walking on the common comes into sight from behind the cottage. He is hardly past middle age, with something of the artist about him, unconventionally but carefully

1. *Mrs Warren's Profession*, 1898.

Shaw's designs on the page of modern drama are well-enough epitomized by the opening page of *Mrs Warren's Profession* (see figure 1), published by Grant Richards in his two-volume set of Bernard Shaw's *Plays: Pleasant and Unpleasant* in 1898. It is a page on which no dialogue appears, indeed nothing about the page – other than, perhaps, the italic typeface and *"ACT I"* – implies that this is a play at all. After failing to persuade John Lane's Bodley Head to take him on, and demurring from Fisher Unwin's invitation to be involved in publishing Ibsen's plays and possibly his own ("if I thought that people were picking up the French trick of reading dramatic works, I should be strongly tempted to publish my plays instead of bothering to get them performed," he wrote to Unwin on 9 September 1895; *Collected Letters* 557), Shaw spent 1897 and much of 1898 cajoling, harassing, and bluntly browbeating Grant Richards to produce his plays in a lucidly Shavian format.[1] Having worked to see his novels into print, Shaw naturally saw the publishing of his plays as a way to a new audience, and as a way to establish himself more fully as an Author (it's hard to imagine a more self-consciously functionalist, Foucauldian site of enunciation than G.B.S.). Noting that "in the present condition of the theatre it is evident that a dramatist like Ibsen, who absolutely disregards the conditions which managers are subject to, and throws himself on the reading public, is taking the only course in which any serious advance is possible, expecially [*sic*] if his dramas demand much technical skill from the actors," Shaw made up his mind "to put my plays into print and trouble the theatre no further with them" (to Golding Bright, 7 May 1897; *Collected Letters* 754). Shaw is more than a little disingenuous here: he continued to mount copyright performances to protect his rights to production, and sedulously pursued plans to stage his plays for actual audiences. At the same time, Shaw's desire to print his plays in a convenient multivolume edition points to an opening that others – Ibsen, most famously, but also Arthur Wing Pinero and Henry Arthur Jones in England – had also seen: the framing of dramatic writing for a mass book-buying public.[2]

How would the plays be done into print? Shaw ostentatiously avoided the model of acting editions with their extensive technical language and abbreviations of stage business, making it a "rule to get away from the old 'Stabs her 2 R C; sees ghost up C (biz); and exit R.U.E.' which made plays unreadable and unsaleable."[3] Shaw's mise-en-page departed significantly from the model already established by other English playwrights, and even by Ibsen's English and Danish publishers. While most of us take the chief oddity of Shaw in print to be his distinctive use of spelling, punctuation, and spacing, what sets Shaw's plays most apart from other modern printed drama is their design and layout. Writing to Richards (on 31 August 1898) of the proof of *Plays: Pleasant and Unpleasant* that "*nothing* could make a page look well with such margins," Shaw complains, "Further, you cannot judge the look of a book by contemplating half of it: the open book presents two pages, which, taken together by the eye, form the complete picture to be aimed at." While Richards was not himself "much attracted by the books for which William Morris was responsible," he saw the value of Morris's aesthetic, its impact on modern book design, and, inevitably, its influence on Shaw (Richards, *Author Hunting* 139).[4] Yet despite Richards's sense that Shaw wanted his books to be hallmark Morris, Shaw pursued a more modern, even modernist, compromise between the material density of Morris's design principles and a more legible typographical style reminiscent of John Lane's Bodley Head, the publisher of *The Yellow Book* and so synonymous with turn-of-the-century modernity.[5]

Needless to say, Shaw was meticulous in his supervision of the proof, insisting that letters be spaced evenly and tightly, rather than justifying the right margin by leading and so increasing white space in the line. Doing so enabled Shaw to distinguish between stage directions (printed in italics) and emphatic speech, indicated by spacing between the letters. He also eliminated what he regarded as excessive punctuation, jettisoning most apostrophes and periods used for abbreviations. Moreover, he insisted that the printer stick to his program of blackening the page. The printer was always to prefer hyphenating words to adding additional spacing as a means to justify the line.

> I return a couple more sheets – all I've got – for press. If you look at pp 17, 25, 6 & 7 you will see that I have made a faint protest against the whiteness of some of the lines. You might suggest to them that they need not justify to avoid dividing a word at the end – that it is better to divide a word than to have a loose line making a streak of whitey grey through the black. Caxton would have printed your name G-rant Richa-rds at the end of a line sooner than spoilt his page with rivers of white. The great thing is to get the color even. Besides, since we are substituting spaced letters for italic in underlined words, it is important that spacing should be regular and rather narrow, so as to make the spacing distinctive. (to Grant Richards, 23 October 1897; *Collected Letters* 816)

Shaw's strictures on hyphenation are played out most visibly on the title pages. Though he may have been tweaking Richards on how Caxton would have broken his name to preserve the evenness of spacing, Shaw clearly prevailed on this point, even when space was not at issue (see figure 2). The title page of *Plays: Pleasant and Unpleasant* sets the author and title information in an evenly-spaced, off-center box at the top of the page, little troubling that the crucial word "Unpleasant" runs to a second line, as does the word "containing." *Three Plays for Puritans* is more emphatic on this score (see figure 3). The desire to preserve an evenly spaced block of type leads to hyphenating the book's title (*Three Plays for Puri-tans*) as well as the titles of all three plays of the subtitle (*The Devil's Dis-ciple, Caesar and Cleo-patra, Captain Brass-bound's Conversion*).[6]

The understanding that the material form of the book substantiates its "literary" or "poetic" meanings is what Shaw most shares with Morris and

Plays : Pleasant and Unpleasant. By Bernard Shaw.
The First Volume, containing the three Unpleasant
Plays.

London : Grant Richards, 9
Henrietta St. Covent Garden, W.C. 1898.

2. *Plays: Pleasant and Unpleasant*, 1898: title page.

Three Plays for Puritans : The Devil's Disciple, Cæsar and Cleopatra, & Captain Brassbound's Conversion. By Bernard Shaw.

London : Grant Richards, 9 Henrietta St. Covent Garden, W.C. 1901.

3. *Three Plays for Puritans*, 1901: title page.

his modernist inheritors. The modernism of *Plays: Pleasant and Unpleasant* might have been more palpable – evocative, for example, of Ezra Pound's decision to publish his wartime volume *Cathay* in khaki covers – had Richards followed through on some of Shaw's more outrageous suggestions: printing the *Unpleasant Plays* "on light brown paper (Egyptian mummy color) in an ugly style of printing, and the pleasant ones on white paper (machine hand made) in the best Kelmscott style" (27 March 1898; *Collected Letters* 740). "Nobody has ever done a piebald volume before," Shaw enthused, but Richards was not to be the first. Shaw's injunction against gilt edging – "I object strenuously to gilt tops" (8 October 1897; *Collected Letters* 811) – was also ignored.

For Shaw, the design of the book was not merely part of its packaging for the market: it was a means both to stage the value of modern drama as print literature, and a means to represent the drama in the form of print, to articulate a sense of the play as writing and performance. Shaw's plays are richly verbal objects, staging their bookishness most visibly in the way they transform that aspect of printed drama most closely associated with the theatre: the stage directions. Shaw's "novelistic," witty account of the environs of the stage plainly asserts the literary texture of the drama, but the extent of the book's absorption of the play emerges considerably more clearly against the background of how other plays of the "new drama" of the 1890s seized the page.

The first edition of Oscar Wilde's *The Importance of Being Earnest* (1899), necessarily identified only as "By the Author of Lady Windermere's Fan" (see figure 4) – was printed in a small run (though not much smaller than the run of *Plays: Pleasant and Unpleasant*). It includes cast lists, is profligate in its use of space, and is at least nominally more "theatrical" (though not particularly technical) in the orientation of its stage directions, which ostentatiously set the theatrical "SCENE – *Morning-room in Algernon's flat in Half Moon Street*" (1) (see figure 5). The play sets both the speech prefixes and the dialogue flush with the left margin, but double spaces around the prefixes; Wilde's page emphasizes the dialogic character of the drama, the movement from speaker to speaker. As with many nineteenth-century plays, in a gesture that seems drawn from the advertising common in play-bills and programs, this edition also contains a page describing "THE SCENES OF THE PLAY" – ACT I *Algernon Moncrieff's flat in Half Moon Street, W.* ACT II *The Garden at the Manor House, Woolton.* ACT III *Drawing Room at the Manor House, Woolton.* – and its "*Time. The Present.*" Pinero's plays also tend to combine the novelistic with the theatrical, deploying extensively descriptive stage directions while retaining

THE

IMPORTANCE OF BEING EARNEST

A TRIVIAL COMEDY FOR

SERIOUS PEOPLE

BY

THE AUTHOR OF

LADY WINDERMERE'S FAN

LONDON

LEONARD SMITHERS AND CO

5 OLD BOND STREET W

MDCCCXCIX

4. *The Importance of Being Earnest*, 1899: title page.

a theatrical nomenclature. *The Second Mrs. Tanqueray* opens with a brief but decisively narrative stage direction, that at once announces the "scene" of the play – "AUBREY TANQUERAY's *Chambers in the Albany*" – and sets the tone of the scene as well: "*Everything in the apartment suggests wealth and refinement*" (*Second Mrs. Tanqueray* 1; see figure 6). Like *Earnest*, this edition recalls theatrical traditions by listing the location of each Act on a

SCENE—*Morning-room in Algernon's flat in Half Moon Street. The room is luxuriously and artistically furnished. The sound of a piano is heard in the adjoining room.*

[*Lane is arranging afternoon tea on the table, and after the music has ceased, Algernon enters.*]

ALGERNON

Did you hear what I was playing, Lane?

LANE

I didn't think it polite to listen, sir.

ALGERNON

I'm sorry for that, for your sake. I don't play accurately—anyone can play accurately—but I play with wonderful expression. As far as the piano is concerned, sentiment is my forte. I keep science for Life.

LANE

Yes, sir.

I   B

5. *The Importance of Being Earnest*, 1899.

separate page – "*The Scene of the First Act is laid at* MR. TANQUERAY'S *rooms, No. 2x, The Albany, in the month of November; the occurrences of the succeeding Acts take place at his house, 'Highercoombe,' near Willowmere, Surrey, during the early part of the following year*" (n.p.) – and by stressing the change in speakers by centering prefixes and spacing after each speech.[7] Both of these texts are explicitly designed for nontheatrical readers, and yet both editions (near contemporaries of *Plays: Pleasant and Unpleasant*) retain the traces of the plays' theatrical origins. Neither play is as thorough in its "novelization" of the scene as Shaw's plays. The traces of a "theatrical" orientation to the work of the page that remain here are just

THE

SECOND MRS. TANQUERAY

THE FIRST ACT

AUBREY TANQUERAY'S *Chambers in the Albany—a richly and tastefully decorated room, elegantly and luxuriously furnished : on the right a large pair of doors opening into another room, on the left at the further end of the room a small door leading to a bedchamber. A circular table is laid for a dinner for four persons which has now reached the stage of dessert and coffee. Everything in the apartment suggests wealth and refinement. The fire is burning brightly.*

AUBREY TANQUERAY, MISQUITH, *and* JAYNE *are seated at the dinner-table.* AUBREY *is forty-two, handsome, winning in manner, his speech and bearing retaining some of the qualities of young-manhood.*

THIS PLAY WAS PRODUCED

AT THE

ST. JAMES'S THEATRE

ON

Saturday, May 27, 1893

6. *The Second Mrs. Tanqueray*, 1895.

2

MISQUITH *is about forty-seven, genial and portly.* JAYNE *is a year or two* MISQUITH's *senior; soft-speaking and precise—in appearance a type of the prosperous town physician.* MORSE, AUBREY's *servant, places a little cabinet of cigars and the spirit-lamp on the table beside* AUBREY, *and goes out.*

MISQUITH.

Aubrey, it is a pleasant yet dreadful fact to contemplate, but it's nearly fifteen years since I first dined with you. You lodged in Piccadilly in those days, over a hat-shop. Jayne, I met you at that dinner, and Cayley Drummle.

JAYNE.

Yes, yes. What a pity it is that Cayley isn't here to-night.

AUBREY.

Confound the old gossip! His empty chair has been staring us in the face all through dinner. I ought to have told Morse to take it away.

MISQUITH.

Odd, his sending no excuse.

3

AUBREY.

I'll walk round to his lodgings later on and ask after him.

MISQUITH.

I'll go with you.

JAYNE.

So will I.

AUBREY.

[*Opening the cigar-cabinet.*] Doctor, it's useless to tempt you, I know. Frank—[MISQUITH *and* AUBREY *smoke.*] I particularly wished Cayley Drummle to be one of us to-night. You two fellows and Cayley are my closest, my best friends——

MISQUITH.

My dear Aubrey!

JAYNE.

I rejoice to hear you say so.

AUBREY.

And I wanted to see the three of you round this table. You can't guess the reason.

MISQUITH.

You desired to give us a most excellent dinner.

that, as we can readily see by looking at a contemporary acting edition –
here of James Albery's *Two Roses* (see figure 7) – which notes the original
production, provides a list of roles and the actors who originated them, a
listing of the scenes, and provides a descriptive account of the setting and
characters conveyed through the technical language of the working theatre.
It is very densely printed (abbreviating speech prefixes) in order to get as
much play as possible on each page.

In several respects, Shaw's mania for blackening the page suggests that
this is a moment of transition in the identity of plays. Other playwrights
equally invested in their pretensions to literary authorship (like Pinero)
chose other designs. Some of those designs, like the multivolume Ibsen
Works published by Gyldendal in Copenhagen in the late 1890s, reveal
their literary pretension in the design of the book: this edition is published
in elegant embossed covers, on heavy paper, and in large type. At the same
time, the Gyldendal Ibsen looks very different on the page from *Plays:
Pleasant and Unpleasant*. Centering speech prefixes and spacing between
the speeches, Ibsen's plays seem to emphasize the dialogic character of the
drama in their layout on the page.[8] William Archer's edition of Ibsen,
published by Walter Scott, was partly a model for Shaw, putting speech
prefixes on the line and not spacing between speeches (see figure 8). Yet this
edition is considerably less dense than Shaw's, tending to justify margins
by spacing rather than by hyphenation ("In Scott's edition the block of
letterpress is not properly set on the page; but otherwise it is not so bad,"
Shaw wrote to Grant Richards, 21 May 1897; *Collected Letters* 767).[9]

Mrs Warren's Profession demonstrates that Shaw's innovations point at
once to the changing social status of dramatic writing, now a potential
mode of literary authorship, and also to a range of differential literacies.
Mrs Warren's Profession ostentatiously rejects the technical literacy of
theatrical production in favor of the interpretive literacy of the home
reader.

In one sense, of course, Shavian design is extremely economical, the
inverse of the Victorian triple-decker novel (three plays in one volume,
rather than one novel in three). In fact, though, Shaw copies the design
of the acting editions here, placing the speech prefix on the first line of
dialogue, indenting it (rather than indenting the speech), and eliminating spacing between speeches in order to get the most play-per-page (see
figure 9). In combination with the choice of typeface, the elegant placement of the block of type on the page, and other design elements (the cover,
the illustration of Shaw facing the title page, much as in Archer's Ibsen),

TWO ROSES.

First performed at the Vaudeville Theatre, Strand, under the Management of Messrs. Montague, James, and Thorne, June 4th, 1870.

CHARACTERS.

Digby Grant, Esq.	Mr. HENRY IRVING.
Caleb Deecie	Mr. THOMAS THORNE.
Jack Wyatt	Mr. H. J. MONTAGUE.
Our Mr. Jenkins	Mr. GEORGE HONEY.
Mr. Furnival	Mr. W. H. STEPHENS.
Our Mrs. Jenkins	Miss LAVIS.
Lotty	Miss AMY FAWSITT.
Ida	Miss NEWTON.

Act I.—AT DIGBY GRANT'S HOUSE.

Act II.—AT WYATT'S LODGINGS.

Act III.—AT D. GRANT DE CHAPERON'S VILLA.

ACT I.

SCENE.—*Room in* GRANT'S *cottage. Window at back, with rose trees shewing on each side; door in flat,* L; *fireplace,* R.; *door,* R.I.E.; *piano,* L. *On the walls framed needlework. Brick floor, with cocoanut matting. Chess table; sewing machine, &c. Everything homely but tasteful.*

GRANT *discovered with a letter and an empty glass on table. He is a tall, well-made man about 48 years old. Hair, somewhat thin at top, brushed straight from back into a bad curl on each side; whiskers bushy, brushed over the finger into a straight curl from top to chin on each side; straight or slightly curved eyebrows sloping down thus* ⌒ ; *large forehead running up at sides; rosy; comedy; well though somewhat shabbily dressed.*

GRANT. *(reading letter)* "Our Mr. Jenkins will have the pleasure of waiting on Mr. Digby Grant, &c., &c., when the favour of his...&c., &c. Skinner, Fox and Eaton," I'm very glad he's coming; the samples, as he calls them, that he leaves here are very useful. *(knocking. Enter* Mrs. Cups) Ah, Mrs. Cups, how do you do?

Mrs. C. *(stiffly)* I'm very well, I thank you.

GRANT. And the "Hen and 'Toothpick" prospers?

Mrs. C. Oh, yes!

GRANT. *(blandly)* That's well.

Mrs. C. *(L. of C. table)* I've called for my little bill, Mr. Grant.

GRANT. *(taking bill, file)* I'm glad to hear it. I was afraid you'd called for the money.

(takes bill off file and hands it politely)

---

7. *Two Roses, from French's Acting Editions.*

THE LEAGUE OF YOUTH.

Characters.

CHAMBERLAIN BRATSBERG [1] (owner of iron-works).
ERIK BRATSBERG (his son, a merchant).
THORA (his daughter).
SELMA (Erik's wife).
DOCTOR FIELDBO (physician at the Chamberlain's works).
STENSGÅRD [2] (a lawyer).
MONSEN (a landowner, of Stonelee) [3]
BASTIAN MONSEN (his son).
RAGNA (his daughter).
HELLE (student of theology, tutor at Stonelee).
RINGDAL (manager of the iron-works).
ANDERS LUNDESTAD (a wealthy farmer).
DANIEL HEIRE. [4]
MADAM [5] RUNDHOLMEN (widow of a storekeeper and publican).
ASLAKSEN (a printer).
A MAID-SERVANT AT THE CHAMBERLAIN'S.
A WAITER.
A WAITRESS AT MADAM RUNDHOLMEN'S.
Townspeople, Guests at the Chamberlain's, etc., etc.

[The action takes place in the neighbourhood of the iron-works, not far from a commercial town in Southern Norway.]

[1] "Chamberlain" (Kammerherre) is a title conferred by the King of Norway upon men of wealth and position. Hereditary nobility was abolished in 1821.
[2] Pronounce Stexngore.
[3] Heire (pronounce Heïré)—Heron.
[4] In the original "Skott."
[5] Married women and widows of the lower middle-class are addressed as Madam in Norway.

Act First.

(The Seventeenth of May. [1] A popular fête in the Chamberlain's grounds. Music and dancing in the background. Coloured lights among the trees. In the middle, somewhat towards the back, a rostrum; to the right, the entrance to a large refreshment tent; before it a table with benches. In the foreground, on the left, another table, decorated with flowers and surrounded with lounging chairs.)

(A Crowd of People. LUNDESTAD, with a committee-badge at his button-hole, stands on the rostrum. RINGDAL, also with a committee-badge, at the table on the left.)

LUNDESTAD.—Therefore, friends and fellow-citizens, I drink to our freedom! As we received it from our fathers, so will we preserve it for ourselves and for our children! Three cheers for the day! Three cheers for the Seventeenth of May!

THE CROWD. Hurrah! hurrah! hurrah!

RINGDAL (as LUNDESTAD descends from the rostrum). And one in for old Lundestad!

SOME VOICES. Hiss! hiss!

MANY VOICES (drowning the others). Hurrah for Lundestad! Long live old Lundestad! Hurrah! Hurrah!

[1] The Norwegian "Independence Day."

8. The League of Youth, 1904.

dressed, and clean-shaven except for a moustache, with an eager, susceptible face and very amiable and considerate manners. He has silky black hair, with waves of grey and white in it. His eyebrows are white, his moustache black. He seems not certain of his way. He looks over the paling; takes stock of the place; and sees the young lady.

THE GENTLEMAN [taking off his hat] I beg your pardon. Can you direct me to Hindhead View — Mrs Alison's?

THE YOUNG LADY [glancing up from her book] This is Mrs Alison's. [She resumes her work.]

THE GENTLEMAN. Indeed! Perhaps — may I ask are you Miss Vivie Warren?

THE YOUNG LADY [sharply, as she turns on her elbow to get a good look at him] Yes.

THE GENTLEMAN [daunted and conciliatory] I'm afraid I appear intrusive. My name is Praed. [Vivie at once throws her books upon the chair, and gets out of the hammock.] Oh, pray dont let me disturb you.

VIVIE [striding to the gate and opening it for him] Come in, Mr Praed. [He comes in]. Glad to see you. [She proffers her hand and takes his with a resolute and hearty grip. She is an attractive specimen of the sensible, able, highly-educated young middle-class Englishwoman. Age 22. Prompt, strong, confident, self-possessed. Plain, business-like dress, but not dowdy. She wears a chatelaine at her belt, with a fountain pen and a paper knife among its pendants].

PRAED. Very kind of you indeed, Miss Warren. [She shuts the gate with a vigorous slam: he pauses in the middle of the garden, exercising his fingers, which are slightly numbed by her greeting]. Has your mother arrived?

VIVIE [quickly, evidently scenting aggression] Is she coming?

PRAED [surprised] Didnt you expect us?

VIVIE. No.

PRAED. Now, goodness me, I hope Ive not mistaken the day. That would be just like me, you know. Your

mother arranged that she was to come down from London and that I was to come over from Horsham to be introduced to you.

VIVIE [not at all pleased] Did she? Hm! My mother has rather a trick of taking me by surprise — to see how I behave myself when she's away, I suppose. I fancy I shall take my mother very much by surprise one of these days, if she makes arrangemunts that concern me without consulting me beforehand. She hasnt come.

PRAED [embarrassed] I'm really very sorry.

VIVIE [throwing off her displeasure] It's not your fault, Mr Praed, is it? And I'm very glad youve come, believe me. You are the only one of my mother's friends I have asked her to bring to see me.

PRAED [relieved and delighted] Oh, now this is really very good of you, Miss Warren!

VIVIE. Will you come indoors; or would you rather sit out here whilst we talk?

PRAED. It will be nicer out here, dont you think?

VIVIE. Then I'll go and get you a chair. [She goes to the porch for a garden chair].

PRAED [following her] Oh, pray, pray! Allow me. [He lays hands on the chair].

VIVIE [letting him take it] Take care of your fingers; theyre rather dodgy things, those chairs. [She goes across to the chair with the books on it: pitches them into the hammock; and brings the chair forward with one sweep].

PRAED [who has just unfolded his chair] Oh, now do let me take that hard chair! I like hard chairs.

VIVIE. So do I. [She sits down]. Sit down, Mr Praed. [This invitation she gives with genial peremptoriness, his anxiety to please her clearly striking her as a sign of weakness of character on his part].

PRAED. By the way, though, hadnt we better go to the station to meet your mother?

VIVIE [coolly] Why? She knows the way. [Praed hesitates, and then sits down in the garden chair, rather discom-

9. Mrs Warren's Profession.

Shaw and Richards achieved, as Katherine E. Kelly argues, "the distinctive look of a mid-priced 'book,' printed reverently in accord with revisionist bookmaking conventions," though adapted to conform to the modern sensibilities of a mass audience, and "lengthened and decorated by prefaces, conclusions, production photographs, and stage directions, and priced to sell to a growing market of book-buying consumers" ("Imprinting" 50). Shaw remained in the forefront of innovation, not only supervising two complete editions of his works, but being involved – through Allen Lane, Chairman of Bodley Head, and also the founder of Penguin books – in the initial stages of mass-market paperback publication. Michael Holroyd notes that one of Lane's riskiest gambles for Penguin was publishing the "Shaw Million" – bringing out ten of Shaw's plays, in editions of 100,000 copies, simultaneously (Holroyd, *Bernard Shaw* III: 374).

"Write nothing in a play that you would not write in a novel; and remember that everything that the actor or the scene-painter *shows* to the audience must be described – not technically specified, but imaginatively, vividly, humorously, in a word, artistically described – to the reader by the author."[10] We tend to think that it's this novelistic character that marks the decisive relationship between print and theatre at the turn of the last century. In part as the result of (moral and legal) censorship, Shaw, Ibsen, and many others wrote for a reading audience, and designed their plays in such a way as to appeal to them. In so doing they incarnated the dominance of the book form of the play over its theatrical representation, confirming a sense of the performed play as an after-effect to its literary, book-bound being. We should recognize, though, how uninfluential Shaw's printing practices were. Shaw's plays are very dense on the page: if one were looking for a way to save paper, Shaw provides it, without having to sacrifice the literary pretension to making fine books. Yet trade publishers have rarely followed Shaw's lead. Play publication has much more often tended either to follow Pinero's plan (centered speech prefixes), or Archer's (large type prefixes, leading the line to justify), or a third model (indenting the speech, rather than the speech prefix, so that the left hand margin consists of prefixes – this is incidentally the model followed in the Penguin paperback editions of Shaw's plays.) All of these alternatives put fewer lines of dialogue on the page, while also marking the movement from speaker to speaker much more visibly, emphasizing the dialogic character of drama as a feature of design and perhaps even in the experience of reading. Shaw's plays take the page as large rectangles of type: they are "novelistic" in their descriptive perspective on the dramatic action, in their physical appearance as type, and perhaps also in their phenomenal apprehension as well.

Moreover, Shaw deployed this novel-like design alongside another strategy for materializing the drama on the page, one he again applied with customary thoroughness: Shaw's stage directions describe the play from the perspective of the reader-as-spectator. Shaw's plays occupy the play much as novels do, as a single block of type, the white page blackened margin to margin. Even their ways of noting speakers (prefixes) and action (stage directions) are subordinate to the act of staging a block of writing, a text unbroken by the white space that might otherwise signal the intrusive temporality of the stage. Shaw is not a man of half-measures. Addressing his stage directions not to production but to consumption, Shaw "directs" the reader to visualize the scene by looking left and right, attending to the hill rising into the distant background and to the bicycle in the foreground (see figure 1). The play opens with a long narrative, but its perspective is hardly omniscient. Shaw insistently situates his reader within the relations of visibility characteristic of his stage, in the perspective of the realistic theatre. And yet the experience of reading a page of Shaw is anything but theatrical, as the page design subordinates the signals of the play's theatrical working, and even the implied spacing of theatrical *duration*, to the assimilation of the play's fictional narrative. Shaw's contemporaries also laminate the theatrical to the narrative elements of the play's design, but the alternation of theatrical and narrative perspectives in the stage directions and the dialogue-oriented layout of the page also trouble the assimilation of the drama to narrative, and constantly foreground the absence of that other scene, the stage, from the page. Shaw's page materializes the play as complete in its reading: reading line to line, margin to margin, the reader enacts the pace of the play.

Shaw's plays energetically avail themselves of the rhetoric of the book. The individualized Author is everywhere in view, from the title page to the extensive prefaces to the idiosyncratic tone with which the stage directions address the reader.[11] Recalling Lukas Erne's sense of Shakespeare as a "literary dramatist," even the unplayable length of, say, *Man and Superman* or *Back to Methuselah* might be a sign of the drama's absorption by the book, and Erne's notion that the apparently "theatrical" signals of stage directions might point to Shakespeare's intentions as a "literary" dramatist apply with evident force to Shaw (*Shakespeare as Literary Dramatist* 222–25). Shaw's descriptive stage directions in *Mrs Warren's Profession* set the play before us without allusion to the stage. Much like the naturalistic theatre itself, Shaw works to render the wheels and pulleys, the flats and batting of the theatrical scene invisible behind or within the illusion they sustain. In many respects this sense of the page also extends to more theatrically oriented elements of Shaw's writing. Shaw excludes "theatrical" discourse from his narrative directions to enable the reader to seize the play undistracted by the signs and signals of its other life.

But a play's language doesn't only live in the mind's eye, it also lives in the ear and on the tongue. Shaw's consistently rhetorical use of punctuation – using punctuation to mark the rhythms of speech rather than the logic of syntax – and his celebrated use of dialect ("Wot prawce selvytion nah?" in *Major Barbara* [107]) might well be read as traces of the stage, or as places where Shaw uses the accessories of the page actually to *direct* the performance. The tension between rhetorical and syntactic pointing is one of the distinctive features of printed drama: punctuation is one of the places where the text's representation of the dramatic fiction joins its implication of performance, its ways of specifying action onstage. But while Shakespeare's or Molière's punctuation, like that of many contemporary playwrights, may work rhetorically to "indicate delivery, not to conform to the rules of grammar" as Sarah Kane puts it (*Complete Plays* 2), Shaw's use of dialect and punctuation is also consistent with his bookish designs on the drama. While dialect and rhetorical punctuation usually point to the play's work on the stage, speaking is how Shaw's characters enact themselves morally and ethically: the sound, shape, and rhythm of speech is, for Shaw, essential to the composition and interpretation of dramatic character. As a director, Shaw was known to score his actors, musically annotating their scripts. But in an important sense, the music is already in Shaw's script. Bill Walker's dialect is, perhaps by design, considerably harder for readers to grasp by eye than for theatre spectators to get by ear. Much as Shaw puts his readers *in* the play by frequently refusing to name characters before they speak onpage, so, too, this kind of naturalism extends to the auditory texture of the play – Bill Walker's cockney forcibly strikes the eye before we can make sense of it. Shaw's rhetorical pointing scores the rhythm and emphasis of printed language in ways that bring the music of the play to book (we might remember that William Archer described seeing Shaw for the first time in the British Library with a copy of Marx at one elbow and a Wagner score at the other – he wasn't listening to headphones). "Well, if youve been waiting, Praddy, it's your own fault: I thought youd have had the gumption to know I was coming by the 3.10 train. Vivie: put on your hat dear: youll get sunburnt. Oh, I forgot to introduce you. Sir George

Crofts: my little Vivie" (*Mrs Warren's Profession* 167). Eliminating casual apostrophes, commas, and periods, Shaw's punctuation brings the effusive logic of Mrs Warren vividly to the page. The points at once embody the character's energy, and her energetic ability to direct the action (and our attention), and so become part of the reader's play. Katherine E. Kelly aptly notes the "performative print style" of Shaw's early plays, but what the plays perform is their bookishness ("Imprinting" 42). The accessories of the page absorb the theatrical drama to the canons of print.

By the end of the nineteenth century, print had achieved a material and ideological dominance over most forms of publication (to protect performance rights, playwrights still had to stage clandestine "copyright performances," morning "public" productions announced only by a single bill, at an absurdly high price, to a well-documented little audience, with a cast usually consisting of the author and friends).[12] Shaw's plays document the ways the accessories of the page can be used to represent the drama: the setting and even the texture of performance are absorbed by how the play is done into print. The accessories of print are deployed so completely in the service of objectifying the fictional drama that the signs of the theatre are very nearly erased. Given the power of print in securing the literary identity of writing, we might expect that Shaw's strategies for occupying the page would be pervasive today, but the pages of contemporary plays have little in common with Shaw's: the white space that Shaw struggled to blacken is, in a sense, constitutive of the action of contemporary drama. Perhaps people today are just not as voluble or as elegant as Hector Hushabye or Jack Tanner or even Eliza Doolittle. Yet while our ways of representing dramatic action have changed, our sense of the mise-en-page has also changed. The page of contemporary drama enacts considerably more anxiety about the possibility of booking the drama than Shaw's pages do. Moreover, between, say, Shaw's pages and Sarah Kane's stands a remapping of the geography of the page. To understand this emerging landscape, though, we have to resist being seduced by dramatic style: the real inheritor of Shaw's absorption of the theatrical into the literary drama is Gertrude Stein.

II. SO MUCH DEPENDS: STEIN'S THEATRE OF THE PAGE

Shaw's Fabian comedies often seem to stand apart from the formal innovations of modernist literature, and to stand apart, too, from the experiments of avant-garde theatre and drama. For all its prescience, *Heartbreak House* is a far cry from *Ubu Roi*, from Meyerhold's biomechanics, from the dada cabaret, even from the delicate inquiry of Yeats's plays for dancers. Nonetheless, Shaw's strategies for objectifying the drama through the accessories of the page stake out one extreme of modern drama's ongoing confrontation with print: the desire to articulate the drama's resistance to the theatre by absorbing the performance into the book. Like Shaw, Yeats, and Beckett, many of the signal playwrights of the English modernist tradition were fully engaged by the stage, but as Martin Puchner has argued, a deeply antitheatrical "stage fright" nonetheless defines modern drama's implication in the theatre. Shaw's absorption of performance to the accessories of print inaugurates, but hardly resolves, the ways modern drama takes the page.

In many respects, the geography of the page – the semantic value of the accessories of print – was most richly explored by modern poetry and poetics. The poetic revolution of the first decades of the twentieth century was undertaken by a generation of writers who conceived their work within the forms of mechanical reproducibility. As the imagists, vorticists, futurists, dadaists, and others recognized, the page could render the text as a visual icon, a different materialization of the text that might prompt materially different acts of reading, might even prompt kinds of reading – as Susan Howe's poems do today – that don't always feel like reading if what we mean by reading is the ability to see distinct, legible, words on the page, and confidently to assemble them in a speakable series.[13] The various uses of capital letters and foreign scripts typical in Ezra Pound's poems is one measure of this tendency; composing on the typewriter is another. Reading T. S. Eliot's manuscript of the poem that became *The Waste Land*, Pound responded to some sections written in longhand, but generally preferred to edit from typescript: "Bad – but cant attack until I get typescript" he wrote over the first draft of "Death by Water" (Eliot, *The Waste Land* 55). James Joyce's *Ulysses* is unimaginable without typographic play – the headlines in "Aeolus," the centered speech prefixes of "Circe" (where the dramatic status of the episode is emphasized by the intrusive, centered speech prefixes, as opposed to the more novelistic blocks of type used in Bernard Shaw's plays), the famous blot at the end of the "Ithaca" chapter. As Jerome McGann argues, implicitly relating Shaw's designs for *Plays: Pleasant and Unpleasant* to the work of a younger generation of poets, a sensitivity to the "visible language of modernism" – print on the page – is the lasting inheritance of William Morris, who "worked to integrate the poem and its performative medium not by seeking a return to oral traditions of production, but by acknowledging the compositional environment as a necessary condition for the creation of modern poetry" (*Black Riders* 46).

The Red Wheelbarrow

so much depends
upon

a red wheel
barrow

glazed with rain
water

beside the white
chickens.

David Antin's talk poems take the page as a means of signifying "speech"; the design of the poem, its ways of occupying the white field of print, and so of transforming that empty space into a field of meaning is one of the achievements of modernist poetics, readily visible even in terse classics like William Carlos Williams's "The Red Wheelbarrow" (*Collected Earlier Poems* 277).[14] In the poem's sixteen words, "so much depends" on how we move from line to line, hanging on the poet's mastery of rhythm and image to give us, finally, something to rest "upon" . . . a mild irony in the poem, in that the word "upon" provides only a momentary rest before we slip into space again toward that part-object, the "red wheel," landing finally on "barrow." So like Williams, so pedestrian, an everyday thing in the workaday world. It seems so solid, that we hardly notice how little realized it is (what color red? wood or metal? large or small? dirty or clean?) until, after a pause (here, the syntax doesn't force us to move on, we have to choose to take action), it's changed (though not in a way that answers any of those questions) by the most unexpected, modestly metaphorical, "poetic" word in the poem, *glazed*, a word which, alongside the whiteness of the chickens (still to come), seems, somehow, without actually putting it into words, to evoke the indelible redness of the red wheelbarrow, upon which so much finally depends. e. e. cummings's "Grasshopper" emblematizes this drive toward iconicity, but Williams is less interested in mimicry than in the poetics of *printed* language, "the *form* into which Williams molds his material, not the material itself," as Henry Sayre puts it (*Visual Text* 65). Later in life, surviving strokes that broke his speech and paralyzed his right arm, Williams composed on the typewriter, guiding his right hand with his left, indenting new lines three spaces, more easily to find them. Williams's famous "three-ply line" is integral to the movement of his later poems, embodying and memorializing the act of writing, white space signaling, and perhaps enacting, forcing us to enact, a kind of duration, suspension, translating Williams's struggle to compose into the force of poetic motion itself.[15] This is nothing new in Williams: the earlier poems dramatize the deft use of print to materialize the movement of language, and to render the space between the words significant, part of poetic *composition*, so to speak.

Free verse at first seems to resist the print traditions of poetry, stanzas disheveling into mere words scattered across the page. Yet, as Marjorie Perloff suggests, free verse is far from free. In its "variability (both of stress and of syllable count) and its avoidance of obtrusive patterns of recurrence," it "tracks the speaking voice"; it's organized by concrete images that provide objective correlatives to the "inner states of mind" of the speaker; while speech-based, it tends toward complete sentences; it has a basically linear, continuous *flow*; its language "depends upon the unobtrusiveness of sound structure in free verse, as if to say that what is said must not be obscured by the actual saying" (as she notes, Gerard Manley Hopkins's verse is the antithesis of the free-verse ideal) ("After Free Verse" 94–95). While Tennyson and Browning and Arnold found the expression of a coherent subject consistent with the regularity of formal, metrical, printed verse forms, modernist free verse breaks less with the purpose of their poetics (expressing a subject) than with the object and vehicle of poetic representation: a more fragmentary and discontinuous subject, registered in a somewhat more relaxed and informal verse. Perloff suggests (reading Henri Meschonnic's magisterial *Critique du rythme*) that "Blank spaces [. . .] would become just as important as the words themselves" in modernist verse, not only within the structure of free verse writing like Williams's, but more fundamentally in the visual experiments of the futurists, and in the page-oriented work of a number of living poets. Modern verse is part of a thoroughgoing "revolution that bred what Meschonnic calls the 'theatre of the page'" ("After Free Verse" 89–90).

It has become conventional, following Fredric Jameson, to describe the postmodern's relation to the modern in spatial terms, as "today dominated by categories of space rather than by categories of time, as in the preceding period of high modernism" (*Postmodernism* 16). But sometimes what may at first seem a rupture or transformation may also seem a continuity: modernist poetics drives the temporality of poetic discourse with the spatializing engine of type, and its beguiling absence from the printed page.

Learning to read, at least learning to read in what Michael Joyce calls the "late age of print," involves learning to read spatially, to account for the rhetoric of typographic space (*Othermindedness* 3). This strategy is visible

in modernist print, and sustains the rhetoricity of the computer screen
and of print-emulating hypertextual writing. It involves learning specific
kinds of reading strategies, even learning to negotiate now-familiar events,
such as punctuation. For as Jerome McGann suggests, punctuation marks
retain a dual function: "We want to recall that this highly evolved set of
marks represent signs that were originally introduced as notations both
for oral articulation and syntactic differentiation, and that they function
in both registers to this day. As a set of oral cues – whether in silent or
articulated reading – punctuation is a foundational element in the affective
(as opposed to the conceptual) ordering of the poem. As a set of syntactic
cues it is also a signifying system foregrounding dominant sets of conceptual relations in the text" (*Radiant Textuality* 156). There are important
distinctions to observe here between the conventions of printed drama and
modernist experiments with the poetics of print. The typographical play of
modernist poetry is often designed to slow reading, to isolate and materialize "language" as an object, to trouble the transparency of the page, even
to prevent the direct assimilation of written language to performance, to
speech. To this extent, the materiality of modern poetry poses problems
for the poetics of performance, at least to the extent that we believe that
a play in print should be designed for ready assimilation to the conventional practices of theatre. As Michael Goldman suggests, "Memorizing
a part is actually a means of freeing oneself from its mere textuality"
(*On Drama* 52).

We will return to the problems of the materiality of poetic language
and its performance in the next chapter. Here, it's important to recognize
that the practices of reading that now seem obligatory for modern poems
could not be created by poems alone. The dialectical interplay between
the structure of the text and the changing practices of its use is readily
observed in the evolution of interpretive practices now seen as not merely
legitimate, but as essential to reading the work of, say, Pound, or Eliot,
or Joyce. It's striking to note a parallel in the history of modern performance, the bafflement not of audiences (they were baffled) but of actors
and directors over what to *do* with plays like *The Master Builder* or *The
Seagull* or *Waiting for Godot*. We don't often take this to be a reading
problem, but it is. How can *we* read this text as theatrically *producible*?
What is it telling us to *do*? How can we apply what we know how to do
to it, in order to make it into a recognizably, effectively theatrical event?
McGann draws an analogy between the "alienation" implied by poetry's
foregrounding of typography and Brecht's similar efforts to alienate theatrical conventions (see McGann, *Black Riders* 168–70). Attending to the

material form of plays in print may also provide a means to "alienate," and so to observe, other aspects of our understanding of dramatic performance, the interplay between the text and the naturalized strategies of its production onstage. Modernist poetry is one of the things that stands between us and the novelistic, even bookish plays of Ibsen and Shaw: it's one of the things that makes Shaw's elegant volumes, to say nothing of the plays they contain, look old-fashioned, positively Victorian in their earnest effort to conquer the page, to expand the imperious, rational eloquence of (Irish?) English to the very margins of discursive space. I want to begin by troubling a common distinction between the printform of modern poetry and that of modern plays: that the typographic "surface" of modern poetry is designed to slow reading, to force attention to the process and materials of the poem, while the accessory typography of modern plays is designed to speed reading, both to objectify the drama as literature and to instrumentalize the play as theatre, so that it can be readily digested for performance. This alimentary sense of drama naturalizes the practices of theatrical reading, and has other implications, too. It implies that modern dramatic writing, unlike other artforms of the modern era, naturalizes rather than foregrounds the materiality of its materials: paint, stone, metal, sound, bodies, words, silence. Shaw used the page to absorb and so to suppress the stage, but when drama participates in this modernist tradition, it typically renders its *theatrical* (rather than its *textual*) materials opaque: think of plays like *Six Characters in Search of an Author* or *The Measures Taken* or *Play*, to say nothing of the immaculate challenge to textuality characteristic of dada, of Artaud, or – in a significantly more compromised way – of performance art. Shaw's plays work to assimilate theatrical play to the page, but most printed drama retains the theatrical complexion of the drama's accessories: *stage* directions seem to direct *stage* action. But Shaw's arrogation of the page to the voice of the author also participates in the sense of the page explored by modernist poetics, which also claims the entire space of the page as the field of authorized writing. While few successful playwrights have so thoroughly followed Shaw's programmatic absorption of the stage, modern drama in print typically frames a dialectical tension between the proprieties of the page and the identities of drama.

If "The Red Wheelbarrow" exemplifies modernist poetry's resignification of the page, Gertrude Stein's plays openly challenge the conventional ways that plays take the page in the age of print. From the outset, Stein's plays addressed, engaged, and troubled the design of printed drama as cognate with dramatic form, as a register of "the play," and so also troubled the ways the space of the page at once implicates and resists the rhetoric of modern performance. Stein insisted that she imagined her writing as a design for performance; as she wrote to Mabel Dodge in 1913, "I do *not* want the plays published. They are to be kept to be *played*."[16] Much as Stein insisted on the theatrical playability of her plays, though, her writing determinedly refuses to "objectify" the drama, to use the "accessories" of the page either to frame the fictive world of the play or to direct how the drama is to be done into theatre. Shaw saw the entire page as the register of authorial agency (type design and layout, the assertively Shavian address of stage directions, the novelized block of type on the page). Stein refuses to distinguish between the registers of the dramatic and the theatrical. Yet while Shaw translates theatrical performance into the narrative fiction of the play, subordinating theatrical discourse to the perspective of a spectatorial novel, Stein openly foregrounds this theatrical discourse. In her plays, the accessories of the printed drama are folded into the poetics of "the play."

Throughout her career, Stein was preoccupied by how plays take the page, and her strategies for enacting this preoccupation remained remarkably consistent. Stein worked to break down the distinction between the drama and its accessories: on Stein's page, it's all *play*. *What Happened*, subtitled *A Five Act Play*, seems to have five – what? readers? speakers? characters? actors? – signaled by the parenthetical prefixes Stein used in her early plays.

ACT ONE

> (One.)
> Loud and no cataract. Not any nuisance is
> depressing.
> (Five.)
> A single sum four and five together and one, not
> any sun a clear signal and an exchange.
> (*Geography and Plays* 205)

Sidestepping the prose itself, with its clear resistance to a sense of dialogic encounter and an increasing emphasis on diegetic narration ("A tiger a rapt and surrounded overcoat securely arranged with spots old enough to be thought useful and witty quite witty in a secret and in a blinding flurry"), Stein's unique treatment of speech prefixes is itself hardly comforting. By the fourth act, speakers (One.) and (Five.) give way to "(Four and four more.)" (208). *White Wines* has "THREE ACTS" which seem to be headed

"1. All together. 2. Witnesses. 3. House to house. (5 women)," as though the play will be performed by five women who will speak "all together" at times, and separately as "witnesses" at other times. Yet, there are only four enumerated Witnesses in the "Single Witnesses" section of the play, though there is a – what? stage direction? narrative description? summons? – for "*More Witnesses*" at one point. Is "*House to house*" a stage direction or a description (*Geography and Plays* 210–14)? *For the Country Entirely* A PLAY IN LETTERS opens strikingly enough:

> Almond trees in the hill. We saw them to-day.
> Dear Mrs. Steele
>   I like to ask you questions. Do you believe that
> it is necessary to worship individuality. We do.
>   Mrs. Henry Watterson.
> Of course I have heard.
> Dear Sir. Of course I have heard.
> They didn't leave the book.
> Dear Sir.
>   They didn't leave the book.
> Yes Yes.
> I know what I hear. Yes sir.
> Dear Sir.
>   (*Geography and Plays* 227)

The deep indentation of Mrs. Henry Watterson's signature line suggests that her "letter" to Mrs. Steele is merely reproduced on the page. While it's possible to hear one "voice" in the letter beginning "Dear Mrs. Steele" and ending "Mrs. Henry Watterson," the design of the text makes the assignment of any number of voices possible here, even in the opening few seconds of the play. Who speaks the opening line? Do the several phrases beginning "Dear Sir" imply a single letter being started, started over, and started over again in a single voice? Does the line "Of course I have heard" belong to "Mrs. Henry Watterson?" The play seems relatively unconcerned, in other words, to assign "speech" to speakers, while enacting a playful obsession with marking the play's processual units. Succeeding sections of the play are headed Chapter 2., CHAPTER 3., *Act 2.*, *Act 3.*, SCENE 2., SCENE 3., *Scene 3.*, *Act 4. Scene 1.*, *Scene 2, Scene 3., Scene 4., Scene 5., Scene 6.*, SCENE 7., *Act 5. Scene 1., Scene 2., Scene 3., Scene 4* (see *Geography and Plays* 227–38). In *Turkey and Bones and Eating and We Liked It*, the page design seems to shift to different conventions, so that it's difficult to tell whether the centered headings – "Polybe and seats." and "Genevieve and cotton." and the like – are narrative markers or speech prefixes, or both: Polybe on

the subject of seats; Polybe (*on the subject of seats*); Polybe: on the subject
of seats.

A PLAY

He was very restless. He does not like to stand
while he picks flowers. He does not smell flowers. He
has a reasonable liking for herbs. He likes their smell.
He is not able to see storms. He can see anything
running. He has been able to be praised.

SCENE I.

Polybe and seats.
Straw seats which are so well made that they re-
semble stools. They are all of straw and thick. They are
made with two handles.
Genevieve and cotton.
I do not like cotton drawers. I prefer wool or linen.
I admit that linen is damp. Wool is warm. I believe I
prefer wool.

(*Geography and Plays* 239)

Even in the many plays like *Mexico*, which merely seem to lay out an
unmarked "conversation," it's not entirely clear how many agents the text
might imply:

Ernestine.
Have you mentioned tracing out California.
I have.
How big is it.
As big as a boat.
What boat.
The city of Savannah.

(*Geography and Plays* 304)

In this sense, the most innovative feature of Stein's drama is not the
dialogue, but the way Stein's writing folds the "accessories," the *didascalia*,
the conventional apparatus that enables the theatre to "objectify" the play
onstage into the play itself, though it might be more accurate to say that
Stein reframes the accessories *as* the play, as part of its verbal identity *as play*.
Stein's winsome approach to her speakers, who seem to dissolve into one
another and into the language they speak is complemented by her treatment
of the formal apparatus of plays as books: act and scene divisions. In *An
Exercise in Analysis*, there are no speech prefixes, only "Acts," which appear

at once to divide the play's action and to articulate its principal claim: "I have given up analysis."

A PLAY

I have given up analysis

ACT II

Splendid profit.

ACT III

I have paid my debt to humanity.

ACT III

Hurry.

(*Last Operas and Plays* 119)

Noting that "It is very strange but anyway there is a difference between act one" (*Last Operas and Plays* 338), *Byron A Play* suggests that the "Act" divisions mark less the narrative progression of a conventional drama than point to a series of "acts," moments in Stein's effort to mark the continuous present of her writing as a visible (theatrical?) *event*: "A play is when there is not only so but also" (336); "A play does not depend upon what not / It depends upon the way a day is made to stay" (337). The formal divisions of the printed play – and we might recall the difficulties that Shakespeare's plays have in maintaining these formalities – became for Stein ways of signifying something else, the events of the page. This reworking of the formalities of printed drama is the burden of the final moments of *Listen to Me*:

Acts
Curtain
Characters
Characters
Curtain
Acts
There is no one and one
Nobody has met any one

Curtain Can Come.
Curtain

(*Last Operas and Plays* 421)

Stein's absorbing obsession with the function of the accessories of printed drama echoes a modern concern for the ways print materializes the authorial, authorized play. For all the pawky pleasure of her plays, Stein's sense of the page of drama seems less to recall Random Cloud than W. W. Greg (nearly her exact contemporary; Stein was born in 1874 and Greg the following year). While Randall McLeod sees typeforms, speech prefixes and the like to mark the play's dispersal of "authorship" among the writing, theatrical, and printshop agents traced on the page, Stein's practice of collapsing the accessories into the drama evokes Greg's sense of the page as the record of the playwright's fundamentally literary conception of the play as a printed thing. For Greg, theatrical discourse is so fully subordinate to the identity of the dramatic writing that it can be altered without changing "the play"; for Stein, theatrical discourse is seamlessly (if sometimes confusingly) merged directly into the play itself.[17]

As Stein suggested in her essay "Plays," written in the mid-1930s, her playwriting can be understood as a flight from the inherent "syncopated time" of performance ("Plays" xxix), the "nervousness of the emotion at the theatre which has perhaps to do with the fact that the emotion of the person at the theatre is always behind and ahead of the scene at the theatre but not with it" (xxxv). Though she had grown up with the operas and melodramas of the San Francisco and Oakland theatre, moving to Paris she "forgot the theatre and almost forgot opera" (xliii); she did not, however, forget "the poetical plays [. . .] that I used so much to read" (xlii). For this reason, when she "all of a sudden [. . .] began to write Plays" (xliii), it's not surprising that Stein conceived of her plays as verbal objects, poems, and incorporated the textual syncopations of the apparatus of the stage *into* the poetry: "Poetry connected with a play was livelier poetry than poetry unconnected with a play. [. . .] In the poetry of plays words are more lively words than in any other kind of poetry and if one naturally liked lively words and I naturally did one likes to read plays in poetry" (xxxix). And to write them.

Stein's conception of "the play" is fundamentally poetic in this sense. Like Yeats and Beckett, and in much the way Greg imagined Shakespeare, Stein sees the page as a unified field of writing, where ink and white space, dialogue and its accessories all identify – and are identified with – the play. This tendency is pronounced even in those plays that have had a regular, if modest, life on the stage, such as *Doctor Faustus Lights the Lights*.[18] The play seems to deploy its "accessories" more or less conventionally at the outset, establishing setting and assigning roles to different speakers, and even identifying the speakers as "characters":

ACT I

Faust standing at the door of his room, with his arms up at
the door lintel looking out, behind him a blaze of electric light.
Just then Mephisto approaches and appears at the door.

Faustus growls out. –	The devil what the devil what do I care if the devil is there.
Mephisto says.	But Doctor Faustus dear yes I am here.
Doctor Faustus.	What do I care there is no here nor there.
	(*Last Operas and Plays* 89)

Hardly a drawing room comedy, in its ways of taking the page, *Doctor Faustus Lights the Lights* nonetheless recalls Shaw. The directions are written in an idiomatic, "authorial" address to the reader, the text marks its theatrical apparatus as distinct from the dialogue, and in its frequent irruption of the diegetic into the dialogue ("The dog says," "The boy says") the text perhaps even novelizes the play from a spectator's perspective. This protocol, however, begins to deteriorate almost immediately.

> Faustus gives him an awful kick, and Mephisto moves away
> and the electric lights thus then begin to get very gay.
> Alright then. (91)

"Alright then?" As in her earliest plays, Stein is attracted by the notion of unassigned language; the phrase seems to belong neither to Faustus nor to Mephisto. Indeed, it seems not so much to operate within the temporality of the play at all, but to mark instead something like "authorial time," representing the temporality of composition in accord with the temporality of reading.

This direction is followed by "The Ballet" – in which dancing is not otherwise indicated – and then by "Doctor Faustus' song."

> Doctor Faustus' song:

If I do it
If you do it
What is it.
    Once again the dog says
Thank you.
    A duet between doctor Faustus and the dog about the electric
    light about the electric lights.
Bathe me
    says Doctor Faustus
Bathe me
In the electric lights
    During this time the electric lights come and go
What is it
    says Doctor Faustus
Thank you
    says the dog.
    Just at this moment the electric lights get brighter and nothing
    comes
Was it it
    says Doctor Faustus
    Faustus meditates he does not see the dog.
Will it
Will it

Will it be
Will it be it.
   Faustus sighs and repeats
Will it be it.
   A duet between the dog and Faustus
Will it be it
Just it. (92)

What's striking, first, about the "song" is that it's hard to know where it begins, or whether it begins at all. Does the song start with the words "If I do it"? Or after the "direction," beginning "A duet between Doctor Faustus and the dog"? When Faustus "meditates" without seeing the dog, is he meditating in song? Does the dog sing (or speak, or bark) after lines like "Once again the dog says" or only when he is described as having a "duet" with Faustus? Do they sing in unison or alternate lines? Or is this duet a spoken duet, the song only beginning after

   A little boy comes in and plays with the dog, the dog says
Thank you.
   Doctor Faustus looks away from the electric lights and then he
   sings a song.

Let me Alone

Let me alone
Oh let me alone
Dog and boy let me alone oh let me alone
Leave me alone
Let me be alone
little boy and dog
let let me alone
   He sighs
   And as he sighs
   He says
Dog and boy boy and dog leave me alone let me let me be alone.
   The dog says
Thank you
   but does not look at Faustus
   A pause
   No words
   The dog says
Thank you (92–93)

Shaw absorbed the stage to the page by narrating the play from a spectatorial perspective that seems to obviate performance. Stein also absorbs the play to the page, but urges a dissonance between "theatrical" discourse and the drama it inhabits. The mise-en-page *is* the site of play:

> The electric lights commence to dance and one by one they go
>   out and come in and the boy and the dog begin to sing.
> Oh very well oh Doctor Faustus very very well oh very well, thank
> you says the dog oh very well says the boy her name her name is
> Marguerite Ida and Helena Annabel, I know says the dog I know
> says the boy I know says Doctor Faustus no no no no no nobody
> can know what I know I know her name is not Marguerite Ida
> and Helena Annabel, very well says the boy it is says the boy her
> name is Marguerite Ida and Helena Annabel, no no no says Doctor
> Faustus, yes yes yes says the dog. (94–95)

The boy and the dog begin to sing, but what do they sing? Do they sing the phrases "says the dog" or "says the boy" (and why isn't it "sings the dog" and "sings the boy"?)? Does the boy report "I know says Doctor Faustus" as indirect discourse, or has the duet developed into a trio? Much as in her earliest plays, Stein's verbal repetitions create the effect of duration, of the "continuous present," by prolonging or even deferring the beginning of action. Yet absorbing the accessories into the action makes the text a surprisingly ineffectual vehicle for "objectifying" the play as narrative and especially on the stage. If there is a play here, that play takes place on the page, and provides at best confusing and inconsistent information about what we might or should *do* with this script. For all the text's emphasis on the authorial control of the mise-en-page, and even of the process of reading ("Alright then"), Stein's script enacts a paradoxical negligence of performance, the sense that she has just altogether suspended the stage.

The mise-en-page stages the play in ways that summon the signs of theatre while simultaneously exhausting their theatrical functionality. Perhaps it's not surprising that Stein's plays have yet to be fully digested either as literature or as theatre. While James R. Mellow introduces the 1998 reprint of *Operas & Plays* by describing Stein's "odd word plays" as "theatrical exercises" that "for all their avantgardism [. . .] often turn out to be parlor dramas," he nonetheless locates them in the principal tradition of modern drama: "Well before Beckett or Pinter, Stein immobilized her characters in talk, talk, talk" ("Foreword" 7–9). Taking the most extreme position, Jane Palatini Bowers argues, "Stein's plays oppose the physicality of performance. Stein's is a theater of language: her plays are adamantly and self-consciously 'literary'" (*They Watch Me as They Watch This* 2). For Bowers, "language" is always "Overwhelmed, transformed, subordinated, menaced, and dissolved" in the theatre (7); as she quite rightly notes, performance necessarily transforms "language," which Bowers understands as the written word, into something else, into speech, behavior, action, *performance* (though we might wonder, with Walter Ong, whether language has this fixity in oral culture, or even in the "secondary orality" of the theatre).[19] While Bowers distinguishes Stein's plays from the work of other modern playwrights, even from those similarly committed to the identity of the text, like Beckett, Martin Puchner more helpfully sees Stein's writing as part of the dominant tradition of modernist drama, enacting as it does "the high modernist values of engulfment and solitary reading, an aesthetics that is directly opposed to the distracting and interruptive nature of the theater as it was systematically celebrated by the avant-garde. Stein's understanding of the work of art and, in particular, her suspicion of the theater put her in the company of Mallarmé, and not of Tristan Tzara" (*Stage Fright* 103).[20]

Stein's hermetic plays also, paradoxically, illuminate the relatively limited force of the text in theatrical production. While Stein's plays define the play as a page- rather than as a stage-event, they have had an important, if marginal, role in the history of modern performance. *Four Saints in Three Acts* and *The Mother of Us All* have, in part through the work of Virgil Thomson, become staples of the modern repertory, and of course Stein's plays have played a foundational role in the American avant-garde, notably for The Living Theatre (which began its career with a production of *Doctor Faustus Lights the Lights*), for the Judson Poets' Theatre, and for Richard Foreman and the Ontological-Hysteric Theatre; they are also regularly performed on college campuses.[21] Yet the textually recondite element of Stein's plays gives even her most ardent defenders some pause. To Richard Howard, Stein is "one of the founders of modern theater, and in America she is one of the three great instigators of that theater," alongside Mae West and Martha Graham. Yet at the same time Howard notes that the "plays are never successful when they are not presented with music. [. . .] There was never a failed musical Stein. Only Stein's plays as plays don't work." For Mac Wellman, too, Stein is "a profound theatrical force," who is "completely ignored," perhaps for reasons suggested by Charles Bernstein: "The play of which Stein speaks has to do with the ethics of reading that her work embodies, which insists that to read we have to perform," to perform *as readers*.[22]

Stein's work is "the purest attempt to call attention to the theater experience which has ever existed" (Richard Howard, "*Operas and Plays*" 128); nonetheless, it has had little impact in the theatre, and its most effective,

even celebrated, stagings have either required Virgil Thomson's sustaining music to succeed, or have been theatricalized by Bowers's "antagonistic avant-garde" for whom "the text is of minimal importance" (*"They
Watch Me as They Watch This"* 131). And yet Marvin Carlson is right to
note that a wide range of contemporary playwrights – he names Sam
Shepard, Adrienne Kennedy, Maria Irene Fornes, Richard Foreman, Eric
Overmeyer, Suzan-Lori Parks, Len Jenkin, and John Jesurun – "share
her indifference to traditional plots and character development," instead
exploring "the structures, sounds, and evocative possibilities of language
itself" ("After Stein" 147). What's at stake here is the ambivalence of
Stein's playful attitude toward the formalities of printed drama. Stein's
anxiety about the nervous syncopation of the theatre is enacted by her
plays' effort to create both an aural and a figural landscape, to arrest dramatic action in the "continuous present" of the reader's experience. This
aspect of Stein's writing is, I think, where her legacy among the theatrically
accomplished playwrights that Carlson lists is the most evident. It surely
underlies Fornes's astonishing and unpredictable *tirades*, and one might
be hard pressed to find a more explicit antecedent to Parks's dialogue in
The America Play than Daniel Webster's first lines in *The Mother of Us
All*, "He digged a pit, he digged it deep / he digged it for his brother, /
Into the pit he did fall in the pit / he digged for 'tother" (*Last Operas and
Plays* 53).

The challenges posed by Stein's plays are essentially the challenges posed
by dramatic writing in the age of print: how to discriminate the agency
of the author, how to mark (and limit) the agency of the theatre, how to
reimagine the play's mise-en-page either as a way to forestall theatricality or
as a means to imagining alternative performativities, even a performativity
solely of the page, where words "do things" only for readers.[23] Stein seems
most directly to infiltrate the dynamic of modern drama in the vexing
ways her plays take the page. Shaw's novelized printform transformed the
playtext from a dramatic to diegetic form. Blackening the page edge to
edge, Shaw insisted that readers enter the book as though they were seated
in the theatre, in effect incorporating and displacing the stage as the site
of drama. But if, following the innovations of modern poetry (or, given
the brilliance of Stein's innovative conversation plays, many of which were
written between 1913 and 1920, *anticipating them*), we regard one of the
achievements of modernist poetics to be the transformation of the page
into a kind of stage, where all elements of the mise-en-page signify as parts
of the poem, then Stein's work takes on a considerably different character.

Stein's plays cannot dictate their incarnation on the stage, no play can. And unless "materializing language" in performance is understood as the projection of words on a scrim, or according to the auratic conventions of the poetry reading (to which we will return), then any performance must materialize "language" as something else: as speaking, as movement, as singing, as acting. To this extent, the performability of Stein's plays and the issues of "fidelity" they raise are consistent with the dominant trajectory of modern drama in the age of print. Chekhov's nugatory dialogue, O'Neill's spoken subtext, Beckett's repetitions of language and gesture, Parks's "rests and spells," Kane's poetic brutalities: the action of modern drama, whether immediately and effectively stageable or apparently just "literary," arises in the conflict between the materialities and mutabilities of the stage and the page.

Alright then.

III. (*PAUSE.*): PINTER'S POETICS

> In *The Birthday Party* I employed a certain amount of dashes in the text, between phrases. In *The Caretaker* I cut out the dashes and used dots instead. So that instead of, say: "Look, dash, who, dash, I, dash, dash, dash," the text would read: "Look, dot, dot, dot, who, dot dot dot, I, dot, dot dot, dot." So it's possible to deduce from this that dots are more popular than dashes and that's why *The Caretaker* had a longer run than *The Birthday Party*.
>
> Harold Pinter, "Writing for the Theatre" (19)

Shaw and Stein evoke complementary strategies for booking the play, what we might call the novelistic and the poetic approaches. Shaw replaces the stage play with the stage-oriented novel; Stein pulls the discourse of the stage into the signifying web of the poem. But the sense that the mise-en-page can have semantic value in the drama need not – as Shaw's plays amply witness – exile such plays from the stage. The accessories of print have also had crucial force in modern drama's life onstage, and in defining the theatrical identity of printed plays.

I want now to look at the opening pages of Harold Pinter's *The Homecoming* (see figure 10).[24] As a book, *The Homecoming* seems to descend more directly from Pinero than from Shaw. Pinter's description of the set combines both literary/descriptive and theatrical/practical stage directions, locating the "old house" at once in the geography of "North London" and in the geography of the stage, mapped for us in practical terms ("a staircase,

The Homecoming was first presented by the Royal Shakespeare Company at the Aldwych Theatre on 3 June 1965, with the following cast:

MAX, a man of seventy	Paul Rogers
LENNY, a man in his early thirties	Ian Holm
SAM, a man of sixty-three	John Normington
JOEY, a man in his middle twenties	Terence Rigby
TEDDY, a man in his middle thirties	Michael Bryant
RUTH, a woman in her early thirties	Vivien Merchant

Directed by Peter Hall

The Homecoming was revived at the Garrick Theatre in May 1978. The cast was as follows:

MAX	Timothy West
LENNY	Michael Kitchen
SAM	Charles Kay
JOEY	Roger Lloyd Pack
TEDDY	Oliver Cotton
RUTH	Gemma Jones

Directed by Kevin Billington

SUMMER

An old house in North London.

A large room, extending the width of the stage.

The back wall, which contained the door, has been removed. A square arch shape remains. Beyond it, the hall. In the hall a staircase, ascending U.L., well in view. The front door U.R. A coatstand, hooks, etc.

In the room a window, R. Odd tables, chairs. Two large armchairs. A large sofa, L. Against R. wall a large sideboard, the upper half of which contains a mirror. U.L. a radiogram.

Act One

Evening.

LENNY is sitting on the sofa with a newspaper, a pencil in his hand. He wears a dark suit. He makes occasional marks on the back page.

MAX comes in, from the direction of the kitchen. He goes to sideboard, opens top drawer, rummages in it, closes it.

He wears an old cardigan and a cap, and carries a stick.

He walks downstage, stands, looks about the room.

MAX. What have you done with the scissors?

Pause.

I said I'm looking for the scissors. What have you done with them?

Pause.

Did you hear me? I want to cut something out of the paper.

LENNY. I'm reading the paper.

MAX. Not that paper. I haven't even read that paper. I'm talking about last Sunday's paper. I was just having a look at it in the kitchen.

Pause.

Do you hear what I'm saying? I'm talking to you! Where's the scissors?

LENNY (*looking up, quietly*). Why don't you shut up, you daft prat?

MAX lifts his stick and points it at him.

MAX. Don't you talk to me like that. I'm warning you.

10. *The Homecoming*, 1997; typography reproduces 1965 Methuen edition.

ascending U.L., well in view. The front door U.R.").[25] The opening page of dialogue also reflects many of the conventions of dramatic publishing today. Stage directions are noticeably spaced out, the two lines "*He wears an old cardigan and a cap, and carries a stick.*" and "*He walks downstage, stands, looks about the room.*" appearing on different lines. While Shaw wanted his plays "set solid," Pinter's page seems considerably less dense, certainly less novelistic, even more iconic, poetic in its use of white space (qtd. Holroyd, *Bernard Shaw* 1: 403). And, of course, there are the famous *Pause*s, here each occupying a separate line, and surrounded by extra spacing above and below. How different our sense of Pinter might be had his plays, and their *Pause*s, been printed more densely, as Doug Lucie's are in *Progress*, for example:

Mark Be making a silly mistake, you go around thinking that. (*Pause.*)
Why don't you come out for a drink with me. (*Beat.*) Take you
somewhere a bit classy. Wine bar. Cocktail bar. You'd like that.
(*Pause.*) No? (*Pause.*) You've got a fantastic body. (*Beat.*) Look at me.
(*She does.*) I mean . . . You could do worse.
(*Plays: 1* 41)

The publishers of contemporary plays tend to be profligate with paper and penurious with ink: Pinter's later plays are even more exemplary of the expense of ink in a waste of shame.

In terms of play publishing, if not much else, the 1950s resembled the 1890s, as first Penguin and then Methuen and Grove began to publish dramatic texts for a general audience, once again dispensing with the technical apparatus of acting editions, as Shaw, Pinero, and others had done a half-century before.[26] Is it possible for us, now, as readers of Pinter – and of course I include actors in that number – to read Pinter as anything other than Pinteresque? This may seem a purely intentional question, but it's not, or not entirely. Pinter's plays are published in a standard format, in paperback, by publishers on both sides of the Atlantic successfully striving to establish a market niche for modern drama. Moreover, the printform of Pinter's plays was apprehended at the interface between two reading practices: the poetics of modernist verse, which renders punctuation, white space, typography all as part of the text's legible signification, and the poetics of modernist acting, particularly acting in the realist tradition, which tends to ignore the material accessories of the printed text (stage directions, the placement of speech prefixes, punctuation) but which, on the other hand, often regards silence – the absence of type, or the space between type – as an especially important instigation of meaning, having the "paralinguistic function" of subtextual "speech."[27] Is it possible for us (*Pause.*) not to see the "*Pause*" (*Pause.*) as one of the features most characteristic of Pinter's dramatic writing, of his use of language? I don't think so, nor was it possible for the first generation of Pinter's directors, audiences, and reviewers. In the first decade of Pinter's real celebrity, the material idiosyncrasies of Pinter's printed texts drove the understanding of Pinter's dramatic writing, and the relation between print and performance they appear to claim.

Martin Esslin's landmark study, *The Peopled Wound: The Plays of Harold Pinter* (1970), is a useful case in point, marking what we might call the normative reading practice for Pinter's plays in the period. Esslin evokes the elegance and mystery of Pinter's often prosaic style. "Basically a lyric poet, Pinter is deeply concerned with words, their sound, their rhythm, their meaning" (44), forging a lyricism carved from silence:

Silence thus is, for Pinter, an essential, an integral part, and often the climax of his use of language. He has been reproached with a mannerism of silence, an excessive use of long pauses. These strictures are true, but again they seem to me to err in so far as they attribute mercenary motives to what is, to this particular playwright, simply part of his creed as a poet and craftsman, a highly personal way of experiencing, and reacting to, the world around him. (46)

In the concluding chapter on "Language and Silence" – the titles of Pinter's most recent plays at the time, *Landscape* and *Silence* – Esslin elaborates the tonalities of Pinter's music. For Esslin, Pinter's "use of language is that of a poet" to the extent that "there are no redundant words in true poetry, no empty patches, no mere fill-ins" (219). But to read Pinter *as* poetry New Critical fashion, to attribute "the density of texture of true poetry" to his page, means reading the "empty patches" as texture, the white spaces, and the *Pauses* they hold, as significant, signifying, not merely as irrelevancies intruding into the dramatic dialogue. How do we know, or why do we think, the *Pauses* are "long," unless it's the space on the page surrounding them that seems to amplify them, translating the space of the page into the imagined time of performance?

Esslin takes what would become a familiar stance: that Pinter's *Pauses* are not merely accessories of the drama's appearance on the page, but part of *the* dramatic text, of the Author's writing.

That is why – as in poetry the caesura, as in music the pause – silences play such a large and essential part in Pinter's dialogue. Pinter uses two different terms for the punctuation of his dialogue by passages without speech: "Pause" and "Silence". In the above example, which has been analysed in some detail, when, at the end of Lenny's first narration, Ruth asks how he knew the girl in question was diseased (and thus reveals her lack of surprise and familiarity with the vocabulary) Lenny's reaction is:

How did I know?
Pause.
I decided she was.
Silence.
You and my brother are newly-weds, are you? (219)

Reading this passage, Esslin notes that the "'pause' bridges the time Lenny needs to take in the whole import of that reaction and to think out his reply. The 'silence' after his reply and before he changes the subject indicates the much deeper caesura of the end of that section of the conversation" (220). Esslin invokes one of the characteristic questions of Pinter criticism, and of the situation of Pinter within the representational horizon of modern theatricality – what's *in* the silence? Is it the site of character revelation, a psychological gap to be filled, Method-style, by motivation, a specific psychological referent? Or is it the location of absence, where we see the blank screen of the subject, an interstitial interruption in the strategic game-playing?

Shaw's plays are nothing if not, to use a favorite undergraduate term, *wordy*: speech is the means of passion in Shaw, so it's appropriate that the page has lots of words on it, words that so densely reify their status as words as nearly to eliminate all non-linguistic space. For all their playability onstage, Shaw's plays frame the dialogue within a diegetic representation of the drama. The layout of Shaw's page – the slightly indented prefixes, dense lines, and narrative directions – makes the plays now seem even a bit antique, too rhetorical to enact in our idiom, in part because we now expect plays to deploy the (white) space of the page to register the drama's theatrical identity, to insert a sense of the temporality of the playing into the readerly text of the play. What would we think of Shaw's plays had they followed David Greig's example, starting a new sentence on a new line, inserting the rhythms of the stage *into* the rhetoric of print (see Greig, *Victoria* 5)? Alternatively, I wonder whether Pinter's *Pauses* and *Silences* would have seemed so freighted with complexity had the plays been laid out differently on the page, which uses the design – now that we are all prepared to read the space of the page as significant – to assign considerable weight to what are, in the theatre, normally considered as moments in which the author is stepping on the performers' prerogatives, their trained ability to decide the pace, rhythm, emphasis, and significance of speech.[28] Shaw used the accessories of the drama to assimilate the temporality of the stage to the pace of reading. Stein's accessories have (at least) a memorial, punning relation to the discourse of the stage, marking her effort to extend the temporality of the playing to the play of the page. Pinter's plays have become widely influential in the ways they take the page and take the stage: they use the accessories of the play at once to objectify the fictive drama and to mark the irruption of the theatre into the proprieties of print.

The complexity of Pinter's occupation of the page is readily visible if we compare the trade and acting editions of his plays. Although many acting editions published today more or less duplicate the text of the trade editions (dispensing with technical jargon and abbreviations, with theatrically oriented stage directions, and with the prop lists, lighting plots, and so on once common in acting editions), acting editions have hardly disappeared. Much as *The Homecoming* preserves some stage lingo in its opening stage direction, the portentously "literary" character of the *Pause* emerges in a very different light if we compare "reading" and "acting" editions of a slightly earlier play, *The Collection*, published by Samuel French (1963), by Grove in *Three Plays* (1962), and by Methuen in *The Collection and The Lover* (1963); the Methuen text was published by Faber and Faber in *Plays Two* in 1991 and reissued 1996. There are several notable differences between the texts. The play opens with two distinct areas represented onstage: a phone booth partly hidden in darkness, and a living room. The Methuen edition is "readerly" in a Shavian manner, not identifying the obscure "*figure* [. . .] *dimly observed*" in the telephone booth, or the "voice" who speaks to Harry on the telephone (Methuen 9, Faber 109); the French edition sensibly identifies the figure in the phone booth as "*JAMES, unrecognized by the audience*" (1), presumably saving the actor the trouble of reading too much of the play before finding out that these are *his* lines (both actors, it may be remembered, are onstage, speaking via telephone). The stage directions in the acting version are also much more explicit about the characters' behavior and costume (James is "*casually dressed*" [2–3]). The Methuen text is, for Pinter, relatively full: "*STELLA enters from a bedroom fixing a bracelet on her wrist. She goes to the cabinet, takes a perfume atomizer from her handbag and uses it on her throat and hands. She puts the atomizer into her bag and begins to put her gloves on*" (Methuen 10, Faber 110). But the acting edition is fuller still:

> STELLA, *a woman in her thirties, enters down* R, *carrying her coat. She drops the coat on the sofa, goes to the radiogram, picks up her gloves and puts them on. She picks up her purse and handbag from the radiogram, looks in the purse, puts it in the handbag then takes a bracelet from the bag, puts the bag on the radiogram and fixes the bracelet on her wrist. She then takes a perfume atomizer from the bag, uses it on her throat and replaces it in the bag. There is a silence.* (3)

There are many differences between the two texts, and the specificity of description is notably less extensive or prescriptive, more Pinteresque in other words, in the trade/"literary" than in the practical/"theatrical" text. But the most suggestive difference between the two versions is the handling of *Pause*. The Methuen trade edition (like the American Grove Press edition in this matter), lays out the page in now-accustomed way, appearing (to us) to mark the density and significance of different kinds of silence by signifying them differently on the page, here as *Pause* and ellipsis:

STELLA: I'm going.

> *Pause.*

> Aren't you coming in today?

> *Pause.*

JAMES: No.
STELLA: You had to meet those people from . . .

> *Pause. She slowly walks to an armchair,*
> *picks up her jacket, and puts it on.*

> You had to meet those people about that order. Shall I
> phone them when I get to the shop?   (Methuen 10, Faber 110)

The Samuel French acting edition tends to place the *Pause*s on the line, sometimes accompanied by a personal pronoun, as in *She pauses*, or with a demonstrative pronoun, producing the arresting phrase, *There is a pause*. Like others in this text, the stage direction concluding this passage is considerably more ample than that of the trade edition used by nontheatrical readers.

> STELLA. I'm going. (*She pauses*) Aren't you coming in
> today?
> JAMES (*after a pause*) No. (*He puts down his cup*)
> STELLA. You had to meet those people from . . .
>
> (*There is a pause.* JAMES *sits still*)
>
> (*She moves slowly to the sofa, picks up her coat, puts it on, then*
> *turns to James*) You had to meet those people about that
> order. Shall I phone them when I get to the shop? (3)

The acting edition, with its weird locution ("*There is a pause*") tends to equate the *Pause* with other stage directions, "*She pauses*." Esslin's sense of the *Pause* as intrinsic to Pinter's poetic writing is muted here, where the *Pause* is pulled toward the practicalities of recording and prompting performance, a text outside the dialogue commanding the actor to *pause, put down cup,* and *sit still*. These material differences don't signify on their own, but gain significance in the ways they are apprehended within different – but, arguably, related – reading formations. In the practice of modernist reading, the isolated *Pause* on the page tends to be absorbed into the functions of action and character, particularly if we are trained to think of that white space as a form of poetic signification, a significance it has gained for actors and directors as well as for general readers. In the "literary" text, that is, the *Pause* seems to mark both the intrusion of a theatrical alterity into the text and the necessity of comprehending that intrusion within the poetic logic of the play, of dramatic "character." Running the *Pause* into the line of stage directions tends to move it, in Pinter's case at least, into a different register, less a theatrical irruption into the poetic text than a merely dispensable part of the *didascalia*, an "accessory" to the "actual text of the plays, in the sense of the matter which is intended to be spoken by the characters," as McKerrow put it (*Prolegomena* 19). Oddly enough, the trade edition absorbs the gaps and ellipses, the *Pause*s and *Silence*s into the drama's poetic design; the theatrical edition maintains theatrical discourse alongside but beyond the drama. Perhaps it's not surprising that the Samuel French edition also contains a full Furniture and Prop List, Lighting Plot, and Effect Plot, texts that also stand apart from the authorized play.[29]

In their material mise-en-page, Pinter's plays appear to inscribe the meaning of performance with a certain temporality, a temporality – and perhaps a psychological complexity – that emerges more palpably from the trade text than from the acting edition, and that emerges finally through the habits of certain kinds of reading, the interpretive practices grooved to the traditions of modern printed drama that legitimate appropriate reading among different interpretive communities. Alice N. Bentson's fine sense of particularities of silence in Pinter dramatizes what has become the critical state of play: "Silences, then, are not the absence of speech but the true, raw, and frequently brutal or vulnerable self. Spoken (heard) dialogue is but a cue to the subtext, which itself is the pure unadulterated thing" ("Chekhov, Beckett, Pinter" 117). Pinter's page is very different from Shaw's, but there's a paradoxical sense here in which the white space, not the density of type, locates Pinter's texts as descendants of Shaw's bookish drama. Shaw's books strive to replace the stage, while Pinter's merely share in the doomed effort to arrogate the actor's freedom to the designs of the printed page.

Niggling about typography and layout in this way smacks of the purely, even comically literary, but in contemporary theatre practice Pinter's *Pause*s are emphatically observed as an essential part of the theatrical texture of the dialogue. Rehearsing *The Homecoming* in 1965, Peter Hall once had "a dot and pause rehearsal," forcing his actors to run their lines beginning to end, reciting where the ellipses, pauses, and silences occurred in the text, and distinguishing between them (qtd. in Lahr, *Casebook* 16–17). Writing in 1988, having just directed *The Birthday Party* at CSC Repertory Theatre in New York, Carey Perloff remarked:

I was not aware in rehearsal that we were "tightening the pauses," but I wanted to make sure that there was a clear distinction between a *pause* and a *silence*. And I wanted to be sure that if a pause was not marked, we didn't take one, no matter how "emotionally true" it might seem. ("Keeping Up the Mask" 64)

It seems unimaginable that *pausing* would be regarded as an illegitimate, actorly intrusion in the plays of, say, Shakespeare, or Ibsen, or Shaw, or even Chekhov. Granted *Pauses* are frequently marked in Pinter, but it's their isolation and emphasis on the page that transforms their status for all modern readers, rendering them not only definitively Authorial, but as part of that part of the text that, in theatre practice, tends to be regarded as the legitimate sphere of the playwright's work – the dialogue – rather than as part of that part of the text contested between playwright and director, the stage directions.[30]

Pinter has often denied the significance of the *Pauses* in ways that confirm the absorption (and irrelevance) of his intentions to the signifying armature of print. Interviewed by Mel Gussow, Pinter confessed,

I made a terrible mistake when I was young, I think, from which I've never really recovered. I wrote the word "pause" into my first play. [Laughter.] I really do believe that was a fatal error because people have been reading my plays and acting my plays most of the time concerned, really obsessed with this pause. I meant it merely as a natural break in the proceedings, or even a breath. [Pause.] But it's become something metaphysical. (Gussow, *Conversations with Pinter* 82–83)

Pinter evokes the *Pause* as a rhetorical marker, recalling one of the original purposes of punctuation that persists to the present day: to mark the manner of speaking the written text. Pinter has also come to describe his composition of *Pauses* and *Silences* as meticulously conceptual, and so to imply that they – again like punctuation – perform important work in the syntax of action and characterization. Revising *Old Times*, Pinter seems to recall Flaubert, said to have spent a full day's writing adding a comma and a second workday taking it out: "I did change a silence to a pause. It was a rewrite. This silence was a pretty long silence. Now it's a short pause." Pinter describes his revisions of *Betrayal* as similarly exacting.

HP: In rehearsal in London, I did three things. I cut one word, "please". I also
    took out a pause and I inserted a pause.
MG: And that made all the difference?
HP: That made all the *damn* difference.   (Gussow, *Conversations* 56–57)

Confirming Gussow's sense that "they stand in for dialogue," Pinter sees
the *pauses* and *silences* as inscribed in and directed by the text (Gussow,
Conversations 36).

My point here is not that Pinter's writing somehow governs theatrical
practice. Rather, it seems to me that the "bibliographic code" of plays like
The Homecoming (and, even more appropriately, *Old Times*) materializes
the play in ways that appeal to certain practices of reading, practices that
legitimate which features of the text appear to signify. The *Pause* seems to
us to participate in the design of modern poetry (we read the space around
it as important). The *Pause* also shares the tension between rhetorical and
syntactic features of punctuation, seeming to mark both a temporal and
affective rupture and possibly a conceptual shift as well. In so doing, and
in clear distinction to its function in acting editions, the *Pause* scores a
theatrical discourse *and* demands its incorporation into the poetic design
of the play. Although stage performance and dramatic performativity have
been decisively altered by print, the theatre remains a space where both the
linguistic and bibliographic codes of printed drama are regularly turned to
other purposes. Stage performance deploys "concrete practices and [. . .]
procedures of interpretation" that sometimes seem – from the partial perspective of textually oriented literary studies – to depart from the (only)
apparently determining order of the text (Chartier, *Order of Books* 2). Here,
though, the material form of Pinter's printed texts participates in the historical forms of modernist print, and so in the historical formation of a
recognizable set of reading strategies, strategies – to judge by the accounts
of Esslin (a literary critic of considerable theatrical experience) and Hall
(a practicing director with a literary pedigree) – that have clearly affected
the productive practices of page and stage. Writing in any form cannot
itself govern or determine performance; in the modern era printed drama
does not exist in an impermeable discursive realm, a cultural space distinct
from the world of theatre practice. To the extent that the materiality of
texts marks their historical formation, they participate in other forms of
meaning-making with which they are contemporary (let alone other forms
of meaning-making that use them). To say that both Esslin and Hall apply a
kind of New Critical poetics to Pinter would be one way of linking the materiality of print in the 1960s to emerging ways of transforming these plays
into theatrically legible objects (as the history of Pinter criticism suggests,

what's *in* the *Pause* – if anything – remains a key interpretive controversy both for literary critics and for performers).

So much depends here on so little. The sense that the placement of the *Pause* marks a tension not only in the use of printed drama but in its cultural identity at a given moment may suggest that the material form of printed drama can tell us something else about the status of writing and performance in our understanding of the work of drama. Although the *Pause* now dwells in the portmanteau of the Pinteresque, Pinter's plays are not unique in galvanizing the interface between print and performance, nor in using the accessories of print to reshape the ambiguous boundary between the authorial and the theatrical. For the past twenty years or so, printed plays have been making much ado about nothing, well about nearly nothing – punctuation. I'm thinking of the famous slash-mark [/] that punctuates the dialogue of many of Caryl Churchill's plays, and that has become more or less conventional in plays developed for the Joint Stock Theatre Company and its successor, Out of Joint. Patrick Marber's *Closer* regularly uses italics, underlining, and underlined italics to signify – well, I think they are supposed to signify – different kinds of emphasis, though what actors are meant to do with these marks is not really clear (describing what "men want" from women, Alice remarks: "she must <u>come</u> . . . like a *train* . . . but with *<u>elegance</u>*") (11).[31] In the collected edition of her plays published after her death, Sarah Kane's *Blasted* begins with this note:

> **Author's note**
> Punctuation is used to indicate delivery, not to conform to the rules of grammar.
> A stroke (/) marks the point of interruption in overlapping dialogue.
> Words in square brackets [ ] are not spoken, but have been included in the text to clarify meaning.
> Stage directions in brackets ( ) function as lines.
>
> *(Complete Plays 2)*

Cleansed, on the other hand, surprisingly notes that, "Where punctuation is missing, it is to indicate delivery" (106). David Greig's *Victoria* comes with a similar caution about how the text must be read spatially, using both punctuation and layout to prompt elements of performance:

> **A note on punctuation**
>
> . . .
> This tends to mean that the character has intended to complete the sentence but is either unwilling or unable to do so.

This tends to mean the character has jumped to a new
thought, or suddenly jumped to silence.

dialogue continues on a new line
This asks the performer to take note of the rhythm of the
speech. It can, but does not necessarily, imply a short beat.

(5)

Despite their distance from the world of Shavian drama, all of these
examples engage the problem Shaw grasped in the 1890s. Yet while Shaw
saw the necessity of reincorporating both rhetorical pointing and stage
directions more generally as accessory to the novelized representation
of the drama, the strategies of contemporary playwrights – following
Pinter – are considerably more complex. Churchill's slash-mark [/] at once
shows performers what to do with the dialogue and represents the interplay of speakers for an audience of readers; the same might be said of
Marber's italics and underlinings. Kane's square brackets supply additional
language that might clarify a character's motives for an actor or for a reader.
The slippage from "character" to "performer" in Greig's note is perhaps
representative: contemporary drama at once appears to value theatrical
discourse more highly (being willing to cede authority in explicitly demar-
cated zones of the text to performers), and yet to locate the discourse of the
stage in specific relation to the literary character of the drama. Such directions are a step, surely, from Shaw's incorporation of description, direction,
and dialect into the diegesis of the novelized drama, but perhaps only a
small step. Judith Thompson's notes to *White Biting Dog* are more urgent,
and more readily visible as part of the literary traditions for booking the
play: "Because of the extreme and deliberate musicality of this play, any
attempts to go against the textual rhythms, such as the breaking up of
an unbroken sentence, or the taking of a pause where none is written is
DISASTROUS. The effect is like being in a small plane and suddenly
turning off the ignition. It all falls down. The play must SPIN, not just turn
around" (n.p.).
  Although it's unlikely that Willy Loman will appear in different parts of
Death of a Salesman as *The Salesman, The Father, The Husband*, many
of the vagaries of early modern printing remain in a general way in
modern dramatic texts. Modern plays – beginning, perhaps, with Shaw's
s p a c i n g and dialects – persist in using rhetorical punctuation, and a kind
of rhetorical orthography, too. In many modern plays, spelling and pointing seem at once to record and to prompt certain elements of performance,
to a much greater extent than other printed genres do, in which the familiar

rules of grammatical or syntactic punctuation predominate. Creatures of print, we sometimes think that the rhetorical use of the page is long past. But much as it is possible to see Shaw assimilating rhetorical uses of print (punctuation, spelling, spacing) to a novelistic strategy for booking the play, so too it's possible to see the efforts of more recent playwrights in two ways: as an effort to resist the "literarization" of the drama by drawing the signals of the stage into the page, where the presence of another shaping discourse interrupts the apparent closure of the literary text, and as a continuation of print culture's efforts to imprint the stage, to locate the signs and signals of appropriate, authorial performance within the text itself. Pinter's *Pauses* and the many conventions to which they give rise participate fully in the unresolved, perhaps unresolvable, tension between the authorized "work," its materialization in print, and its subsequent performance that sustains modern drama's ongoing colloquy with print. As the eminent poet Susan Howe might put it, "I can underline letters and use **bold** and *itals* for emphasis, but a person cannot be two places at once, such marks are only acted charades" ("Ether Either" 120).

IV. WHAT'S IN A NAME?: *THE LARAMIE PROJECT*, THE AUTHOR, AND COLLABORATION

> Authorship is a special form of human communicative exchange, and it cannot be carried on without interactions, cooperative and otherwise, with various persons and audiences.
>
> Jerome J. McGann, *The Textual Condition* (64)

> . . . the play, even in print, is always a process
>
> Stephen Orgel, "Macbeth and the Antic Round" (159)

The desire to mark the oral, rhetorical force of drama in print is surprisingly widespread in recent published plays, and I think we have to read that persistence both as nostalgia for the waning power of print to determine performance (it may signify that fiction, too), and as a sign of the contested ground of dramatic writing today. Printed drama is oddly marginal to the canons of print and its academic offspring, the study of literature, to the practices of the theatre, with their emphasis on the authorizing role of the director, and to the burgeoning importance of nonverbal, physical, and/or collaborative theatre work, often grouped together as (perhaps only apparently) unscripted "performance." While the accessories of the page locate the contested authority of the drama between stage and page, they also enact something else, a nostalgic desire for the proprieties of print authorship. This nostalgia is also emblematized by Shaw's plays, and persists in a somewhat surprising arena of contemporary printed drama: the plays of collaborative or collective theatre companies.

The Laramie Project provides a useful example of how the printform of recent plays might be seen to express an anxiety about the loss of print's authority, its cultural centrality, and so about the loss of a certain dimension of the identity of dramatic writing, its identity as print literature. As a book, *The Laramie Project* dramatizes some of the ongoing concerns of the slippery relationship between print and performance culture, concerns about how – or whether – the accessories of print objectify the play. *The Laramie Project* is a distinctive object: a paperback book of 13 × 20.5 cm, it's slightly smaller than the Grove playtexts (today 14 × 21 cm, though older editions were 14 × 20 cm) and considerably larger than the typical Methuen plays (11 × 18 cm); notably, it's exactly the same trim size as much popular fiction (Don DeLillo's recent novel, *The Body Artist*, published by a different press, is the same size). The trade edition is visually much more striking than most playtexts published today. The cover is a full-color reproduction of the striking poster for the show, featuring a brilliant blue sky, a long shot of the highway leading into Laramie, only the roadsign ("LARAMIE POP 26687 ELEV 7165") breaking the bleak horizon (see figure 11). The photograph is framed by a narrow white border and the title, also in white, floats in block letters just above the clouds. The book's theatrical status is underscored by the blurbs gracing the front – "'ONE OF THE TEN BEST PLAYS OF THE YEAR' – TIME" – and back covers: "'Astonishing. Not since *Angels in America* has a play attempted so much [. . .]' – ASSOCIATED PRESS"; "'Kaufman is pioneering a new genre of theater. He aims for a radical redefinition of what theater is capable of' – TIME"; "'This play is *Our Town* with a question mark, as in "Could this be our town?"' – THE NEW YORK TIMES." The back cover also describes the Matthew Shepard murder and trial, and the process that Kaufman and the Tectonic Theater Project used to interview townspeople in Laramie and to devise the show: "using eight actors to embody more than sixty different people in their own words." As is often the case with celebrated novels (again, see *The Body Artist*), the blurb on the front cover is accompanied by a leaf of "Acclaim" from the press that precedes the title page, acclaim that fails to make it clear whether the New York or Denver production is being described (though since the bulk of the blurbs are from New York papers, it's probably New York acclaim). Published by Vintage, a division of Random House – a much larger house than Grove or TCG or Methuen or Nick Hern, the principal publishers of contemporary drama, but with a rich history of literary publishing – the text contains

"ONE OF THE TEN BEST PLAYS OF THE YEAR" —TIME

THE
LARAMIE
PROJECT

A PLAY BY

MOISÉS KAUFMAN

AND

THE MEMBERS OF TECTONIC THEATER PROJECT

LARAMIE
POP   26687
ELEV   7165

A VINTAGE ORIGINAL

11. *The Laramie Project*, 2001: cover.

an introduction by the author, which provides the date and place of the
Denver and New York openings, and some general information about the
staging. While the first printing does not list "credits" – director, designers,
producers, etc. – nor provide a listing of which of the original actors played
which characters, by the sixth printing (still copyright September 2001) this
information is included, without changing the numbered pagination.

In many respects, of course, *The Laramie Project* is not a very experimental play on the page or on the stage. It's divided into acts and scenes
(the scenes are called "moments"); it proceeds in a straightforward, linear
narrative that uses the Company's interviews with townspeople to tell the
story of Matthew Shepard, the murder, the court trials, and the various civic
and media events surrounding them; its use of a restricted, always visible
cast onstage to enact a series of roles takes advantage of the conventions
of fluidity and openness to the audience common on the contemporary
stage – even common in Shakespearean theatre today.[32] On the page, the
layout and design of the play work both to reveal and preserve these elements of the performance structure. The actors of the original production
sometimes describe meeting the various citizens of Laramie before they step
into "character," as "Greg Pierotti" (played by Greg Pierotti) does at the
beginning of the play:

> GREG PIEROTTI: My first interview was with Detective Sergeant
> Hing of the Laramie Police Department. At the start of the
> interview he was sitting behind his desk, sitting something
> like this *(he transforms into Sergeant Hing)*:
>
> I was born and raised here
> My family is, uh, third generation. (5)

On the other hand, sometimes the actors merely appear onstage, or onpage,
as the characters they play.

MOMENT: JOURNAL ENTRIES

NARRATOR: Company member Greg Pierotti:

GREG PIEROTTI: We arrived today in the Denver Airport and drove
to Laramie. The moment we crossed the Wyoming border I
swear I saw a herd of buffalo. Also, I thought it was strange
that the Wyoming sign said: WYOMING – LIKE NO PLACE ON
EARTH instead of WYOMING – LIKE NO PLACE ELSE ON EARTH.

NARRATOR: Company member Leigh Fondakowski.

LEIGH FONDAKOWSKI: I stopped at a local inn for a bite to eat.
And my waitress said to me:

WAITRESS: Hi, my name is Debbie. I was born in nineteen fifty-
    four and Debbie Reynolds was big then, so, yes, there are a
    lot of us around, but I promise that I won't slap you if you
    leave your elbows on the table.

MOISÉS KAUFMAN: Today Leigh tried to explain to me to no avail
    what chicken fried steak was.

WAITRESS: Now, are you from Wyoming? Or are you just passing
    through?

LEIGH FONDAKOWSKI: We're just passing through

NARRATOR: Company member Barbara Pitts:

BARBARA PITTS: We arrived in Laramie tonight. Just past the WEL-
    COME TO LARAMIE sign – POPULATION 26,687 – the first thing
    to greet us was Wal-Mart. In the dark, we could be on any
    main drag in America – fast-food chains, gas stations. But as
    we drove into the downtown area by the railroad tracks, the
    buildings still look like a turn-of-the-century western town.
    Oh, and as we passed the University Inn, on the sign where
    amenities such as heated pool or cable TV are usually touted,
    it said: HATE IS NOT A LARAMIE VALUE.

NARRATOR: Greg Pierotti:

MOMENT: ALISON AND MARGE

(13–14)

This constant textual reference to the research and performance work of the
original cast is a familiar dimension of contemporary performance writing,
but it is embodied in the printform of *The Laramie Project* in distinctive
ways. Anna Deavere Smith's plays, which are created in a generally similar manner, are printed in such a way as to foreground the "character"
Smith (or another performer) plays. In *Fires in the Mirror* and *Twilight:
Los Angeles, 1992*, the function of *The Laramie Project*'s Narrator – providing the *name* of the actor, actor/character, or character – is taken over by
projecting names on a scrim above the stage. This effect is represented on
the page by a bold-face headline giving the character's name and a scene
title – "The Reverend Al Sharpton Me and James's Thing," for example,
in *Fires in the Mirror* – followed by a brief description of the circumstances
of the interview: "Reverend Sharpton's face is much younger, and more
innocent than it appears to be in the media. His humor is in his face. He
is very direct. The interview only lasts fifteen minutes because he had been
called out of a meeting in progress to do the interview" (Smith, *Fires in the
Mirror* 19). These names and titles are preserved on the page, where they
precede each speech; the speeches are laid out phrase-wise, something like

controlled free verse on the page, and each new speech begins on a fresh page. Smith's plays, both in performance and on the page, tend to emphasize their continuity with the traditions of dramatic publishing, incorporating the agents of the play as "characters" with *names* that erase the actor – no *Enter Will Kemp* here. *The Laramie Project*, though, works to keep the transformation of actor-to-character visible as part of the play's mise-en-page. It presents its agents as subjects of transformation – writers, dramaturgs, actors, townspeople, characters – while expressing a desire to legislate those relationships. Perhaps it takes a New York actor to find the drama in the lesson that people in Wyoming are, well, people after all. While dramatizing the shifting boundaries of sympathy and identity seems to be the point of *The Laramie Project*, the fact that the "identities" of performance *can* be so readily marked on the page points, I think, to the fundamentally literary design of this apparently "new genre of theater." In a sense, *The Laramie Project* is a performance-work imagined as a book.

Despite these claims for the play's innovative character as drama, as a book, *The Laramie Project* takes a strikingly retrospective stance toward the theatre. Its apparatus foregrounds the text as the record of an important social and theatrical event, both the Matthew Shepard case and the play's creation and performance. The elaborate description of the process of creation, and even perhaps the bios of Kaufman, the writers, and the dramaturgs that follow the text frame *The Laramie Project* in print less as an instigation to future performance than as the record of past life (the novelistic elements of the book's material production would be consistent with this, too). Even the dialogue, with its effort to bring the "actors" into view as they become "characters" might be seen as an effort to put the whole play, including its performance, between the covers of the book, as "an actor-driven event" (xiv). To this extent, even while it brings the agents of the play's research and performance to the page, *The Laramie Project* reifies a kind of anxiety about the loss of print, the desire to retain the stabilizing function of print, its imagined – and, finally, imaginary – ability to fix the work as a textual object, to fix it in the commodity form of the trade book. This anxiety is most visible at that moment where the ideology of print is most characteristically made visible: the Author. Does a performance need an Author? I'm not certain, but it is clear that in the economy – and for the time being, in the ontology – of printed drama (and perhaps of performance) plays don't merely need writers (as film and television do). They need Authors.

AUTHOR'S NOTE

The Laramie Project was written through a unique collaboration
by Tectonic Theater Project. During the year-and-a-half-long
development of the play, members of the company and I traveled
to Laramie six times to conduct interviews with the people of the
town. We transcribed and edited the interviews, then conducted
several workshops in which the members of the company presented material and acted as dramaturgs in the creation of the
play.

  As the volume of material grew with each trip to Laramie, a
small writers' group from within the company began to work
closely with me to further organize and edit the material, conduct
additional research in Laramie, and collaborate on the writing of
the play. This group was led by Leigh Fondakowski as head writer,
with Stephen Belber and Greg Pierotti as associate writers.

  As we got closer to the play's first production in Denver, the
actors, including Stephen Belber and Greg Pierotti, turned their
focus to performance while Leigh Fondakowski continued to
work with me on drafts of the play, as did Stephen Wangh, who
by then had joined us as an associate writer and "bench coach."

                                                              (ix)

The Laramie Project begins with an "Author's Note" – that's Author-
apostrophe-s, in the singular, referring to Moisés Kaufman, who alone holds
the copyright to the play. The note describes the collaborative process of
the play's production, and explains the daunting complexity of attribution
played out on the book's title page (see figure 12), with its authorial by-line,
secondary by-line in smaller type, and list of head writer, associate writers,
and dramaturgs – to say nothing of the "bench coach." What a struggle here
to register the process of theatrical production within the representational
structure of print and the legal structure of copyright. Remember: there
may be writers and dramaturgs, actors and characters, Laramieites and New
Yorkers, but *The Laramie Project* is "by Moisés Kaufman."

  Perhaps it's not that surprising that the company and its trade publisher would deploy the book's bibliographic codes in this way. The book's
memorializing gesture is confirmed in several small ways by comparing the
Vintage trade edition with the acting version published by Dramatists Play
Service. Also published in 2001, the Dramatists Play Service edition naturally materializes a different sense of the text's use. The book, like all acting
editions published by DPS, and resembling those published by Samuel
French, is a much plainer object; though nearly the same trim size as the

THE
LARAMIE PROJECT

by Moisés Kaufman
and the members of Tectonic
Theater Project

Head Writer	Leigh Fondakowski
Associate Writers	Stephen Belber, Greg Pierotti,
	Stephen Wangh
Dramaturgs	Amanda Gronich,
	Sarah Lambert, John McAdams,
	Maude Mitchell, Andy Paris,
	Barbara Pitts, Kelli Simpkins

VINTAGE BOOKS | A DIVISION OF RANDOM HOUSE, INC. | NEW YORK

12. *The Laramie Project*: title page.

trade edition (it is 1 cm shorter), it is printed much more densely (and so is about half as thick as the trade edition), and is bound between buff-colored heavy paper covers, with a standard design (no photo). The text contains the same paraphernalia contained in the trade edition, though organized a bit differently. The dedication (*"Dedicated to the people of Laramie, Wyoming and to Matthew Shepard"*) has a separate page (in the Vintage edition it appears above the copyright notice); the play is preceded by the Acknowledgments, Author's Note, Introduction, the Denver and New York cast lists, and the list of Characters (the trade edition opens with the Introduction, followed by the Author's Note, Denver and New York cast lists, and Characters, printing cast biographies and the Acknowledgments at the end of the volume).

Yet while the DPS text does not have ground plans or prop lists, as many acting editions do, it does point to the practices of performance, informing potential producers that the proprieties of *The Laramie Project* extend considerably beyond the dialogue. Although the title page of the acting edition is considerably less complex than the trade edition – THE LARAMIE PROJECT | by MOISÉS KAUFMAN | and the MEMBERS of TECTONIC | THEATER PROJECT – and omits the list of writers, associate writers, and dramaturgs, this ancillary information is provided on a page immediately following the copyright page, which warns that the by-line, and listing of Head Writer, Associate Writers, and Dramaturgs "must appear in all programs distributed in connection with performances of the Play," with the further specification that in addition to naming the "Authors" [Moisés Kaufman and the Members of Tectonic Theater Project] on all programs and advertising, "The names of the Authors must appear on a separate line, in which no other names appear, immediately beneath the title and for 'Moisés Kaufman' in size of type equal to 50% of the size of the largest, most prominent letter used for the title of the Play and for 'Members of Tectonic Theater Project' in size of type equal to 25% of the size of the largest, most prominent letter used for the title of the Play." Although such specifications are typical in acting editions, the variety of writing functions significantly complicates them; moreover, while the Head Writer, Associate Writers, and Dramaturgs have been removed from the title page and from any stage production's formal billing ("The billing must appear as follows: THE LARAMIE PROJECT | by Moisés Kaufman | and the Members of Tectonic Theater Project"), the acting edition is nonetheless traced by their potential absence from printed materials surrounding a production. For while it's not unusual to detail the arrangement and proportionality of billing for advertising purposes, it's notable that "the 'Author's Note' included in this book and biographies for Moisés Kaufman, Leigh Fondakowski, Stephen Belber, Greg Pierotti and Stephen Wangh must appear in all programs distributed in connection with performances of the Play," particularly since the biographies do not appear in the Dramatists Play Service edition (see 2–3).[33]

The play's collaborative creation instigates problems for *The Laramie Project*'s print identity that also spill over into the printed materials ancillary to stage production, materials which are enjoined to preserve the hierarchies of print authorship: posters, programs, marquees. And while there are many changes in wording between the trade and acting editions, the bibliographic codes of the two editions also distinguish the two plays in important ways.

MOMENT: JOURNAL ENTRIES

NARRATOR: Company member Greg Pierotti.
GREG PIEROTTI: We arrived today in the Denver Airport and drove to Laramie – The moment we crossed the Wyoming border I swear I saw a herd of buffalo. Also, I thought it was strange that the Wyoming sign said:
THE COMPANY. WYOMING – LIKE NO PLACE ON EARTH.
GREG PIEROTTI. Instead of WYOMING – LIKE NO PLACE ELSE ON EARTH.
NARRATOR. Company member Leigh Fondakowski.
LEIGH FONDAKOWSKI. I stopped at a local inn for a bite to eat. And my waitress said to me:
WAITRESS. "Hi, my name is Debbie. I was born in 1954 and Debbie Reynolds was big then, so yes, there are alot of us around, but I promise that I won't slap you if you leave your elbows on the table."
MOISÉS KAUFMAN. Today the company tried to explain to me to no avail what chicken fried steak was.
WAITRESS. "Now, are you from Wyoming? Or are you just passing through?"
LEIGH FONDAKOWSKI. "We're just passing through."
NARRATOR. Company member Barbara Pitts.
BARBARA PITTS. We arrived in Laramie tonight. Just past the "Welcome to Laramie" sign – "Population 26,687" – the first thing to greet us was Walmart. In the dark, we could be on any main drag in America – fast food chains, gas stations. But as we drove into the downtown area by the railroad tracks, the buildings still looked like a turn-of-the-century Western town. Oh, and as

we passed the University Inn, on the sign where amenities such as heated pool or cable TV are usually touted, it said. HATE IS NOT A LARAMIE VALUE.
NARRATOR. Greg Pierotti.

MOMENT: ALISON AND MARGE
(Dramatists Play Service 27–28)

There are a number of substantive differences between the DPS text and the Vintage text. The DPS text gives the line "Wyoming – Like No Place on Earth" to the "Company," and "Moisés Kaufman's" line is slightly different, too, making "the company" rather than "Leigh" responsible for the "chicken fried steak" joke. But the principal differences between the two texts lie in their bibliographic encoding of the drama. DPS, like Samuel French, uses a dense and simple page design. Margins are justified left and right, speech prefixes are simply capitalized, are neither hanging nor indented, and are separated from the dialogue by a simple period. In itself, the density of the page is notable; one might have expected more white space for notes, but efficiency is the premium here. Like acting editions in the nineteenth century, DPS offers an inexpensive delivery system for the play's dialogue, particularly avoiding the white space between speeches that bulks up the trade edition. The acting edition's punctuation is notable, too. The trade edition follows the speech prefix with a colon, and follows the Narrator's introductions with a colon as well – "Company member Greg Pierotti:" – where the acting edition uses a period. In a sense, the Vintage edition's effort to absorb the performance extends down to its points: in both the speech prefixes and the Narrator's introductions, the words are encoded as a kind of gesture, a deictic pointing, where the acting edition simply marks a transition from one use of words (speech prefix) to another (dialogue). Placing the exchange between the Waitress and Leigh Fondakowski in quotation marks, the DPS edition also seems to remind the actors of the pluperfect character of this moment, a past prior to the past performed in the rest of the scene.

This tension between memorializing and instigating performance is, perhaps more predictably, enacted by the stage directions, which are often much more extensive in the trade text.

ACT THREE

The stage is now empty except for several chairs stage right.
They are all facing the audience and arranged in rows as if
to suggest a church or courthouse.

(Dramatists Play Service 71)

(The stage is now empty except for several chairs stage right. They occupy that half of the stage. They are all facing the audience and arranged in rows as if to suggest a church or a courthouse. As the lights come up, several actors are sitting there dressed in black. Some of them have umbrellas. A few beats with just this image in silence. Then MATT GALLOWAY *enters stage left. Looks at them and says:)*
(Vintage 75)

The Vintage text (which places the "Act Three" on the previous leaf) not only specifies the geography of the stage (*"They occupy that half of the stage."*) but also of course inscribes the design and direction of the original stage production (are these authorial?), a moment in which the play's performance design unmistakably alludes to the classic drama of small-town life as national allegory, Thornton Wilder's *Our Town*.

The two editions of *The Laramie Project* dramatize the extent to which print's closure on the materialization of dramatic writing is far from complete. The challenges of encoding authorship, the ways actors and readers might be signaled in different ways by the accessories of the bibliographic code, point to the challenges of objectifying the drama in print, and to the ways the problematic identities of drama continue to trouble the play's place on the page. Whether the play is conventionally authorized, whether it appears to incorporate the stage (as Shaw's plays do) or to direct it, how the various discourses of the drama's identity are registered, refined, distinguished: these problems persist, even at the moment that print seems to be challenged by other more mutable and multiple means of perpetuating writing.

Margreta de Grazia and Peter Stallybrass note that the use of Shakespeare's name on title pages "may reflect not his authorship, in any traditional sense, but rather his centrality to the company in multiple capacities (as playwright, actor, shareholder), not to mention his distinctive loyalty to that company for which he wrote exclusively" ("Materiality" 275–76). While replacing the Author with a diversified set of writing functions might seem to provide credit where credit is due, I'm not sure it really resolves the issue. In the theatre, as in television, there may be many writers and many acts of writing behind a given production, but a book (and a play?) apparently needs an Author. Many of the most celebrated and influential works of the past half century pose similar problems: the plays of Caryl Churchill that were developed with the Joint Stock Theatre Company, but published under her name; the collected *Early Works* of Luis Valdez, published under his name but devised in collaboration with members of

El Teatro Campesino, some of whom were illiterate; even the close collaboration of directors and writers (Elia Kazan and Tennessee Williams, Anne Bogart and Charles Mee, Liz Diamond and Suzan-Lori Parks, Samuel Beckett and Samuel Beckett), collaboration that occasionally, invisibly, makes its way into the published texts of plays – or in Beckett's case, was explicitly forbidden (at least until Beckett agreed to collaborate on the "revised texts" for *The Theatrical Notebooks of Samuel Beckett*).[34]

There are alternatives, of course. *The Farm Show: A Collective Creation by Theatre Passe Muraille* is "© Canada 1976/Theatre Passe Muraille/Paul Thompson," expressing a sense of propriety well suited to Paul Thompson's notion that "The play was not written down; it developed out of interviews, visits, and improvisations. Most of the words used were given to us by the community along with their stories. [. . .] I'm not sure how much of this will come through the printed word" (Theatre Passe Muraille, *The Farm Show* n.p.). Similarly, Passe Muraille's widely produced *The Farmers' Revolt* is published as an impressive volume, *1837: William Lyon Mackenzie and the Canadian Revolution*, by Rick Salutin and Theatre Passe Muraille. Here, while the title page perhaps collapses authorial functions, the copyright page works to clarify: "*1837* © Copyright 1976 Part I by Rick Salutin | Part II by Rick Salutin and Theatre Passe Muraille" – part I is an extended historical essay "1837: Mackenzie and Revolution," while Part II is the play, *1837: The Farmers' Revolt*. While the "Note on the script" of Complicite's *Street of Crocodiles* marks the company's inventive adaptation of Bruno Schulz's stories by including "quotations which will point the reader to the textual inspiration at the origin of each scene" (*Plays: 1* n.p.), the plays collected in *Plays: 1* appear under the headline "COMPLICITE," and both "Introduction and collection" are "copyright © Complicite 2003." The title page of the single-volume text of *Mnemonic* takes a similarly straightforward approach: "**Mnemonic** *devised by* the Company."[35]

This compositional quandary points directly to the literary implications of stage drama, for however unusual it may be as an aspect of published *plays*, the distinction between the Author (Kaufman) and "writers" is surprising only if we segregate theatrical drama from the sphere in which most of today's drama gets written, by individuals who typically function as a team of "writers" without the pretension to (or possibility of) print Authorship: the writers of film and television scripts. And while it's critical to recognize that the book has been responsible for the persistence of dramatic writing, and for its partial incorporation within the canons of literature and literary study, we are only beginning to understand the consequences of print as a delivery system for works of art in general, and for dramatic writing in particular. Charles Mee's brilliant plays are notable for their palimpsestic, collage-like incorporation of a wide range of contemporary writing. Mee has published many of his *History Plays* in a trade edition, which contains the usual copyright information and directions for obtaining performance rights, and also publishes them on a website, which contains the following invitation:

Please feel free to take the texts from this website and use them as a resource for your own work: cut them up, rearrange them, rewrite them, throw things out, put things in, do whatever you like with them – don't just make a few cuts or rewrite a few passages, but pillage the plays and build your own entirely new piece out of the ruins – and then, please, put your own name to the work that results.

But, if you would like to perform the plays essentially or substantially as I have composed them, they are protected by copyright in the versions you read here, and you need to clear performance rights. (Mee, *The (Re)Making Project*)

Mee's invitation is at once provocative and less provocative than it may appear. Mee seems to invite appropriation and so he does; but the specified appropriations are restricted to textual revision. Change the text, put your name to it, great. But what does it mean "to perform the plays essentially or substantially as I have composed them," given that so much in the sphere of performance is not and cannot be pre-scribed?

More to the point, especially given the degree to which Mee's writing embodies a "digital" sense of the mobility and malleability of writing, this proviso also seems to articulate an anxiety and nostalgia for the identity and propriety of the printed work. As Mee suggests here, the page is no longer the alternative, the "other" platform of the drama. Much as digital technology now provides a means to analyze writing and print through nonwritten, nonprint technologies, I think we can anticipate new opportunities, challenges, models for our understanding of the interface between writing and performance, challenges that will be made visible through the accessories of the page (most software gives writers a much wider and more dynamic array of symbols, fonts, and designs). Indeed, they are already emerging, not only in the theatrically oblique printform of Suzan-Lori Parks's plays, or Sarah Kane's, but also in the different position of writing in emerging forms of play, in ubiquitous or immersive gaming, for example. These new ways of materializing writing – or is it virtualizing writing? – will bear on the shape of drama. How the digital text will change the unstable interface between dramatic writing and performance is hard to say. Will it close the book on that tale a last time told? My guess is that there will be something "left to tell" and that much as they were in the opening of the print era, our ways of imagining the use of this technology to create, record, represent and instigate performance will again enact, and perhaps dissimulate, the work of drama.

CHAPTER 3

Something like poetry

Speaking teaches us what our natural "literature" is. In fact, everyone, in a given amount of time, will say something that is like poetry.
Anna Deavere Smith, *Fires in the Mirror: Crown Heights, Brooklyn and Other Identities* (xxxi)

For the record: Speech is writin**G**
writin**G** speech. That is the lesson
the body waits to hear with
every word it reads.
Bob Perelman,
"An Alphabet of Literary History,"
(*Marginalization of Poetry* 149)

The printing of modern plays is, for the most part, highly conventionalized. Playtexts are divided into acts and/or scenes, speakers are noted more or less consistently; the book – whether an acting or a trade edition – usually contains some ancillary information about the playing, cast lists, dramatis personae, notes on the premiere production, or, minimally, where to apply for the rights to stage the play. As we have seen, though, the various accessories that bring the play to book provide an index to larger questions of the identity of drama: how the drama is engaged in and by print, how booking the play represents the drama at the intersection of literature and theatre. Some playwrights are clearly invested in the regime of print, working to shape the play as a specific kind of book (Shaw's stage directions are echoed, in this sense, by Tom Stoppard's), or to reshape the page to signal new possibilities of dramatic action and theatrical performance (Pinter's *Pauses* are part of this trend, and both Suzan-Lori Parks and Sarah Kane come to mind here, too). While many "accessory" experiments seem designed to identify the drama with print literature, the page can and does have different uses, and retains the potential to point to the signifying possibilities of that other stage.

Performance art seems to oppose the deterministic reproduction of texts with the fashioning of something different, to avoid the logocentric mastery of a dramatic script, an antecedent verbal order that prescribes the force of the performance. What should we make, then, of the publication of "performance" texts? If the text does not govern the performance, if – as in the case of Spalding Gray, Guillermo Verdecchia, Holly Hughes, Tim Miller, Guillermo Gómez-Peña, Carmelita Tropicana, to take several familiar examples – the staging of the work seems to depend on the individual authority of the writer/performer, then the publication of the text seems to have an obscure or at least ambiguous purpose. It makes no real gesture to *record* the performance nor can it really impel authentic future performances, yet it also seems to represent performance on the page. Performance writing sometimes dramatizes a startling use of print: it seems to resist the conventional forms of printed (and stage) drama by adopting the familiar strategies of printed poetry. The figuration of the page as a field of performance that links, say, Pinter's *Pauses* to the suspensions of Williams's lyrics provides a rich and unacknowledged backdrop for the printing of performance texts, at least for those texts principally associated with the theatrical stage. In this chapter, I take a different perspective on modern drama's performance in print, setting several plays alongside the practical and theoretical concerns of contemporary poetry and poetics, especially the questions about the materiality of language on the page and in the materialized "sounding" of the principal form of performed poetry, the poetry reading. Reading poetry and plays reciprocally provides a final sense of the modern drama's encounter with the page: how the mise-en-page of dramatic language defines modern drama's poetics of agency.[1]

Widely performed on stage, broadcast on television, disseminated on video and DVD, and published by a major trade publisher, Anna Deavere Smith's plays – *Fires in the Mirror: Crown Heights, Brooklyn and Other Identities* and *Twilight: Los Angeles, 1992* – at once mark and challenge conventional categories of dramatic writing, registering an anxiety about the implication of print and contemporary performance. Smith's writing and performances provide an index of the pressure on the interface between print and performance exerted by writing for solo performance today. Based on transcripts of interviews conducted live and/or on the telephone, Smith's working methods for the "series of theater (or performance) pieces called On the Road: A Search for American Character" are now familiar (*Fires* xxiii). She creates these works by "interviewing people and later performing them using their own words," and closely imitating their habitual gestures and mannerisms; her "goal has been to find American character in the ways that people speak" (xxiii). In preparing a piece, Smith uses audio (and sometimes videotape) recordings of the interview to help her reproduce each speaker's distinctive vocal rhythms, emphasis, and gestural punctuation as well. She then arranges the monologues thematically – in *Fires*, for instance, under headings like "Hair," "Mirrors," "Identity." Smith developed this technique explicitly to avoid a Method-inspired psychological identification with her subjects' emotional life, working to bring a more public rhetoric of "character" to the stage.

Garrick will put his head between two folding-doors, and in the course of five or six seconds his expression will change successively from wild delight to temperate pleasure, from this to tranquillity, from tranquillity to surprise, from surprise to blank astonishment, from that to sorrow, from sorrow to the air of one overwhelmed, from that to fright, from fright to horror, from horror to despair, and thence he will go up again to the point from which he started.

Like David Garrick in Diderot's famous recollection, Smith's performance asserts itself as an art of mimicry, formalizing the signals of social discourse in a way that appears to mark them for observation, discussion, and critique (Diderot concluded, by the way, "Can his soul have experienced all these feelings, and played this kind of scale in concert with his face? I don't believe it; nor do you") (Diderot, *The Paradox of Acting* 38). Smith's search for "American character" avoids the practiced regime of individual emotional or psychological identification that sustains the dominant forms of American acting. Imitating the external features of everyday behavior (speech patterns, gesture, posture), Smith locates "character" in the citational register of public identity, framed as an explicitly "performative" strategy for inhabiting the vocal and physical regimes of social discourse.[2]

Portraying a range of raced, classed, and gendered subjects, Smith has been duly celebrated for her efforts to represent the complex exchange between identity and politics expressed by important social controversies in the United States: the Crown Heights riots in New York in 1991, the Los Angeles uprising following the verdict in the Rodney King police-beating trial in 1992, gender equity on college campuses, the relation between the press and the presidency during the Clinton administration. Smith's means of engaging social identities have themselves generated controversy, controversy that helps to frame the problematic ratio between dramatic writing and theatrical performance, as it is embodied in Smith's work and more generally in performance writing. Some viewers of Smith's performances have seen her refusal of sympathetic "identification," the quasi-Brechtian distance or gap between Smith and the role or "character" she plays, as

parody, the gesture of the minstrel show, of misogynist travesty, of the ethnic slur (Smith's performances of white Jewish women in *Fires* and *Twilight*,
or of Korean women in *Twilight* are typically liable to this resentment).
While this offense may be inevitable, it also reflects a sense of the implicit
textuality of Smith's work, an accommodation of "performance writing" to
the regime of scripted "dramatic theatre." For to protest Smith's enactment
in this way is to regard her portrayal of the script of "character" as illicit,
unauthorized, faithless, to argue that "Anonymous Lubavitcher Woman"
(*Fires*) or "Mrs. Young-Soon Han" (*Twilight*) would inhabit her script, her
language, more sincerely, without the irony that appears in the gap between
"actor" and "character" in Smith's lucid performance. Yet "fidelity" of this
kind depends on a modern, print-derived understanding of theatre: only
when the identity of the play is assigned to its bookish form does theatrical "fidelity" to "the text" become imaginable. In this sense, modern
dramatic theatre is always "performative" in J. L. Austin's sense. Its force
arises from the way we *do* things with words, the ways we attribute potential
action to them and so evoke what kinds of meanings they might have *as*
performance.

New forms of playwriting – Ibsen in the 1880s, *Waiting for Godot* in the
1950s, autoperformance in the 1980s and 1990s – often point to lacunae
in contemporary performance practice, as the available conventions of the
stage may seem inadequate to the demands made by new writing: what or
how to *do* this text, or some elements of this text, is not self-evident in the
contemporary practice of theatre. Smith's gestural mimicry is an instance
of this kind of innovation, particularly as it falls across liberal notions of the
(im)proprieties of racial or ethnic marking in performance. Is Smith's performance, we might ask, akin to Fredric Jameson's account of postmodern
pastiche, "like parody, the imitation of a peculiar or unique, idiosyncratic
style, the wearing of a linguistic mask, speech in a dead language"? Is *Fires
in the Mirror* "a neutral practice of such mimicry, without any of parody's
ulterior motives, amputated of the satiric impulse, devoid of laughter and
of any conviction that alongside the abnormal tongue you have momentar-
ily borrowed, some healthy linguistic normality still exists" (*Postmodernism*
17)? Probably not; while Smith's imitation seems value-neutral, as a whole
each of her plays and performances are full of conviction, even tenden-
tious. Instead, like Brecht, Smith abrades the interface between empathy
and demonstration, and enacts a particularly gritty instance of the general
problem of dramatic performativity, a moment in which the transformation of writing into representational action gains social traction in the world
beyond the stage.[3]

Isn't Mel Gibson's Hamlet too thoughtless? Ethan Hawke's too callow? Isn't Smith's "Anonymous Lubavitcher Woman" too trite? Despite the innovative character of her working methods, Smith's performance activates interpretive habits long associated with dramatic performance in the age of print: the desire to measure the performance against another (more) authorized site of the work's perdurable identity, the script. And what provokes this anxiety in Smith's performance is her use of language. Smith's ironic distanciation emerges less from the narrative juxtaposition of different speakers and perspectives ("The Reverend Al Sharpton" and "Rikvah Siegal" on the meaning of "Hair") than from the way Smith's vocal imitation, her studied attention to the shaping and emphasis of individual gestures and syllables, foregrounds the character's practice of *speech* – its accents, rhythms, clichés, and even its implicit "poetry." Onstage, Smith's attention to physical and verbal gesture recalls Richard Schechner's definition of performance as "restored *behavior*" ("Collective Reflexivity"). Yet her forceful marking of the character's speech underscores the textual element of the performance, the illusion that what is being "restored" – as is perhaps always the case in print culture – is the antecedent text, at once the text of the interview and the script of character it records. Transcribing live behavior into live acting, Smith's performance nevertheless stages its dependence on writing.

For this reason, Smith's plays have also proven controversial as they have moved from the stage into a different arena of production, print. Although Smith's work is hardly representative in method or style of the wide diversity of "performance" practice (much of which owes its lineage to the visual arts and to dance, and does not involve a script or writing in any direct way), it raises an important set of questions about writing in contemporary drama, theatre and performance.[4] Is this kind of work *drama*? Is Smith a *writer*, or a *playwright*? What is the ratio of script to performance in the identity of Smith's work? While Smith's performances have been widely discussed, the distinctive appearance of her works in print – their mise-en-page – has not drawn much attention, despite the fact that the design of Smith's page is commonly thought to bear directly on performance. The visual layout of the speeches appears to phrase a gestural punctuation, marking the rhythm, pacing, emphasis, and significance of utterance in the formalities of print. Smith's page locates a different kind of genre instability, too. For while her solo performances draw Smith's *plays* (notably, her preferred term) toward the regimes of "performance art," their lineated appearance on the page draws her books toward the print regimes of contemporary poetry, a field in which performance – particularly performance by *actors* – is regarded with an irritable skepticism. Smith's sense that her work preserves "something that is like poetry" gestures in this direction, too, as does her presiding concern with the forms and rhythms of language. Here, I want to attend to the work of Smith's page in recalling, legislating, and enacting a performance of language, a possibility which has been one of the dominant dimensions of modernist poetry, and which has – since the "performance poetry" movement of the 1970s – led to a critical interrogation of the relationship between the poem on the page and the poem in performance. Smith's page, and the page of performance writing more generally, materializes a searching anxiety about the relationship between the printform of the drama and the ethics of enactment in the late age of print.

I. PRIZING THE PLAY: PERFORMANCE, PRINT, AND GENRE

> L'opposition du poète et de l'acteur en est toute contaminée.
> Henri Meschonnic, *Critique du rythme* (280)

As printed books, Smith's plays locate two instabilities lurking in the assimilation of drama to print, instabilities noted ever since Ben Jonson published his plays among his *Works* in 1616: the place of dramatic writing in the canons of print authorship, and the bearing of performance on the print identity of drama. Print's bearing on the social identity of Smith's work is illuminated by a small but revealing controversy, the Pulitzer Prize jury's decision to drop *Twilight: Los Angeles, 1992* from consideration for the 1994 prize.[5] The Pulitzer Prize is a prize for *writing*: prizes are awarded in various categories of journalism, in fiction, poetry, drama, musical composition, and, perhaps revealingly, in photo-journalism and editorial cartooning. Prizes are not awarded in theatre, choreography (how can we know the dancer from the dance?), or musical *performance*, and the prize in drama is "For a distinguished *play* by an American *author*, preferably original in its source and dealing with American life" (Pulitzer Prize website). Although *Fires in the Mirror* had been a "Nominated Finalist" in 1993, the 1994 Pulitzer committee noted two reasons for removing *Twilight* from consideration: the "language of the play is not invented but gleaned from interviews" and "the play is not reproducible by other performers because it relies for authenticity on the performer's having done those interviews" ("Rebutting").

The Pulitzer committee's comments direct our attention to the awkward assimilation of drama to the authorized canons of print literature in two ways. What does it mean to represent others' language within the structure of an authorial work? And to what degree do the competing claims of "performance" as a mode of production undermine the print-inflected sense of the drama's identity as "writing"? William A. Henry III, chair of the Pulitzer jury, reports that "What Anna said to me was that doing the interviews was integral to performing the piece, that she couldn't imagine what it would be like to have someone else doing her work, and that it wouldn't be the same thing. [. . .] Plainly, it was a creative act. But it's not fiction" ("Rebutting"). A play can be recognized as *writing* only when, like a poem or a novel or even an editorial cartoon, its originating agent can be recognized as an Author responsible for the words on the page (well, at least for the dialogue; the committee isn't very picky about the provenance of other elements of the page, as stage directions, layout and design, punctuation and so on are either assumed to be authorial or to be irrelevant to authorship). Writing down, organizing, assembling, and shaping a collage of interview material, Smith's "writing" has operated as an act of construction and selection, but not – to the Pulitzer committee, at least – as an inscribed act of invention. The Pulitzer committee are no Foucauldians: whether or not *Hamlet* would meet these criteria for original authorship, to date the prize has not been awarded for work that distinguishes the dramatic author-function from the individualized "author" typical of other literary modes. Musicals have won the prize on several occasions – *South Pacific* in 1950, *Fiorello* in 1960, *How to Succeed in Business Without Really Trying* in 1962, *A Chorus Line* in 1976, *Sunday in the Park with George* in 1985 – but in all cases, the committee has been able to individuate and authorize each element of the script, even in the case of *A Chorus Line* clearly apportioning the disciplines of "writing," naming and distinguishing the creator of the performance – "Conceived, choreographed and directed by Michael Bennett" – from the more conventional authors and composers – "with book by James Kirkwood and Nicholas Dante, music by Marvin Hamlisch, and lyrics by Edward Kleban."[6] Musicals are richly collaborative works, but are, however inaccurately, readily represented as having a clear division of creative labor. The prize has rarely been given for adaptations (to Albert Hackett and Frances Goodrich, for their adaptation of *The Diary of Anne Frank* in 1956), and has sidestepped collaboratively scripted work like *The Laramie Project* and other solo works like Eric Bogosian's *Talk Radio* (nominated in 1988), though the prize for fiction has been given for works that raise analogous complications – Norman Mailer's *The Executioner's Song* in 1980 and Michael Cunningham's *The Hours* in 1999.

Genres and the ways we define them are always under the pressure of new creation: the Pulitzer Prize for 2004 was awarded to Doug Wright for his one-man autobiographical play, *I Am My Own Wife* – a play in which "Doug Wright" appears as a character, but which was neither performed by nor directed by Wright. The Pulitzer committee's decision to dismiss *Twilight* not only points to the ongoing challenge of assimilating printed drama to other forms of literature, but also underscores a regulatory relationship between dramatic writing and theatrical performance. Performance is an important element in the Pulitzer Prizes: both musical and dramatic compositions must have been performed (and, usually, have been performed in or near New York, where the committee is based) to be eligible for consideration. But the sense that Smith's performance is intrinsic to the work itself, and so eliminates *Twilight* from consideration as "drama," is revealing. This line of thinking implies that however important performance may be to the full realization of the work, the work is finally, ineffably embodied in the script or score. A scripted work dependent on a specific performer would not be a work of *writing*, and so would not fall within the committee's purview (stand-up comedy, for example; presumably a musical composition which could be performed only by its virtuoso composer would be similarly excluded). Performance may realize the work but should have no real bearing on the intrinsic public identity of the writing. Regarding dramatic writing much as it regards musical composition, the committee takes the printed text to contain and regulate the full and precise realization of the work. Performance can be neither re-creation, co-creation, nor transformation, but only a form of "derivative creativity."[7] *Twilight* is not individuated enough to qualify as Smith's unique *writing*. *Twilight* is too closely identified with Smith's unique individuality as a performer to qualify as *dramatic* writing.

It's important not merely to dismiss the Pulitzer jury's thinking in our enthusiasm for Smith's work, in part because Smith's account of her writing seems to echo the jury's conventional understanding of drama and performance. Answering to the sense that the writing is actually predicated on her personal skill or charisma as a performer, Smith has insisted that her plays can and should be performed by others. She pointed out that a full-cast version of *Fires in the Mirror* had been performed by the Mixed Blood Theater of Minneapolis, saying, "I *want* other people to do the acting, to experience what it is to be in somebody else's shoes" ("Rebutting"). Smith's work has proven attractive for full-cast performances, particularly on college campuses, and *House Arrest* was workshopped by a full cast leading up to Smith's later solo performances.[8] Smith argues that the multiplicity of voices she brings together in "my work" *should* be enacted by a full cast: "As for 'she didn't write a word of it,' that's beside the point. [. . .] I deliberately positioned myself across from that kind of theater, that has a single voice. It's political, yes. It's anti-traditional, yes. But I feel we desperately need bigger voices, and that's why, you bet, I want fifth graders performing my work" ("Rebutting"). And yet it's not the representation of "multiple voices" that's at issue: Tony Kushner's *Angels in America* (which won the 1993 prize in drama) not only represents a wide range of "voices" but also stages historical figures like Roy Cohn. The committee's decision rests on the assertion that *Twilight* is not authorized in a conventional sense, as either an individual or a corporate "work." While Smith chose interview subjects, wrote the monologues down, edited them, and gave them dramatic form, activities fully consistent with individual "writing" (it's "*my* work," after all), Smith's account of the collaborative nature of this kind of writing also confirms the committee's hesitations. In the interviews, Smith's "goal was to create an atmosphere in which the interviewee would experience his/her own authorship. Speaking teaches us what our natural 'literature' is. In fact, everyone, in a given amount of time, will say something that is like poetry" (*Fires* xxxi). Perhaps they speak something "like poetry" that Smith transforms into drama, writes as *her* play; perhaps the words remain their own property, despite appearing under the sign of *Twilight*.

Like the committee, Smith values drama as principally a form of writing, introducing the published version of *Twilight: Los Angeles, 1992* with this statement:

This book is first and foremost a document of what an *actress heard* in Los Angeles. The performance is a reiteration of that. When I did my research in Los Angeles, I was listening with an ear that was trained to hear stories for the specific purpose of repeating them with the elements of character intact. (*Twilight* xxiv)

Since Smith is concerned to establish her works as *plays* in a conventional, literary sense, it's not surprising that she refers to the published form of her play as a "book," a "document" of which the "performance is a reiteration." While this sense of performance as reiteration jibes with the jury's literary understanding of drama (an authorial text that others can reiterate without fundamentally altering it, because its identity is not finally implicated in its embodiment, as performance), Smith also implies that this form of social drama depends on *her* ability to lend voice to what she heard, to how she heard the stories, and to her process as a writer and performer: "the specific purpose of repeating them with the elements of character intact" absorbs the interviewing, writing, rehearsing, and performing into a single indivis-ible process. The jury's decision to bypass *Twilight* for consideration, its effort to come to grips with the genre of Smith's work is not just benighted aestheticism. Insofar as the jury's categories of judgment resonate with the tensions in Smith's own account of her work, this decision evokes a more general problem. How do we understand dramatic writing under the pres-sure of new forms of writing, performing, and printing plays? What's at stake in the material form – print, performance – of this form of dramatic writing, the autoperformance text, a text that seems, in its connection to the identity of a given performer, to complicate a conventional understand-ing of text and performance, writing and enactment as distinct modes of production?

Since the Author is one of the principal ideological and material effects of print in the modern era, it's perhaps not surprising that the controversies about the identity of Smith's work take place at the multiplex interface of agency: author/writer/actor/character. Although much of the theatri-cal criticism of Smith's work has focused on the externality of her acting practice and its distance from the character-oriented, realistic traditions of the American Method, Smith describes her career as involved with "the pursuit of the authentic with the use of acting," a search "specifically to find America in its language," a language that is conceived *as* writing, even *as* print (Smith, *Talk to Me* 35, 12). As she reports in her memoir *Talk to Me*, Smith became interested in speech and character as part of her training at the American Conservatory Theatre in San Francisco in the 1970s. In addition to various movement, speech, and acting classes, she was required to take a Shakespeare class, which opened with an empha-sis on rhythm, stressing a distinction between iambic and trochaic meter. Smith's teacher maintained that "if you got a trochee in the second beat, a character was really 'losing it' psychologically, and this 'loss' made it pos-sible for you to really know something about that character, if you wore his or her words" (36). King Lear's entirely trochaic "Never, never, never, never, never" provides the "classic example of everything falling to pieces rhythmically" (36).

The desire to find clues to "character" in the printform of Shakespearean verse is long-standing, expressed in Folio-based practices of actor training associated with Neil Freeman and others who find a kind of psychological import in the meter, punctuation, capitalization, and other formalities of early modern print.[9] What is striking here, though, is less Smith's predica-tion of her work on Shakespeare than her sense of a determining relation-ship between the imprint of speech and the inner workings of character.

"Character, then, seemed to me to be an improvisation on given rhythms" (36), and can be seized by focusing on the rhythms of speech. "Character depends a great deal on trochees" (40), so much so that Shakespeare "broke through accepted rhythms," proving "that accepted rhythms were too restrictive to hold humanity" and so bringing us "human character that has lasted centuries" (41). Unlocking the secret character of her interview subjects involves a Shakespearean attention to the trochee – "What would it take now to bring across some trochees in the second beat" (41)? What it takes is learning to wear the language of others, to inhabit their "rhythmic architecture" (36), rather than being distracted merely by the words themselves. Smith shifts the purpose of her performance from a Method-inspired attention to discovering the character's inner "self" to a more engaged, even dialogic relation to "character." Her acting is less an identification *with* the psychological coherence of "character," than an identification *of* the (in)coherence of his/her public performance, the formal rhythms of speech: "It's in language that I think I can find the other. If I can get people to that moment that they're digging deep, and then I repeat what they have done, I should actually end up seeming quite like them" (53). Smith's attention to the word provides a point of identification: "My paternal grandfather had told me when I was a child, 'If you say a word often enough, it *becomes* you'" (37).

Speaking teaches us what our natural "literature" is (*Fires* xxxi) – Smith's apparently "oral" sense of theatre is, as Walter Ong might point out, more akin to "secondary orality," evidently assimilated to the canons of print literacy that have arisen since, say, Shakespeare's era.[10] Inarticulate poets that we are, our speech should be preserved in print precisely because it is our native "literature." Despite its apparent investment in speech, Smith's theatre is a theatre of writing, a "dramatic theatre" in a relatively conventional modern sense, a stage predicated on print: "People seem to be looking beyond the spoken word. The word is not enough. When was the last time any of us accepted a person's 'word'? We need contracts, we need laws, we need evidence" (*Talk to Me* 39). We need books, we need printed plays. It may be that speaking teaches us the rhythms of our natural "literature," but it is only in print that this speech emerges *as literature*, as "something that is like poetry." In its dual materialization – as printed text, as solo performance – Smith's work dramatizes a cultural confusion that even the august Pulitzer jury could not really be expected to resolve. How do we understand the auratic work of performance in the age of mechanical reproduction? Do we assign authenticity to the reproducible and reproduced text, located as the origin of the work? Or do we value the evanescent performance as the work's essential materialization, even if – as Smith herself seems to think – that performance is a kind of reiteration?

What to call it? Writing or wrighting? Drama, theatre, performance art? What to call Smith? A writer? A playwright? An author? A performance artist? When she's performing *Twilight* should we call that *acting* in the same sense that we might call her work in *An American President* or *The West Wing* acting? Smith regards "*performance art*" as "a catchall phrase meant to serve a variety of people in a variety of art forms, not just theater, who cannot be easily categorized," and so prefers the term *playwright*: "I like to think of a playwright in the old way. The word, as you see, is spelled play-w-r-i-g-h-t. It's not w-r-i-t-e. That's not a typo. *Playwright* is like *wheelwright*. A wheelwright makes wheels. A playwright makes plays" (*Talk to Me* 198). A teapot tempest, perhaps, but the definitional problems swelling around Smith's work dramatize the challenge of writing and performing now, in the late age of print, at a moment when – despite the rise of new forms of performance, new modes of theatricality, and the urgent calls to displace both writing and theatre with alternative modes of live and/or digital performance – print seems to continue to exert a powerful, if nostalgic, force on our sense of the cultural identity of an important mode of representation: dramatic performance.

II. THEATRE OF THE VOICE: ANNA DEAVERE SMITH'S LYRIC PAGE

> Le lien entre la poésie et la page comme théâtre porte plusieurs questions. Quelles interactions entre le visuel et l'auditif? Le visuel, transcription? La poésie, spectacle? Oui, si le spectacle est l'actualisation, dans un lieu, du subjectif, et la poésie l'aventure du sujet – transsujet dans le langage. La poésie: théâtre de la voix.
>
> Henri Meschonnic, *Critique du rythme* (308)

The Pulitzer debate frames several crucial issues – the status of dramatic authorship, the function of writing in the theatre, the relationship between writer and performer and between writing and performance in locating the identity of the drama – and constellates them around the materiality of the printed play. On the page, Smith's plays have a distinctive look: a series of monologues, grouped under different headings ("Prologue," "The Territory," "Here's a Nobody" and so on in *Twilight*). Each monologue opens with a title ("My Enemy," the first monologue of *Twilight*), a speaker "Rudy Salas, Sr. Sculptor and painter," and a description of the subject and scene of the interview.

My Enemy
Rudy Salas, Sr. Sculptor and
painter

> (A large very warm man, with a blue shirt with the
> tails out and blue jeans and tennis shoes. He is at a
> dining-room table with a white tablecloth. There is a
> bank of photographs in frames on the sideboard
> next to the table. There is a vase of flowers on an-
> other table near the table. There are paintings of his
> on the wall. Nearest the table is a painting of his
> wife. His wife, Margaret, a woman in glasses and a
> long flowered dress, moves around the room. For a
> while she takes photo albums out of the sideboard
> and out of the back room, occasionally saying
> something. She is listening to the entire interview.
> He has a hearing aid in his left ear and in his right
> ear. He is sitting in a wooden captain's chair, me-
> dium-sized. He moves a lot in the chair, sometimes
> with his feet behind the front legs, and his arms
> hanging over the back of the chair. He is very warm.)
>
> (*Twilight* 1)

While some of these introductions are extensive – the account of Rudy
Salas provides a detailed description of his clothing, character, the room
in which the interview took place, his wife, and his movements – others
are quite brief (the interview with Josie Morales: "In a conference room
at her workplace, downtown Los Angeles" [66]). Smith does note when
she conducts an interview by telephone – as in the case of Homi Bhabha
("Phone interview. He was in England. I was in L. A. He is part Persian, lived
in India. Has a beautiful British accent" [232]). The page takes a striking
stance toward performance, in part because it is not clear how much of
this material should or might be evident in performance. As it turns out,
onstage as well as in the television broadcasts, the written headings – section
headings, heading of the individual monologue, name and occupation of
the speaker – are part of the show: onstage, they are projected during the
scene; on film or video, they are inserted as titles between scenes. Writing
visibly articulates the structure of the performance.

On the other hand, the sketch of the scene and character clearly serves
a different purpose, informing the reader about the circumstances of the
interview, and occasionally providing an index of some possible gestures in
performance (Rudy Salas's feet and arms). While these accounts resemble

stage directions, providing some signals for future performers, they are in a sense part of the "novelization" of modern plays in print. While Shaw's directions enact the play for a spectatorial reader, Smith's descriptive directions seem to do something else, something perhaps even more literary. Rather than enfolding a potential performance into narrative form, Smith's directions appear to narrate, to memorialize a past moment of performance, describing a moment in the history of the play's development. As they appear in print, the descriptive passages mark an anomaly in how the print-work embodies, represents, or signals the performance-work. The headnotes provide diegetic information that will not be used in theatrical performance, information that speaks to the writerly origins of the script (Smith's actor-centered performance uses only minimal costume and set elements, and generally refuses to place the character in an explanatory naturalistic setting). To the extent that they seem to record the performance of the play's writing, *Fires* and *Twilight* might seem even more bookish than other printed plays, a suggestion underlined by the amount of ancillary information these books contain: in *Fires*, a page of "acclaim," a dedication page, table of contents, acknowledgment pages, a Foreword by Cornel West (six pages), an Introduction by the author (nineteen pages), "The Crown Heights Conflict: Background Information" (three pages), "Crown Heights, Brooklyn A Chronology" (seven pages), a listing of "The Characters" (three pages), and finally a full "Production History" (two pages) (*Fires* ix–lx).[11] *Twilight* opens with acknowledgments, an introduction, and a production history, twenty-eight pages in all. How these elements instantiate the play as a book is confirmed by the acting edition of *Fires in the Mirror* published by Dramatists Play Service. Although the acting version has a brief, untitled paragraph describing the collaborators of the original 1991 production at The Festival of New Voices at the New York Shakespeare Festival, its prefatory material is otherwise limited to a dedication, table of contents, and list of characters (eight pages). Notably, this absence of "narrative" or historical texture is supplemented by the presence of a specifically theatrical text: the acting edition contains a property plot and list of sound effects.[12]

The stabilizing rhetoric of the book extends to a critical aspect of the printform of Smith's drama, the layout of the monologues on the page. Although they might be printed as paragraphs – in the manner, for example, of ethnographic reports, which they resemble to some degree, or of Tim Miller's monologues – Smith's work is represented on the page "performance-wise," or perhaps "poetry-wise."

> So I don't know what kind of crap is that.
> And make me say things I don't wanna say
> and make me do things I don't wanna do.
> I am a special person.
> I was born different.
> I'm a man born by my foot.
> I born by my foot.
> Anytime a baby comin' by the foot
> they either cut the mother
> or the baby dies.
> But I was born with my foot.
> I'm one of the special.
> There's no way they can overpower me.
> No there's nothing to hide,
> you can repeat every word I say.
>
> (*Fires* 139)

The final monologue of *Fires*, "Carmel Cato: Lingering," dramatizes both Smith's rhetorical use of print conventions, and their implication of performance. Although Smith's characters are represented on the page as speaking in sentences (their utterances begin with capital letters, are marked with punctuation and are completed with a period [.]), the rhythm of their utterances seems to be marked by the page design, which aligns the text flush left but leaves a ragged right margin, using the page design to suggest the rhythms of speech: lineation as rhetorical punctuation. This layout implies "speech," but does so with considerable ambiguity. Are these rhythms a record of the interview, a record of Smith's performance, and/or directions to a performer? The layout on the page represents performance at the intersection between the narrative or diegetic and the theatrical or productive functions of dramatic writing, a tension characteristic of the drama in the era of print. The spatial dynamics of lineation mark considerably more than breathing pauses. The formal construction of the page according to the conventions of lyric poetry renders the bibliographic code of *Fires* significant, and materializes the play's meanings in specific ways. Read as a poem, the lines mark a poignant insistence on the individual "I" with the claim to a "special" status, using repetition to sustain and enlarge the force of that identification ("I'm a man born by my foot. / I born by my foot."), framing a stark alternative between the life of the mother and of the child, and of course giving a special prominence to Cato's rejection of "The Jewish people" who "told me / there are certain people I cannot be seen with / and certain things I can not say" (138). Cato's deft, and deftly metatheatrical, embrace of Smith stands pointedly on its own as well: "you can repeat every word I say." Whether imposing the rhetoric of the lyric poem on Cato's speech, or discovering this rhetoric in his speaking, Smith's writing does much more than merely represent casual utterance as something like poetry. Materializing the words as a poem, Smith materializes Cato's language in a distinctive genre, identifies it with and through a specific form and practice of cultural meaning.

David Brooks ridicules this element of Smith's writing as a merely pompous inflation of everyday "banalities" produced by "randomly striking the return key on the keyboard" ("Ms. Smith" 36). Nonetheless, the implication of the semantic design of the poem in its material form on the page situates Smith's plays in the dominant tradition of modern American poetry, reaching back to Ezra Pound and the imagists, to William Carlos Williams, and perhaps most immediately to Charles Olson's "projective" poetics and the poetry it has inspired. Olson's "Projective Verse" (first published in 1950) collocates the material form of the poetic line and the "field" of the page with an organic (heartbeat, breath) process of poetic composition, and articulates Smith's poetics in a surprisingly thorough way.[13]

Olson urges "COMPOSITION BY FIELD, as opposed to inherited line, stanza, over-all form, what is the 'old' base of the non-projective," a sense of "the *kinetics* of the thing" ("A poem is energy transferred from where the poet got it [. . .] by way of the poem itself to, all the way over to, the reader"). The "projective" poet orchestrates the formal elements of writing directly with the sense perception and organic process of the poem's development ("Projective Verse" 239–40). The "two halves" of the poem's "intelligence" are the relationship between the ear/syllable and the breath/line:

> the HEAD, by way of the EAR, to the SYLLABLE
> the HEART, by way of the BREATH, to the LINE
> (242)

This formulation connects oral and written poetics, but the characteristically modernist formality of the line arises more vividly as a consequence of mechanical reproducibility: "It is the advantage of the typewriter that, due to its rigidity and its space precisions, it can, for a poet, indicate exactly the breath, the pauses, the suspensions even of syllables, the juxtapositions even of parts of phrases, which he intends" (245). Typewriting materializes both words and the space around them, formally sustaining Olson's notion that the spatial form of the line on the page can signify the breath and the pause as crucial elements in the poem's *verbal* design. "For the first time the poet has the stave and the bar a musician has had. For the first time he can, without the convention of rime and meter, record the listening he has done to his own speech and by that one act indicate how he would want any reader, silently or otherwise, to voice his work" (245). The typewritten or printed line has a dual status, perhaps less immediately akin to traditional dramatic writing than to performance writing like Smith's: it represents performance at the intersection of the past of composition and the future of the poem's readings, its directed performances.

Olson's account of projective verse has become the common currency of poetry, so it's hardly surprising that many "performance" texts, and a surprising number of plays, evoke this implicitly organic rhetorical punctuation, the punctuation of the breath reified as the line on the page. Nor is it surprising that Smith's plays evoke Olson, given her investment in reproducing the formal elements of speech (the trochee). For Olson, though, the formality of typewriting is not simply a means to preserve an innately "oral" act in the visual design of the printed page. Instead, typewriting enables an understanding of poetic communication that is at once "restorative" and "performative." According to Olson, type arrestingly restores poetry to the order of the ear – so that the "intervals of composition" heard by the poet can be transmitted to the reader – rather than the formal ordering of the eye insistently evoked by the oppressive designs of official verse forms. What Williams, Pound, cummings, and others discovered in their exploration of free verse was that they could compose "as though verse was to have the reading its writing involved, as though not the eye but the ear was to be its measurer, as though the intervals of its composition could be so carefully put down as to be precisely the intervals of its registration" (246). Poetry is oral and organic, composed along the breath. The formal designs of the ear – "rime & regular cadence" (246) – that were the oral poet's means of composing and preserving his work have at once "merely lived on" after the rise of print and yet have also subtly transformed the practices of writing and reading. The poet of traditional verse shoehorns inspiration into forms that may no longer have expressive value, forms which now register print's emphasis on the visual over the oral, writing over speech, reading over performance. The typewriter – and, of course, the entire revolution of modernist book printing – enables the poet to register the organic process of composition, and to transmit it to the reader.

Despite its "performative" character (for Olson, both words and white space "do things"), projective verse articulates seamlessly with a "literary," even perhaps New Critical, understanding of dramatic performance. A literary valuation of the drama tends to see its performance as licensed and constrained by the text, so that a staging that seems to depart from such fidelity becomes something else, a betrayal of the work. Similarly, although print enables Olson's poet to write for the ear, to record the juncture of head and heart, syllable and line, it also enables the poet to instigate the reader's "performance" in the design of the poem on the page. Projective verse does not, in this sense, make a text available for new, altered, reimagined performances, it does not make the text available for new performances at all. Projective verse *projects* the poem *into* the reader.

Lineation appears at once to reenact the process of the poem's composition, to embody the semantic content of the poem, and to enact its rhetorical address to the reader: the rhetoric of the projective line both transmits the poem and claims to govern its proper performance. Nonetheless, projective lineation also appears to challenge the organic connection between subject, writing, reading, and (re)performance, and so to challenge the conventional sense of the stage's dependence on the page. Like Smith, Olson pins the revolution of modernism to the trochee: "The revolution of the ear, 1910, the trochee's heave" (239), echoing Pound's Canto 81, "To break the pentameter, that was the first heave" (Pound, *Cantos* 518).[14] But if Pound and Williams are the touchstones of Olson's effort to define projective verse, the task of locating "the degree to which the projective involves a stance toward reality outside a poem as well as a new stance towards the reality of a poem itself" appears to demand a dialogue with Euripides and Zeami and Elizabethan drama, and even with T. S. Eliot's plays. Like his modernist predecessors, Olson is invested in a poetics of the "Direct treatment of the 'thing,'" a poetics in which the concreteness of verbal expression asserts a (more than) metonymic relation to the concreteness of social reality (Ezra Pound, "A Retrospect" 3). In Olson's *objectism*, a word is considerably more than an individualized exhalation; it is "taken to stand for the kind of relation of man to experience which a poet might state as the necessity of a line or a work to be as wood is, to be as clean as wood is as it issues from the hand of nature, to be as shaped as wood can be when a man has had his hand to it" (247). For the poet to issue a word with this kind of cleanness requires an effort of self-displacement: "Objectism is the getting rid of the lyrical interference of the individual as ego, of the 'subject' and his soul, that peculiar presumption by which western man has interposed himself between what he is as a creature of nature (with certain instructions to carry out) and those other creations of nature which we may, with no derogation, call objects" (247). This abnegation, essential to the poet's representation of an objectified world in words, is sustained in the essay through Olson's encounter with drama, which exemplifies the act of "getting rid of the lyrical interference of the individual." To Olson, drama does not register an emanation of individual sensibility, but a world of its own: "It is projective size that the play, *The Trojan Women*, possesses, for it is able to stand, is it not, as its people do, beside the Aegean – and neither Andromache or the sea suffer diminution" (248).

This attention to the objective nature of the drama amplifies and specifies the work of projective poetry as a theory of writing and performance. "Such works" – and here Olson refers at once to Euripides and to Homer – "could not issue from men who conceived verse without the full relevance of human voice, without reference to where lines come from, in the individual who writes" (248). The "lines" are not merely the self-expression of the "individual who writes"; the writer must displace the individual ego to allow that larger language, the full relevance of human voice, to emerge. Unlike the dominant mode of modern American poetry, the lyric, dramatic writing is crucial to Olson because it clearly locates the individual, expressive voice of the writer within a fully socialized, objectified language, a language inherently set apart from the spontaneous overflow of individual feeling. The dramatic poet (multiplied and concealed behind the characters) shares with the epic poet (multiplied and concealed behind the supra-individual sweep of the narrative) the ability to "carry much larger material" because the language he uses, the language that arises on his breath, is not individual, not his language alone. For this paradoxical reason, "the *Cantos* make more 'dramatic' sense than do the plays of Mr. Eliot" (248). The *Cantos* strive to represent, projectively, *language* with the full relevance of human voice, while Eliot "fails as a dramatist":

in his listenings he has stayed there where the ear and the mind are, has only gone from his fine ear outward rather than, as I say a projective poet will, down through the workings of his own throat to that place where breath comes from, where breath has its beginnings, where drama has to come from, where, the coincidence is, all act springs. (249)

Olson's "Projective Verse" is often taken as a paean to the breath, to the poet's organic expression, but the poet's breath sustains Olson's larger project only when it bears the public resources of language, when it stages a world by "getting rid of the lyrical interference of the individual." Olson's poetics articulate the defining tensions animated by dramatic writing in print culture, and "Projective Verse" locates the theoretical and practical context for the mise-en-page of writing like *Fires in the Mirror*, *Twilight*, and a wide range of performance writing. Smith's investment in the trochee, the sense that her writing begins as an act of listening, the apparent representation of the breath in the lyric design of the page, even her emphasis on dialect, on the precise shaping of the *syllable*, involves a virtuosity of absence as a means to embodying "the full relevance of human voice," on the stage. Smith's writing and performance are deeply implicated in the trajectory of (post)modern poetics, and poetics provides the means to read the tension between the organic and the objective staged on the page of her plays.

"Projective Verse" implicates Smith's writing in the context of contemporary poetics, and foregrounds the materiality of Smith's lineation: does it really matter, really signify like verse, *mean as* poetry? Is there more than a passing, superficial similarity between Smith's practice and the discourse of modern poetry? Much as the different "lyrics" that Smith assembles encode a diversity of languages and speakers within a single formal design, the modern English free-verse lyric is hardly without conceptual and formal conventions. It's worth recalling Marjorie Perloff's characterization of the formalities of free verse at greater length again here:

(1) The free verse, in its variability (both of stress and of syllable count) and its avoidance of obtrusive patterns of recurrence, tracks the speaking voice (in conjunction with the moving eye) of a perceptive, feeling subject, trying to come to terms with what seems to be an alien, or at least incomprehensible world. [. . .] (2) Free verse is organized by the power of the Image, by a construct of images as concrete and specific as possible, that serve as objective correlatives for inner states of mind. [. . .] (3) Although free verse is speech-based, although it tracks the movement of the breath itself, syntax is regulated, which is to say that the free-verse "I" generally speaks in complete sentences. [. . .] (4) A corollary of regulated syntax is that the free-verse poem *flows*; it is, in more ways than one, *linear*. [. . .] (5) As a corollary of feature 4, the rhythm of continuity of which I have been speaking depends on the unobtrusiveness of sound structure in free verse, as if to say that what is said must not be obscured by the actual saying. In this sense, free verse is the antithesis of such of its precursors as Gerard Manley Hopkins's sprung rhythm. [. . .] (6) Finally – and this accords with the unobtrusiveness of sound – the free-verse lyric before us is remarkable for its lack of visual interest. ("After Free Verse" 94–95)

As a formation in the history of writing, free verse instantiates a certain range of subjective experience. Of course, Smith's writing begins as speech, which may in part account for its unobtrusive rhythms, its regulated *flow*. But the visual design of her page also seems to provide that speech with *more* interest, to lend its rhythms additional, spatial punctuation and emphasis, to make its subdued native imagery stand out *as* imagery, to impose new meanings by imposing a specific visual form. In this sense, the design of the writing, its bibliographic code, reinforces the ideology of the lyric "I" in ways that throw the conventionality of Smith's representation of her speakers into much sharper relief. The multiplex arrangement of "characters" in *Fires* tends to emphasize their individual perspectives, to differentiate them sharply according to distinctive social, racial, gender, and class positions. By framing their language on the page according to the conventions of the contemporary lyric, Smith also subordinates such distinctions to a lyric valuation of the subject. After all, Smith's speakers recognize an alien world ("So I don't know what kind of crap is that"), through the organizing power of the image ("I born by my foot"), delivered through a casual-but-nonetheless-sentence-structured imitation of speech ("And make me say things I don't wanna say/and make me do things I don't wanna do), arrayed in linear fashion to represent a linear process of thinking in unobtrusive language with unobtrusive rhythmic effects, in ways that use the page (however modestly) to emphasize the homely idiosyncrasy of the imagery. Like Olson's, Smith's lineation appears to be based on the breath, and as a writer Smith tends to disappear behind her "voices" (since her own breathing in performance usually departs from the line breaks, it might be fairer to say that this lineation represents a breathing subject rather than determining one). The design of the page locates the writing relative to the ideology of lyric poetry, asserting a fundamental, sympathetic, even sentimental *likeness* among the characters, a likeness in the ways they engage with the social world represented in the continuity of their engagement with language. The tension between "the full relevance of human voice" on the one hand, and the breath whence "all act springs" on the other is replayed in Smith's work, reenacted in the gap between print and performance. For while Smith's solo enactment of a range of characters works to stage the political distinctions of speech and speaking, tracing individual difference through the common resources of language and gesture that frame identity as public discourse, her page stages the lyric "I" in its unique isolation, alone on the page, an individual subject nonetheless bound to and by the common conventionality of the breathing word.

"L'opposition du poète et de l'acteur est en toute contaminée" (Meschonnic 280). To say that Smith's conception of character, as it is registered both on the page and in performance, jibes in some way with the dominant conventions of modern poetry is surprising only if we regard genres as impermeable, only if we accept the boundaries (or *Borders*) of print culture (poetry on this shelf, drama on that, cookbooks over there). It's hardly surprising that Smith's writing is evocative of "performance poetry" in general, and more specifically of plays and performances that were developed in the performance-poetry scene of the San Francisco Bay Area in the late 1960s and 1970s: Ntozake Shange's choreopoem, *for colored girls who have considered suicide / when the rainbow is enuf,* first produced in

1974, comes immediately to mind as a precursor to Smith's drama.[15] But to train our attention on the materiality of the poem, on the political consequences of the lineated subject so to speak, is also to frame Smith's work in the context of critical avant-garde poetics of the 1980s and 1990s, a critique most familiarly associated with the L=A=N=G=U=A=G=E movement. Some sense of this critique can be gained from Bruce Andrews's brief essay, "Lines Linear How to Mean":

> Lines linear outline, clear boundaries' effect, notice the package from its perimeter, consistency, evenness, seemingly internal contours which end up packaging the inside so that they can react or point or be subordinated, as a homogenized unit, to what's outside. Lines as signatures of meaning by inscription "relationships by force" – after the fact, marking off an internal hierarchy of value identified with parts or tags, disciplining the already-constituted body. Too late. How far inside are we? Boundary as dividing – "you step over that line & you're asking for trouble" – privatizing property, without (internal) authority. Territorial markers and confinements, ghost towns, congested metropolis on a grid. (Andrews, *Paradise & Method* 119)

Reading the materiality of the page across genres may alert us to unsuspected features of the work, arising from the way its historicity is registered materially in the context of other printforms. To take the lyric line and the subject of capital as rhymes invites us to resituate Smith's page, to place the politics of performance alongside the politics of poetics. For Andrews, the line is part of an Althusserian understanding of ideology, the "body of sense & ideology [that] works to socialize" the subject by acting "on meanings the way it acts on individuals" that a radical approach to the materialization of poetry might resist, "alienate" in a specifically Brechtian sense (*Paradise & Method* 53). Whether we take Language writing, as Steve McCaffery suggests, either as "a partial critique of language inside the commoditarian experience of a bourgeois ideology," or as capitalism's "perfected simulacrum," Language writing objectifies the uses of language through a specifically Brechtian gesture, a gesture that extends the critique of the page to the stage of its enactment (*North of Intention* 25).

Andrews's critique of the proprietary character of the poetic line broadens the colloquy between performance writing and lyric poetry. Using a variety of forms that stage the interpenetration of genres (verse essays, theoretical poems), often through an absorbing fascination with the materiality of the word and its potential to be objectified – even spectacularized – on the page, Language writing brings into focus three distinct but related elements of

Smith's mise-en-page, and of experimental dramatic writing more generally: the potential alienation of (performed) language from its systematic
overdetermination by commodity culture; the political necessity of leverag-
ing the subject out of the poem, to disidentify speaker/speech/monologic
subject; and a formal attention to the ways the page might and might not
enable some of these dislocations and their enactment by readers and/as
performers. Attending to Smith's poetics, we can pinpoint a tension at the
heart of her work, between the rhetoric of "diversity" implied by the plays'
multiplication of subjects, and the constraints of the relatively homogenized
acts of lyric subjection performed by her verse.

III. LINES OF SUBJECTION: LANGUAGE WRITING, POETRY, AND PERFORMANCE

> The sentence and the line have different ways of bringing meaning
> into view.
>
> Lyn Hejinian, "Language and Paradise,"
> *The Language of Inquiry* (60)

To set Smith's writing in the context of Language poetics may seem at
first perverse: the densely theoretical concern with the objectified status of
the *word*, of language on the page characteristic of Language poetics may
seem poles apart from a form of writing that appears to arise directly from
speech, to be so fully, if unconsciously embedded in that commodified
social language that Language writing works to resist. Yet Language poetics
is fully engaged with the materiality of "something that is like poetry," and
so provides a dynamic explanatory context for the printform of Smith's
bookish plays. The social critique embodied in Language poetics opens
from a rich engagement with the performance of language (on the page,
in poetry readings), an account that resonates sharply against the material
mise-en-page of much performance writing, and against the social critique
embodied by Smith's performance.

As Bob Perelman argues in "Language Writing and Literary History," the
diverse group of writers labeled "Language" writers, while never producing "a uniform literary program" can be seen to have "a loose set of goals,
procedures, habits, and verbal textures," habits and textures also reminiscent of contemporary performance: breaking the automatism of the poetic
"I" and its naturalized voice; foregrounding textuality and other formal
devices; using or alluding to Marxist or poststructuralist theory in order
to open the present to critique and change (*Marginalization of Poetry* 12–
13).[16] Contesting "the expressive model emanating from workshops and

creative-writing departments" (15) through a theoretical and pragmatic commitment to the "material bases of writing" (14), the program of Language writing is pursued through an effort to see the social and the literary arenas as interpenetrating, to understand the act of writing as a means of exploring – and often alienating, in an explicitly Brechtian sense – the overdetermination of language by conventional social values. Despite the difficulties of encapsulating this wide range of poetries and poetics, Perelman does sketch some of the identifying marks of a Language poem:

> A neutral description of language writing might attempt to draw a line around a range of writing that was (sometimes) nonreferential, (occasionally) polysyntactic, (at times) programmatic in construction, (often) politically committed, (in places) theoretically inclined, and that enacted a critique of the literary I (in some cases). (21)

Insofar as more conventional lyrics regard the page as the transparent embodiment of sensibility, Language writing tends actively to imprint the page as the site of spectacle: it is the stage where words, objects, referents engage one another, often refusing the synthesis of a mastering lyric voice. This strategy is self-evident even in less rebarbative Language poems, such as Lyn Hejinian's *The Beginner*:

> This is a good place to begin.
> From something.
> Something beginning in an event that begin-
> ning overrides.
> Doubt instruction light safety fathom blind.
> In the doorway is the beginning thus and
> thus no denial.
> A little beat of time, a little happiness quite
> distinct from misery as yet.
> The sun shines.
> The sun is perceived as a bear, then a boat,
> then an instruction: see.
> The sun is a lily, then a whirlpool turning a
> crowd.
> (*The Beginner* 9)

Whether in the justified-left-and-right format of prose-appearing poems like Ron Silliman's *Tjanting* or Hejinian's groundbreaking *My Life*, the lapidary sentence/couplets of Barrett Watten's "Complete Thoughts" or Susan Howe's extraordinary experiments with overprinting, Language writing pays self-conscious attention to the mise-en-page and its effect on the work of the reader. Here, for example, the "sentence and the line have different ways of bringing meaning into view," particularly as the beat of declaration ("This is a good place to begin") at once raises the question of what's not declared (where, exactly, are we beginning? *in medias res*? where, exactly, is "This?"), and seems to be countered by "sentences" (begin with a capital letter, end with a period) that operate according to nonsyntactic, associative logics, the logic of poetic "lines" perhaps. "Doubt instruction light safety fathom blind" is not only not a sentence (no subject, no verb), but is a (blank) verse line that emphasizes its formal complexity: ten syllables, its basic iambic pentameter thrown off kilter by the trochee in the first syllable, a sharp caesura falling dead center, marked by a double stress (the spondee *light safety*) that neatly divides the line into two metrical halves. (Or maybe it *is* a sentence, or sentences, in the imperative: *Doubt* instruction *Light* safety *Fathom* blind?) The indicative mood of *beginning* is sustained by the narrative consequentiality of the sentence, whose subject happens in time, is placed by demonstrative adjectives (This) and prepositions (from, in), does something to its object, an object it can't seem to control, can't quite rein into the restrained gallop of the (non)syntax. Once begun, the narrative implies a cause and its effects. In a world of "thus and thus" there can be no "denial," and yet that "little beat of time" points to a cause that remains grammatically obscure while nonetheless inscribing a momentary consequence, a little happiness, "quite" (completely? almost?) distinct from a misery still offstage, ominously enough "as yet." The final three lines here enact a kind of poetics of the sentence and the line, moving from a subject/verb sentence perhaps definitive of "what is" ("The sun shines"), through an account of the process of metaphor, to the creation of metaphor itself. As in many of her poems, Hejinian's tone is a critical problem. How to take "The sun shines"? As the modernist "thing itself"? A cliché? Ironic deflation? Jameson's blank parody? And does it demand to be read differently than "The sun is a lily, then a whirlpool turning a / crowd"?

Finally, the layout of the words on the page enacts the poem's concern with beginning, sequence, consequence, place and time: only with the third "sentence" ("Something beginning") do we realize that the spatial point of the poem's beginning is not the margin, the edge. "This," marked as the beginning even with its large initial capital T, turns out to be indented, already *in* the space of the poem. It may be that we come to understand the formal structure of the lines *as* sentences only when the third line is urgently not enjambed as a line of poetry, but merely broken, apparently striking an unseen margin mid-word (a limit to beginning? an invisible barrier to the poem's extensiveness?), throwing us back to a different, unrecognized point of beginning, a left margin we had not yet understood as the page's (the poem's?) true point of origin. And when we turn the page, we might be surprised to find the poem discandying into what looks like prose, or at least like paragraphs.

The Beginner is far from the most idiosyncratic poem in its visual design, but what I mean to illustrate here is the way that Hejinian frames the poem's occupation of the page as a strategy of performance, a performance in which the "bibliographic" elements of the poem – those "accessories" of layout, design, typography, even punctuation – don't merely sustain the semantics of the poem, but are the materials from which the poem urges its fundamental meanings, the materials which must be encountered and performed by the poem's readers. Despite its resemblance to free verse, the formal structure of Hejinian's lineation frames an opposition between the organic breath and the enactment of language, a tension between the line and the sentence that evokes the strain between the lyric and the dramatic in Olson's "projective verse" and that continues to animate writing more explicitly connected to the stage of dramatic performance.

We could recall David Antin's "talk poems" again here:

> [. . .]   writing is a form of fossilized talking   which gets put
> inside of a can   called a book   and i respect that can   its a
>   means of preservation   or maybe we should say in a frozen food
> container called a book   but on the other hand if you dont know
> how to handle that frozen food container that icy block will never
>   turn back into talking   and if it will never turn back into talking
> it will never be of any use to you again
>   ("is this the right place?" 45–46)

While Antin's work falls squarely into an oral tradition of poetry, it is important to recognize that this oral tradition is, in Ong's sense, now secondary, fully imagined through the impress of print, not least because Antin's "highly particularized format: unjustified left and right margins, lowercase letters, spaces (usually five or six characters) between phrases, and the absence of all punctuation except – intriguingly – the question mark," is an emphatically *print* object, a "calculated" means of representing speech in the materiality of the page (Marjorie Perloff, "Talk Poem" 125). In an extended conversation with Antin, Charles Bernstein noted that there "is some connection to the practice of lineation suggested by Olson in 'Projective Verse'" in Antin's poetry, provoking Antin to account for his various experiments with the mise-en-page. While we might think that Antin's distinctive layout is supposed to provide instructions for performers (breathe in the gaps), Antin sharply distinguishes between the notion of a musical score and the material design of the talk poems on the page. A score is "a kind of transducer, allowing 'the music' to be stored, transmitted and distributed by other means than live performance, and to enable reperformance by oneself or by other performers," but the talk poems "weren't designed for other performers or for reperformance in general." Antin points to a persistent problem in contemporary poetics, and marks a palpable anxiety shared by both poetry and performance writing: how are we to calibrate the materiality of the text with the materialities of speech, of acting, of performance? Is speech governed from the page? How does the charisma of the poet, or of the actor, engage, represent, and/or displace the authority of the poem? While Antin had no "textification" in mind when he started doing talk poems, when he turned to transcribe and publish his talk poems from tape recordings (like Smith in this regard), he worked "to confront the textual discourses, which were generated at a desk in the language of textification, with a text that was generated by talking, that derived its life and its mode of thinking from talking and carried the trace of its origins into the world of the text" (Antin and Bernstein, *A Conversation* 62). In this sense, the spatial form of Antin's writing – which, as Bernstein carefully notes, more resembles word "clusters" than poetic "phrases" predicated on the breath (61) – anticipates the paratactic logic of "The New Sentence" of Language writing, even of non-talk-poems like *The Beginner*.[17] Such writing uses the mise-en-page to represent performance, perhaps even to create a kind of textual performance, inscribing events which have a complex, indeterminate, ambiguous relation to the actual or embodied performances of readers.

Given this programmatic commitment to the space of the page as a stage for an alienated, objectified language, and so to "an alternative language system" that resists the "voice" or charisma of the performer, it's perhaps not surprising that Language writing has a complex ambivalence toward the performance of poetry, particularly toward *speech*. In 1986, Ron Silliman introduced his landmark anthology of Language writing, *In the American Tree*, with Robert Grenier's celebrated declaration, "I HATE SPEECH" and went on to reject a "speech-based poetics" less because performance was the enemy of poetry than because "speech" seemed to naturalize language to the charismatic agency of the poet's voice (Silliman, "Language" xvii, xviii). Grenier argues that speech frames poetry in a persistent "reiteration of the past dragged on in formal habit. I HATE SPEECH" ("On Speech" 477), but Silliman is more expansive:

```
. . . composition itself
is a means of thinking,
an active process
        not necessarily
        the sort of "organic" mimicry
                of thought or of speech
    we associate with the Projective Verse of the 1950s
but sharing with that tradition
a recognition
of the poem's intimate entanglement
with consciousness as such.

This ineluctable involvement precisely
gives the work –
that finished published Thing –
the potential to engage a reader
not as consumer
but as a participant,
someone who in the most literal sense
struggles with the text.          (Silliman, "Afterword" 582)
```

Rejecting the "organic" expressivity of projective verse, Silliman nonetheless echoes Olson's call for an objectified, worldly sense of language, where the materiality of the word, its thing-ness, transforms the reader from a consumer of consciousness to a contestatory performer, struggling to engage with the poem as a participant in its materialization of meaning. In this sense, "I HATE SPEECH" marks the poem's resistance to the voice, while at the same time urging the ineluctable implication of performance in the ontology of the poem.

Language poetics attends at once to the materiality of the poem and to the suppression of the lyric voice: perhaps inevitably, the "poetry reading" emerges as a significant point of contention. In fact, the vivid antitheatricality animating the controversy surrounding the proprieties of reading poetry aloud is largely cognate with the concerns animating performance writing for the theatrical stage, and of course with the antitheatrical anxieties sustaining modern drama itself. How can the performance of language on the page – both the mise-en-page and the enactment of reading – extend into the social world without reinserting language into the narcotic (or worse, histrionic) lyricism of the speaking voice? Many of the principal writers associated with Language poetics are splendid readers, and several – Bruce Andrews, Carla Harryman – are also involved with experimental performance. In a series of critical verse essays reminiscent of Brecht's dialogues or Edward Bond's poems and songs, Charles Bernstein attempts to coordinate the performance of the poem with the poem as performance in ways that dramatize an evolving, sometimes grudging, effort to come to terms with performance itself. Taking his cue at once from Brecht and Michael Fried, Bernstein urges lyric poetry to resist a use of language that merely mediates an "artifice of absorption," the dreamy identification between the lyric voice and the reader that replicates the modernist effort to "absorb the reader in the poem" ("Artifice of Absorption" 35). Instead he calls for the alienated deployment of language, language traced by its own means of "Unfamiliar-ization," its own "*verfrem*dumdum*den* effect." Bernstein's account of Brecht models his sense of the possibilities of performed poetry:

> Brecht used his techniques
> in conjunction with a
> [bracketed]
> subject matter
> & this subject
> matter tended
> to be in
> the form of
> melodrama,
> a form which
> exaggerates
> absorptive dynamics.
>
> (66)

Absorption has its problems, but so does theatricality. Bernstein is suspicious of the "absorptive dynamics" of emotional engagement, which he associates with the theatrical seductions of lyric speech, typified here by the emotional exaggeration of Brechtian melodrama. But we might think that Bernstein's surprisingly antitheatrical impulses lead him to misread Brecht in important ways. The melodramatic elements of Brecht's theatre are at once the moment of a suspiciously emotive absorption, and the elements that enable an alienating experience, one in which Brecht's "truly rending contradiction between experience and portrayal, empathy and demonstration, justification and criticism" can emerge as part of theatrical experience (*Brecht on Theatre* 277). In performance, Brecht cannily produces the "absorptive" dynamics of melodrama – Kattrin drumming on the roof, Grusha's escape with the infant, Galileo's delayed recantation – as part of a larger, alienating purpose. Engaging the theatrical spectator through the emotive conventions of melodrama, the epic theatre forces that narcotic identification with the narrative back on the viewer, alienating not so much the action onstage as the spectator's desire for it to happen in a

particular way. Mother Courage is not changed by Kattrin's sacrifice, carefully counting the pennies for her daughter's burial; Galileo's recantation
enforces a specific unhappiness on the deflated audience, the unhappiness of
wanting, needing a hero.[18] Brecht's alienation makes palpable the theatre's
ability to (de)construct the spectator's apparently individual, transcendent
"subjectivity" by implicating individual desire in the externalized process of
the stage. The process of Brecht's theatre – narrative absorption, theatrical
alienation – obsessively teaches us that desire, the desiring subject, is what
the theatrical mode of production *produces*.

This relatively "textual" form of alienation can be inscribed in the dynamics of the poem. To Bernstein, the poem's alienated embodiment on the
page foregrounds the objectivity of language, its dissociation from a merely
individual experience. This mise-en-page enforces the reader's alienated
embodiment of the poem in the act of reading, a performance that similarly dislocates the comfortable assimilation of the poem to the lyric practice of subjection, the emotive or "melodramatic" identification with lyric
"speech." Susan Howe's overprinting, Michael Palmer's or Bob Perelman's
paratactic dis/connections, the way the intensity of imagery dislocates narrative in Leslie Scalapino's work: the impermeable materiality of the poem,
its evident staging on the page, marks the "outer limit" of the reader's
"absorption in the poem."

> . . . The tenacity of
> writing's thickness, like the body's
> flesh, is
> ineradicable, yet mortal. It is
> the intrusion
> of words into the visible
> that marks
> writing's own absorption in the world.
> (Bernstein, "Artifice" 87)

Charles Altieri refines this Brechtian tension as a dimension of the poem's
politics of reading, arguing that Bernstein frames a contrast "between the
romantic desire to become absorbed within the comforting emotions established by the text's representational field and the anti-absorptive work performed by self-conscious attention to the rhetorical structures and construc-
tive energies that absorptive art tries to conceal" ("Some Problems" 186).
Despite Bernstein's effort to distance it from Brechtian melodrama, this
anti-absorptive dimension of the poem's enactment is achieved through an
explicitly Brechtian process. In both its bibliographic ("writing's thickness")
and linguistic dimensions, the poem seduces the reader with its rhetoric

(who doesn't want Kattrin's drumming to save the village, knowing it won't change the war? who doesn't want Galileo to resist the instruments of torture, knowing that he will not?). The poem enforces a recognition of the rhetoricity of that seduction, alienating, so to speak, the reader's absorption in the poem through the process of his/her engagement with the poem's materiality, its means of production. This alienated rhetoricity also sustains the poem's claim to perform a kind of critical ideological work, work akin to the work of epic theatre. For the poem is at once an object in the world and a means of rehearsing our relation to the world through its language, the design of its rhetoric. The promise of poetry, as Altieri puts it, is that "the play of absorption and anti-absorption becomes our means of positioning the text not as object but as interface between selves and worlds" (189). To Altieri, reading is a form of deep play, in which readers struggle to adopt the forms of lyric agency opened by the poem's design: "Lyric agents are those who are learning how to let themselves explore agential forces that they neither control nor even quite contain within their individual psyches" (192). This form of fictive agency has little to do with the role playing we might associate with reading a Browning monologue, or early Eliot, or even strongly "voiced" poetry like Yeats's, or Stevens's "The Emperor of Ice Cream." This poetry resists modeling a single lyric voice, and the politics of its rehearsal model a multiple, alienated sense of agency.

Perhaps one has to speak here of the reader as self-conscious locus of possibility. His or her pleasure resides in pushing the self into an "open" where thinking and feeling find new directions. Not organized by the forces of gravity set in motion either by representational structures or by heroic self-reflexive constructions, the syntactic intricacy of the work becomes an actual willing presence in a world otherwise driven by ideology. (190)

As an object in the world, writing's materiality at once enables and resists the reader's absorption in the poem, and so also enables the reader's resistance to absorption in the ambient ideology of language itself: "Where 'meaning' and 'will' had been, there readers can now focus on those energies put into play by the imagination's capacities to register overtones, trace connections, and lose (loose) itself in shadows" (190).

The political force of lyric agency depends precisely on Brecht's most critical insight, an insight that is usually ignored in the effort to locate the politics of the spectacle as an epic lesson. If alienation *effects* are to occur, they will occur in the dynamics of subjection, in the zone in which attentive audiences – audiences for whom pleasure and instruction are dialectically inseparable, audiences whose thinking is driven by the pleasure of the spectacle – will become strangers to themselves, be driven from the self into an "open" where the imagination of alternative identities, alternative ways of taking agency, can take place, where alternative ways of taking agency are enforced as the affective price of participation.

Although the silent reader, bravely confronting the tenacious thickness of words on the page seems considerably removed from the cigar-chewing, punch-throwing spectator of Brecht's pugilistic playhouse, Bernstein's poetics shrewdly seize on Brecht's central insight: social change begins by alienating the "ordinary man's calm and incorruptible eye" (*Brecht on Theatre* 10). Many writers conventionally grouped under the sign of poetry – Bruce Andrews, for instance – are energetically involved in experimental performance projects as a means of incarnating the politics of poetry: "*Translation – how to get from one to the other; how the compositional principles can share a common concern for the production of meaning (and therefore, the constitution of the social body).*"[19] And yet Bernstein labors to keep Brechtian "theatricality" at bay, and to keep "theatricality" from becoming the positive antonym of narcotic "absorption." As Martin Puchner argues in his deft critique of Michael Fried's foundational dichotomy between "absorption and theatricality," the modernist colloquy between writing and performance (poetry or drama and the theatre) is predicated on a deeply antitheatrical skepticism arising from the "perceived affinity between the theater and the public sphere." Both the collaborative agency of actors and the interference of the social public trouble the writer's (or the painter's) ability to implement a complete "control over the external circumstances of reception," and so finally impede the unmediated *absorption* in the work, that "intense concentration on works that conform to the modernist ideal of difficulty" that has become "the sine qua non of modernism" (Puchner, *Stage Fright* 10).[20] Bernstein resists the "artifice of absorption," but extends a modernist sense of the incompatibility of the poem and the stage by refusing to take Brechtian "theatricality" as its salutary alternative: the "*verfrem*dumdum*den* effect" of Brechtian "melodrama" must be distinguished from the alienated work of anti-absorptive poetics.

Despite the apparent effort to collocate "writing's thickness" with the "body's flesh," the performance of poetry must be protected from the apparently distasteful dissimulation of the stage. David Antin confesses, for instance, that he took up "talk poetry" because the poetry reading made him feel too theatrical, lapsed, secondary: "when I got to the reading all the work was done, and I was reduced to being an actor in an experimental play that I'd already written. And I didn't want to be an actor. I didn't want to illustrate the way I had worked" (Antin and Bernstein, *A Conversation*

42). Much as Antin wants to resist the absorptive dynamics of the conventional lyric, and of the conventional poetry reading, the scene of the "talk poem" is nonetheless authentic, even absorptive, precisely because it resists the discourse of theatricality, especially *acting*. Opposing "absorption" but resisting "theatricality" leaves little ground to stand, or read aloud, on: what does this anti-performative performance *do*? This question is especially troubling the more urgently these poetics claim a political force for anti-absorptive reading. As Thulani Nkabinde Davis reminds us, performance poets – the progenitors of slam – "tried to close the distance created by printing and to give the audience a sense of community not possible in the individual experience of reading"; since poets were explicitly engaged in an oppositional politics, "A 'poetry reading,' or even poetry, had to reach out of printed pages and become physical" ("Known Renegades" 75). Yet this physicality tips the reading toward the "theatrical," the "performance factor," which "led to confusion as poets worked for punch lines and calculated appeals to ideological imperatives," violating the absorptive dynamics that authenticate the poem as performance (Henderson, "Worrying" 77). Not surprisingly, Bernstein emphasizes the danger that the theatrical stage poses to the enactment of poetry: "No art form (the combination of hyperbole and truism is an illustration of theatricality) is as pulled toward its own trivialization as is performance art, for this trivialization – of gestures, of time, of communication – is inherent in the medium. The presence of an audience to the artist is like the song of the Sirens to the sailor: its attendance not only distracts but destroys" ("On Theatricality" 206).

Public means breed public manners: performance enables the poet to reach an audience that is immediate, to lay evident claim to the social function of art. Nevertheless, to *do* something, the enactment of poetry must inevitably encounter the stage, the bodily flesh of actual bodies, of acting. "The basis of the poetry performance is in fact hostile to the presence, the manner of the professional actor" (Jerome Rothenberg, "Poetics of Performance" 122–23). Although Jerome Rothenberg and others are at pains to distinguish the performance of poetry from the tawdry effects of (ugh!) theatre, the terms they use to distinguish poetry from the stage often explicitly recall the distinctive innovations driving American performance in the 1970s and 1980s, forms which also marked their distance from (ugh!) theatre: Jerzy Grotowski's poor theatre, and its descendant, the autoperformance monologue.[21] For Rothenberg and for Bernstein, the actor always diminishes the work of poetry by displacing the absorptive character of language behind the charismatic artifice of its embodiment.

For Grotowski, the poetry of Marlowe or Calderón can only do its work when it occupies the disciplined, sacrificial body of the actor: the actor, not the text, becomes the site of authentic absorption. It is, perhaps, a testament to the impermeability of genre that Rothenberg's notion of the identity of text and performance in poetry readings – the poet as charismatic, even shamanistic witness – may have cost Anna Deavere Smith the Pulitzer Prize in drama, but would not, presumably, have had similar consequences for Charles Bernstein, or Bruce Andrews, or Lyn Hejinian, or for a recent winner like Paul Muldoon, a celebrated reader of his poems. Again, but in a rather different sense, "L'opposition du poète et de l'acteur en est toute contaminée" (Meschonnic 280).

Like Rothenberg, Bernstein also resists poetry read by actors: such acting "frames the performance in terms of character, personality, setting, gesture, development, or drama, even though these may be extrinsic to the text at hand. That is, the 'acting' takes precedence over letting the words speak for themselves (or worse, eloquence compromises, not to say eclipses, the ragged music of the poem)" ("Introduction," *Close Listening* 11). Whether it is possible for words to speak "for themselves" or not, what is clearly at stake for Bernstein is a rhetoric of performance, a fidelity effect, an enactment of the dialectical tension between "absorption" and "impermeability" that should transpire in the encounter with the printform of the poem, an effect that can take the stage in "the profoundly antiperformative nature of the poetry reading, the poetry reading as radically 'poor theater,' in Jerzy Grotowski's sense" ("Introduction" 10).[22] But while Grotowski understood the actor's work as a disciplined surrender to the physical, immediate fact of performance, Bernstein's nontheatre of the poem emphasizes "the acoustic production of a single unaccompanied speaking voice, with all other theatrical elements being placed, in most cases, out of frame. The solo voice so starkly framed can come to seem virtually disembodied in an uncanny, even hypnotic way" (10). This hypnotic, disembodied, objectified, absorbing voice evokes Beckett's theatre (*hypnotic* is a long way from Brecht!), and Beckett's famous resistance to the personality of performers, but Bernstein has another agenda in mind. Beckett's disembodied voices tend, paradoxically, to witness the actor's virtuosity, the technical accomplishment required to speak Beckett's "toneless" jackhammer delivery, to retain the trace of stage presence in the disappearing-machine of Beckett's drama. Bernstein, however, imagines the "anti-expressivist poetry reading" as "an oasis of low technology that is among the least spectaclized events in our public culture" (10). For Bernstein, the low-tech anti-glamor of the poetry reading enables a kind of alienation of the mediagen(et)ic "I" of the contemporary culture of spectacle. Sidestepping the means of theatre, the poetry reading enunciates the words for themselves.

While this sense of the textually determined performance, of performance as transparent to the text, extends modernism's antitheatrical dream of a literary stage (Yeats's barreled, Beckett's jugged speakers), it plays a distinctive role in Language poetics. For the sounding of the poem is crucial because "sound registers the sheer physicality of language. [. . .] Sound is language's flesh, its opacity as meaning marks its material embeddedness in the world of things" ("Introduction" 21). Sound has an "Iconicity" (21) associated with the materiality of writing that Bernstein connects to Jerome McGann's sense of "textual performances": the sense that the bibliographical code of the work's materialization provides the signifying platform for its linguistic code, its meaning. McGann dislocates the authorizing force of the original in the process of the work's manifestation in history, and Bernstein also wants to see in "these multifoliate versions *performances* of the poem; and I would add the poet's own performance of the work in a poetry reading, or readings, to the list of variants that together, plurally, constitute and reconstitute the work" (8). While sounding the poem operates, as writing does, as a means of "'thickening the medium'" (21), some soundings are nonetheless more authoritative than others. "An actor's rendition, like a type designer's 'original' setting of a classic, will not have the same kind of authority as a poet's own reading or the first printing of the work. But the performance of the poet, just as the visualization of the poem in its initial printings, forever marks the poem's entry into the world; and not only its meaning, its existence" (8–9). Bernstein evokes the question of the identity of the work, the problem that the Pulitzer jury faced when it considered Smith's *Twilight*. If the poetic text is paramount, then all soundings are potentially authoritative, and so equally (in)authentic: the priority of authentic meaning reserved for the text and then mediated by subsequent performance is, of course, the conventional understanding of dramatic writing in the theatre. Yet if performance is critical to the identity of the work, then what is the originary, authoritative force of the writing?

Language writing works to preserve the poem's disruptive, material entry into the world as an element of its social and political utility. In this sense, performance cannot be merely deflected as a derivative after-effect, and so the poem must have "a fundamentally plural existence" ("Introduction" 9). Yet "while performance emphasizes the material presence of the poem, and of the performer, it at the same time denies the unitary presence of the poem, which is to say its metaphysical unity" (9), a unity more palpable, more unified when the poet reads the poem than when an actor does. The

"bodily grounding of language" (22), its "*animalady*" is the condition of
poetry, a bodily grounding found in performance art too – in the gestural
structure of Smith's work, or in the fact that Guillermo Gómez-Peña often
reads from the text during his performances, enacting the performance's
dependence on writing (Gómez-Peña is in fact a superb reader of his poems;
what is striking is that he is not "off book" in many of his most celebrated
performances). "Yet, in the present cultural context of the late twentieth
century, this animalady loses its force as concrete experience when reified
as (represented) speech or sentimentalized as (a return to) orality," or, we
might suspect, when sentimentalized as acting (22). Sentimental speech is
something we listen to, but the *animalady* of performed poetry is something
we hear, something that resists our abilities to decode, and that forces us to
a different strategy of apprehension. To learn to "stop listening and begin
to hear; which is to say, stop decoding and begin to get a nose for the sheer
noise of language" lies at the heart of the politics of poetry in performance
(22). The materiality of the poem on the page alienates language from
its typical, commodified usage. Negotiating this alienated language, the
reader hypothesizes, occupies, however briefly, alternate modes of agency.
Sounding the poem gives it a different order of material existence in the
world. Its animalady promotes a distinctive form of attention and interpretive action or participation. Actors, trained to transform language into
character, too often recommodify language, package it as the wrong kind
of performance.

The animalady of performance cannot finally be ascribed to, or be contained by, the text. Performing a poem makes it "a physically present /
acoustic event, to give bodily dimension – beat – to what is / otherwise
spatial & visual" ("Thelonious Monk" 21). No longer seeing performance
as merely additive to the poem's cultural work, "suggesting one way that
a work might be / read" (18), in "Thelonious Monk and the Performance
of Poetry," Bernstein has come to see performance as a way to disentangle
poetry from the commodified charisma of speech.

> [. . .] In
> performance, it becomes possible to lay down a rhythmic
> beat, a pulse, that is otherwise more speculative or tenuous
> in the scoring of words on a page. For me, this pulse is
> constructed around "nodal" points of pauses or silences or
> breaks – a *point* I want to put as technically as I can to
> distinguish this from notions of breath or speech rhythms or
> other notions of an unconstructed or unimposed reading style.
>   (21)

The live reading becomes a way to materialize the poem's oppositional character, to mark "breaks" and to resist their assimilation to "breath or speech rhythms or / other notions of an unconstructed or unimposed reading style" (21). To see this materialization, this performance, as a legitimate instance of the poem, however, can happen only if we disentangle the reading from the "remnant of Romantic ideology that still / haunts that performance styles of poetry readings," in which

> the acting style is to pretend that there is no
> acting, where the performance style is to feign
> that no performing is going on
>
> (22–23)

Bernstein calls for the poetry reading to *space* the text, create a gap, a gestural punctuation much like the gap opened by Smith's mimic gesture, a sounding that marks the difference between writing and performance. Yet, if

> To deny the performative
> aspect of poetry is to repress
> its most literally political dimension

so too

> To deny the rhetoricity
> (rhetoricalness?)
> & theatricality of a poem is to idealize a
> literary space outside of ideology & history.
>
> (23)

Sensitive to the connection between embodiment and politics, Bernstein finally edges toward a kind of complementarity here, in which the performance of poetry seems to verge, if only just, on that other stage, where theatrical action can sustain the "theatricality of a poem."

The densely theoretical orbit of Language writing is not only inflected by Barthes and Derrida and Foucault but insists on a rematerialization of writing cognate with the work of textual theorists like McGann and even with practical textual work like the editing of Shakespeare's plays. Calling for modes of writing that enact a different kind of relation between text and reader, Language poetics implies a critique of the subject, and urges alternative means to realizing the subject at the interface between writing and performance. In this sense, Bernstein's and Rothenberg's emphasis on "sounding" the poem can be seen to complicate and also to extend what we might take, alongside Charles Altieri's brilliant and impassioned summons, as one of the purposes of lyric poems. For as Altieri argues,

"Physically sounding the sounds gets us in contact with poetry's material presence in our bodies," and an imaginative sounding, a sounding in which the multifoliate potentialities of the writing enable a "sensuous indulgence that overflows into the luscious delights of being able to stage ourselves as different identities or at least as having rich experiences not readily available to us without the texts" ("Taking Lyrics Literally" 262). While this experience should be one of the delights of reading *plays*, it is in fact the disembodiment of the voice of lyric poetry, its construction as a kind of pure "articulateness" – "articulateness as a condition of constantly flirting with the inchoate factors making us dissatisfied with what we can say about what we feel" (263) – that seems to enable this vision of lyric agency. This essentially dramatic sense of the lyric, a sense that is strangely protected from the demands of the theatre's ways of treating the text's use-value for actual performance, draws us back to writing more explicitly engaged with performance, the mise-en-page of performance writing and contemporary drama. "For there is no better access to other identities, or to who we become because we can take on other identities, than giving ourselves over to a range of speaking voices. Then we are not watching characters on a screen or a stage; we are actually becoming the voices through which they live" (262). As Smith might put it, "the word becomes you."

IV. SPACES OF GESTURE: THE POETICS OF THE PAGE IN SMITH AND KANE

> An actor must be able to space his gestures the way a typesetter produces spaced type.
>
> Walter Benjamin, "What Is Epic Theater?" (151)

As Henri Meschonnic suggests in his magisterial *Critique du rythme*, "Toute page est un spectacle: celui de sa pratique du discours, la pratique d'une rationalité, d'une théorie du langage" (303). Language poetics articulates a densely theoretical account of the alienated work of material language at two sites of production: the page and the stage. The effort to find a bridge from the materiality of print to the embodiment of performance evokes an anxiety about the unregulated charisma of the performer, charisma that threatens to naturalize the alienated language of the Language poem to the narcotic, culinary discourse of theatrical character, the hypnotic allure of the poetic subject that Language poetry works otherwise to resist. While it seems to me that Language poetics tends more successfully to rephrase than to resolve the problematic tension between writing and performance, this detour into Language poetics alerts us to an alternative modeling of that relationship. To what extent can the rhetorical, alienating means of the mise-en-page find an adequately alienating mode of production in the mise-en-scène? Rather than conceiving the page/stage along an axis of determination (either the page determines stage meanings, or stage practice determines the page's possible signification), Language poetics suggests a third possibility: the materiality of the mise-en-page, the precise construction of printed words in space, does not operate as a kind of stage direction, an authorized and authoritarian effort to govern subsequent performance (though some authors may intend it that way), nor is it complete in itself, a container or "can" of perfected meanings waiting to be emptied by performance. Instead, Language poetics implies the incommensurability of these two modes of writing's "thickness." The poem's physical design on the page, and its physicalized performance cannot be collapsed into one another so that the script grounds the performance or the performance realizes the script. Hejinian's sentences, Howe's overprinting, Antin's spacing don't tell an actor, or a reader, what to *do* in order to unfreeze the fossilized poem. Language poetics reframes the page as a distinctive field of play, insisting that words can and must be joined in ways beyond the habits of conventional speech. *Sounding* (recalling Grenier) should not be confused with the SPEECH that claims to reproduce the poem in the actorly charisma of the performer's determining presence.

The controversial status of the poetry reading resonates with the contemporary scene of dramatic writing, particularly the scene of autoperformance. Although autoperformance depends on the personal style, sometimes the peculiar virtuosity, of the performer, what is usually at stake in autoperformance is the authenticity of language. Of course, autoperformance tends to reverse the priorities of "poetic" performance: the poetry reading emphasizes the sounding of the *word*, while autoperformance works to lend the word an embodied *sound*. The reframing of the mise-en-page as a field of play locates one place where poetry joins a dominant tradition of modern dramatic writing. The mise-en-page represents a field of performance – adopting a strategy familiar in plays throughout the modern canon – by framing a performative syntax that seems to repudiate or just ignore the normative practices that transform words into language, and language into the representation of a subject, identity, character, action. The performance represented by the mise-en-page may well not have, or not yet have, a familiar practice of realization, either in the theatre or in the more downbeat theatricality of the live poetry reading. The challenges to sounding a poem are in this sense much like the challenges first posed by the intermittencies of Chekhov's characterization, by Beckett's brutal negation of the actor's embodiment, or by Parks's "rests and spells" today. Writing and performance resist assimilation; yet one way to regard the history of dramatic theatre is as an ongoing effort to strike a plausible, if provisional, accommodation between page and stage, a way to satisfy our desire to find or express that *animalady*, the restless infection of language, the desire to enact words as deeds.

Language poetics adapts, extends, and counters the modernist emphasis on the signifying visuality of the page. Many contemporary plays and performance texts seem equally to deploy the design of the page to destabilize the dynamics of performance, doing so at just the moment that "drama" is advertised as disappearing from the scene of consequential performance, slipping into the grave of history alongside that other corpse, print. To read the page of Anna Deavere Smith's writing, and of much recent drama, as a kind of spectacle is to ask in part how the mise-en-page of *Fires* or *Twilight* contributes not merely to the subsequent execution of the work on the stage, but also what it contributes to our understanding of the drama that is precisely *not* translated to the stage. Because Smith's work already exists across several platforms of production – as writing, as Smith's live solo performance, as Smith's video performance, as solo performance not involving Smith, and as cast performance – it provides us with an unusual chance to recalibrate the operation of the mise-en-page against its transformation into performance. Despite the disarming simplicity of the writing, the visible effort to assert the page merely as the record of speech, there is a surprising asymmetry between the design of the page and the rhetoric of Smith's performance.

Smith's performances provide a striking opportunity to engage the bibliographic and performative "accessories" of the writing, to place typographical (mise-en-page) and gestural (mise-en-scène) into dialogue. Given Smith's emphatic, precise mimicry, we might expect the rhythms of her performance closely to approximate the "projective" implications of the text's visual design. Yet, much as David Antin's talk poems are recomposed for print, so too there's a significant gap between the rhetoric of Smith's performance and how the words take the page. Laying out the monologues verse-wise, Smith complements grammatical punctuation with the palpably rhetorical effects of verse lineation, encoding her writing both with the trace of the "projective" breath and simultaneously with the alienating potentiality of Brechtian *spacing*. Can we take the mechanical design of the page at once to assimilate language to the expressive "I" of the contemporary lyric *and* to isolate the word, dramatize its *thingness* in the economy of language production? It may seem implausible at first to locate this alienating potentiality in the mild lyricism of Smith's writing, with its evident coordination of coherent, expressive subjects. Yet this ambivalence helps to account for a crucial problem in Smith's work, one familiar to anyone who has ever followed the video of *Fires* or *Twilight* with the text in hand: the language and rhythms of the page provide an inaccurate, even deceptive, record of Smith's actual performance. Smith frequently alters the ordering of the selections in her works in stage performance, and naturally has had to reshape her work for television. Since actors necessarily alter small passages of dialogue in performance, it's not surprising that there are a number of differences, large and small, between the words spoken on the *American Playhouse* broadcasts and the texts published by Anchor Books.[23] But it's not merely the fact that the "characters" are shuffled into a different order, or that their speeches are slightly cut or reshaped in the same way that, say, Macbeth's or Hamlet's lines might be cut for a performance of Shakespeare's plays. Departing from the apparently "projective" implications of the "free verse" page, Smith's performance invites us to reread the page for the alternative poetry that takes shape there.

To think of Smith not as acting the text – transforming the language into the vehicle for her personal charisma – but as *sounding* it, working (as Rothenberg describes the performing poet) "to renew it by sounding," is particularly attractive (Rothenberg, "Poetics" 121). For although Smith is an unusually charismatic performer onstage, the point of her performance is to suppress "the lyrical interference of the individual" (Olson 247) in order to let the verbal and gestural "poetry" of her subjects emerge. In this sense, we might think that Smith's performance, despite its theatrical virtuosity, its "acted" quality, also enacts a kind of *sounding*, a vivid and experimental effort to renew the subject's language but to renew it as something else, as poetry. Onstage, Smith systematically departs from the implied rhetoric of her subjects' printed verse, sounding what seems to be an alternate poetry. The gestic "spacing" of Smith's familiar gestural punctuation, not only marks or estranges "language" and "character" (it certainly does do that), but also marks her subjects' speech as distinct from the "spaced type" of the page. *Sounding* the writing, Smith performs a rival materialization, encoding language in an epic performative that is neither determined by, nor a simple embodiment of, the material design of the words on the page.

If *this* page were a digital screen we could now open a window and run Smith's video alongside the published text. Instead, we have to resort to a lower-tech strategy. To compare the structure of the monologues in performance with their bookish "origins," we have to transcribe them back into the form of the book, into print. This transcription has a surprising value, though. Smith's performances assert an extraordinary subservience to "the text," claim to be inspired, *driven* by the text to a degree that goes well beyond the most traditional sense of a normative theatrical fidelity to the written play. Transcribing the performance back into the rhetoric of the page enables us to see that the "text" of Smith's performance verbally, rhetorically, and materially resists the implications of the printed mise-en-page. Let's look at two brief passages from *Fires in the Mirror* alongside a transcription of Smith's performance. First, "The Reverend Al Sharpton: Me and James's Thing" as printed:

> I just came home from spending a weekend with him now,
> uh, uh,
> I think James deserved that.
> And just like
> he was the father I never had,
> his kids never even visited him when he went to jail.
>
>   (*Fires* 21)

The page design sets each line *as a line*, a unit, implying a rhetorical and conceptual unity to each phrase. Textually, "Al Sharpton" is a man of short, pithy phrases; each phrase seems marked by a pause at the end, a kind of landing or momentary completion. To my ear, Smith's performance not only changes several phrases, but her breathing transforms the "projective" relationship between line and breath. In performance, Smith's sharp intake of breath seems less to mark the end of a line than to begin a new line, to impel a new continuity. The performance not only uses a slightly different set of words, but it breaks them into a different rhythm, a rhythm that materializes a different "Al Sharpton" (I will mark Smith's breathing with *, and indicate pauses as Smith's texts do, by starting a new line):

> *I just came back from spending the weekend with him now
> *I think James Brown deserved that tribute
> *and just like he was uh uh uh uh uh uh father
> *I never had
> his kids
> *never even came to visit him
> when he was in jail
> *so I was the son
> he never had
>
>   (George C. Wolfe, dir., *Fires in the Mirror*)[24]

The "accessories" of performance represent a rather different speaking subject than the one encoded by the "accessories" of print alone. In print, "The Rev. Al Sharpton" is a somewhat more disjointed speaker than he is in performance: the referent for "that" in the sentence "I think James deserved that" seems to dangle, while the printed page uses spacing to make a kind of sense out of the nonsequitur "And just like / he was the father I never had / his kids never even visited him when he went to jail." In performance, though, Smith adds the word "tribute" to clarify the demonstrative adjective "that," perhaps even transposing the "uh uh" of the second line into a more grammatical utterance, an indefinite article modifying "father" (it could easily be represented as "a a a a a a father"), the repetition emphasizing the force of "father," and breaking the line about the children into three parallel phrases: "his kids / never even came to visit him / when he was in jail." Smith's performance transforms the implied rhetoric of the page, representing a different, more coherent "Al Sharpton." His speech patterns gain energy and urgency from where the breathing falls, which may or may not be well suggested by lineation. "Al Sharpton" is two "projective" poets: on the page, "Al Sharpton" pauses for effect; on the stage, "Al Sharpton" exhales language.

The second passage is from "Angela Davis: Rope":

> So when I use the word "race" now I put it in quotations.
> Because if we don't transform
> this intransigent
> rigid
> notion of race,
> we will be caught up in this cycle
> of genocidal
> violence
> that
> is at the origins of our history.
> So I think –
> I'm convinced,
> and this is what I'm working on in my political practice
>   right now –
> that we have to find different ways of coming together
> (Fires 30–31)

> umm *
> and so
> when I use the word race now*
> I put it in quotations
> umm eh
> *because I am interested in community that is not static in that way*
> and this is what I am working on in my political practice right now* is
> trying to find ways of coming together* in a different way
> (Wolfe, Fires)

This passage is considerably more difficult to compare, not only because Smith has so extensively cut and rewritten the text for television, but also because her performance seems so far removed from the rhetorical implications of the page. Nonetheless, both on the page and in performance, "Angela Davis" alternates between short, punctual phrases and longer, more periodic sentences. Yet while both page and stage present "Angela Davis" as speaking in a variety of rhythms, they mark that distinction differently. On the page, Davis says, "So when I use the word 'race' now I put it in quotations," but in performance this passage is more broken, beginning with "umm," and is interrupted by pauses and breaths in several places before flowing into a longer, more continuous "speech."[25] On the page, "race" is succeeded by a series of short phrases, and the words *cycle, genocidal, violence, history* develop rhythmic and conceptual force as modifiers of *racism*, framing "Angela Davis" as a speaker who gives each word its due, even marking the *that* that shifts gears into the crucial, suspended subordinate clause "that / is at the origins of our history." In performance, Smith cuts this passage, but she transforms the implications of the writing more significantly by emphasizing "Angela Davis's" more periodic sentence-like phrasing. While the printed text moves from short to longer phrases, Smith's performance seems to represent "Angela Davis" speaking not in phrases but in paragraphs.

Conducting an interview on the telephone may affect how Smith takes in the poetry of speech, but we might wonder why words that seem in performance to be delivered as paragraphs, extensive rhetorical periods, appear on the page poetry-wise, broken into lines. "Minister Conrad Mohammed," in the celebrated "Seven Verses" monologue, speaks in longish, continuous sentences, too; I would have been tempted to represent his first long sentence – "The condition of the Black man in America today" – as a paragraph (*Fires* 52). Similarly, "Angela Davis" moves from short to long phrases that are difficult to break into "lines" at all, despite their layout on the page. This periodicity is marked in Smith's performance, where her intake of breath is not only more punctual, more audible than in "Al Sharpton," but also seems to happen in the middle of phrases. Smith's act of speaking does not seem to break the sentence into "projective" lines at all. Instead, the force of the language seems to drive through the breathing. In performance, "Angela Davis" seems to resist the implications of the poetic line, its ways of "marking off an internal hierarchy of value identified with parts or tags, disciplining the already-constituted body," perhaps, in favor of delivering a clear, argumentative "speech" that subordinates the logic of performance to the logic of sense (Andrews, *Paradise & Method* 119).

In the "General Production Notes" to *House Arrest*, Smith takes a playwright's stance toward the limits of the actor's freedom: the "process of playing the play and speaking the words in their exact presentation is the core of the technique of performing the play" ("General Production Notes" 5). Hamlet would approve. Yet Smith's inability to follow these instructions herself suggests that the "relationship of language to identity" is evoked differently in different practices of identification, that her subjects materialize different identities as their language is materialized in different ways. When compared to Smith's actual performance, then, the lineation of *Fires in the Mirror* emerges as a distinct visual strategy, representing "character" in the discourse of lyric poetry in ways that are often clearly at odds with the ways language is materialized in the discourse of her performance. "Al Sharpton" live is considerably more emphatic, his phrasing more coherent, more grammatical; the performance-text realizes a more persuasively coherent and conventional "character" than the bookish play does. "Angela Davis" is more varied, beginning with some thoughtful hesitations, but then leading into an extended prose mini-lecture; the performance-text in this case resists the coherence of "something that is like [lyric] poetry," to emphasize instead the instrumental character of language, language as a vehicle for *doing* not *being*. To compare the text and the performance in this way is not to ask Smith to have performed the play more accurately. I think we have to assume that Smith's live performance is where her mimetic faculties are most urgently and accurately at work. Rematerializing the performance on the page dramatizes the work that the distinctive layout and design of the mise-en-page of *Fires in the Mirror* is always, already performing. The bibliographic code of the play on the page, in this case, may well provide an inaccurate, deceptive, even (perhaps in the case of "Angela Davis") politically retrograde index to the articulation between language, speech, and subject that sustains Smith's sounding on the stage.

Attending to Smith's plays in this way alerts us to the complexities of *sounding* as a representation of writing, and of ways the "accessories" of the play's occupation of the page might be absorbed by, or resisted by, the conventions of performance. We might wonder whether the printform of Smith's plays betrays the "animalady" of her performance, the ways her precise and gestural "sounding" of language transforms the dynamics of the page. Predicated on her interviews, Smith's writing asserts the page as a direct transcription of lyric speaking. Yet Smith's reanimation of that fossilized talking dramatizes a resistance to the rhetoric of the page, a desire to retain and to represent an alternative agency. To read the slippage between Smith's writing and performing in this way requires us to take the printform of the play seriously, to attend to, to give value to its lyric design.

In the rigor of its ethnography, the alertness of the writing, the scrupulous refinement of the performance, Smith's work is unique. Nonetheless, the interplay between Smith's writing and enactment dramatizes a problematic that sustains contemporary performance writing, not only in more formal works like *The Laramie Project* or the rich collaboration of Complicite's plays, but also in the looser sphere of solo performance. One of the most visible conventions of solo performance today is the series of invented "characters," a form linking, say, Danny Hoch's *Jails, Hospitals & Hip-Hop* and *Some People* to Smith's plays. Despite the fact that Hoch invents his monologues ("I don't tape-record or interview people to play them onstage" [*Jails* xiv]), he, too, "trained as an actor, to play everything from Molière to Tennessee Williams to Sam Shepard to Samuel Beckett to Shakespeare, even Neil Simon" (xi), before becoming frustrated with the theatre's repudiation of "the rich language that was my whole cultural foundation" (xi). Yet while Hoch shares the sense that "Theatre is *about* language. Oral, physical, and spiritual language" (xii), his series of portraits derives from a process perhaps more reminiscent of David Antin than of Anna Deavere Smith. He began by composing his "stories, voices, and characters" improvisationally, "onstage. I 'wrote' it all orally in front of audiences," and then eventually came to write/revise a script, refining "the visceral fragmented storytelling riffs into clarified visceral stories that *sounded* like riffs" (xii, xiii). For Hoch, though, verse seems to be reserved for characters who speak/perform in hip-hop riffs, as in "Message to the Bluntman" in *Jails, Hospitals & Hip-Hop* (3), or "Roughneck Chicken" – "a mythical character somewhere between Jamaican dub poet, Yiddish sage, and chicken" – in *Some People* (145). As in the majority of performance writing, Hoch's plays are mainly written in prose. Autoperformance asserts its essentially "theatrical" character against the tired conventionality of "theatre."

Perhaps for this reason it's not surprising that the printed texts of many monologues have a prosy, instrumental character: the text is merely the pretext for the performer's enactment. Guillermo Verdecchia's superb plays (*Fronteras Americanas*, for example), Sandra Tsing Loh's *Aliens in America*, even Spalding Gray's celebrated monologues seem not to contest the materiality of the performance with the rival materiality of the page (we might recall Gray's worn spiral notebooks in performance: Gray typically enacted the still-essential inflection of manuscript culture in the era of postmodern print performance). Guillermo Gómez-Peña seems to see the page as a crucial site of his work's materiality: some works – *Border Brujo, Califas, Sin/Translation* – are designed on the page as poems, and retain the rhythms of ritual speech in his performance, while others – *Naftazteca: Pirate Cyber-TV for AD 2000* – appear as prose.

Smith's plays are part of a widespread effort to use writing, the material design of the page, to open if not to prescribe alternative performances.[26] I would like to conclude here by considering the page design of Sarah Kane's *4.48 Psychosis*, a play that clearly uses the page to interrogate the status and staging of dramatic subjects. Kane typically uses lineation and punctuation to urge a more-or-less "rhetorical" approach to reading her plays. Representing speeches on the page line-wise, and deploying a range of modestly idiosyncratic punctuation, Kane at once urges actors to read the plays anti-grammatically, and suggests that the proper performance is nonetheless visible in the printed text. Kane specifies that "Punctuation is used to indicate delivery, not to conform to the rules of grammar," and that "Where punctuation is missing, it is to indicate delivery" (*Complete Plays* 2, 109). Kane's characters are often represented speaking in paragraphs, but she does on occasion (like David Greig in this respect) represent "character" more "projectively":

> **Tinker**   You'll get used to him.
> Can't call you Grace any more.
> Call you . . . Graham. I'll call you Graham.
>   (*Complete Plays* 146)

While Kane's earlier plays are distinguished by their elegant, terrifying visuality, the ways they seem at once to compress a meticulous and intense naturalism with vivid and disorienting, surreal imagery, her last plays are formally inventive in a different way, more often beginning with their strategies of occupying the page.[27] The absence of character "names" in *Crave* – where the speech prefixes are simply A, B, and C – and the absence of prefixes altogether in *4.48 Psychosis* at once suggests Kane's inquiry into a "wider concept of performance," though to a kind of performance – like Beckett's – in which stage action arises from an essentially poetic engagement between writing and performance.[28] Reviews of *4.48 Psychosis*, both of the 2000 premiere and the 2001 revival as part of the Sarah Kane season at the Royal Court Theatre, dwell on the poetic character of the language and its implication, for better or worse, in the poetry of theatre. *4.48 Psychosis* is a "fragmented prose-poem for various voices" that is "underlaid with liturgical rhythms" (Kate Bassett, Rev. of *4.48 Psychosis*); the "spirit of T. S. Eliot, though not his poetic gift, hangs over the piece" (Robert Hewison, Rev. of *4.48 Psychosis*); it "is not a play in the familiar sense of the word. It is more, in the manner of Kane's penultimate work *Crave*, a dramatised poem" (Michael Billington, Rev. of *4.48 Psychosis*); it "turns out to be not a play, but a raw, intense, free-form dramatic poem, for an indeterminate number of voices" (Joyce McMillan, Rev. of *4.48 Psychosis*).

The appearance of the play on the page, its non-narrative organization, and the elegance and rhythmic quality of the language push the play toward "poetry," a poetry that to some reviewers has little to do with the stage. Yet as Benedict Nightingale notes, while this "posthumous text [. . .] reads as if it wasn't designed for performance," it resembles a specific genre of notoriously challenging, writerly, stageworthy texts: "Yet Beckett's *Not I* and *That Time* work better on the stage than on the page, and that's also the case here" (Nightingale, Rev. of *Crave* and *4.48 Psychosis*).

Beyond noting how far the theatre reviewers' sensibilities are determined by their reading of the text, does this "poetic" dimension of the printed page bear any material freight into the performance? Rather than asking how theatre embodies the text, might we ask how the text's poetry resists assimilation to the normative conventions, and normalizing psychologies, of the stage? Noting that the "play reads like a long poem, even using indentations and line spacing to give the words a specific look on the page like a lot of modern free verse," David Chadderton also remarks that the 2000 Royal Court production brought Patsy Rodenberg, one of the most prominent of English-language voice teachers, in to work with the actors, with the result that the cast's "speaking of the verse – sometimes spoken individually, sometimes spoken in chorus by two or all three – was clear, precise and had a feeling for the sound of the language rarely seen in modern theatre" (Chadderton, Rev. of *4.48 Psychosis*). How might Kane's page be seen as a document of *animalady*, a use of language that resists the conventions of "(represented) speech" or being "sentimentalized as (a return to) orality," but that urges actors, spectators, readers to "stop listening and begin to hear; which is to say, stop decoding and begin to get a nose for the sheer noise of language" (Bernstein, "Introduction" 22)? Is there a distinction between lyric and theatrical agency?

Perhaps in the manner of some poetic sequences, from Shakespeare's sonnets to John Berryman's *Dream Songs* or James Merrill's *Changing Light at Sandover*, *4.48 Psychosis* articulates different acts of subjection, different positionalities or sites of speech, without assigning any portion of the text to a given speaker, or to a fixed number of voices. James Macdonald, who directed both the 2000 and 2001 productions at the Royal Court, finds that "basically there is only one voice in the piece – or one central voice, although there is also the doctor/lover voice" (qtd. Saunders, *'Love me or kill me'* 123). Nevertheless, he chose three performers, who used the rehearsal to explore the text, without deciding which actor would own which lines until well into the process, with the result that the actors had all explored a range of subjectivities before the assignment of given speeches was fixed for the performance. We might think, though, that Macdonald's procedure here, however successfully it engaged with the very challenging task of theatricalizing this text, is allegorized, and perhaps resisted, by the play's materialization in the mise-en-page, which seems to use the space of the page to enact the subject's terrifying inability to find herself in a single voice.

One of the techniques used to help severely depressed patients to focus their thoughts is to count backward in increments of, say, 7: 100, 93, 86, and so on. This technique is evoked in *4.48 Psychosis*, and displayed in a way that evokes Kane's larger writing strategies.

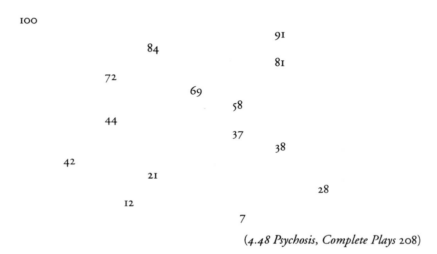

(4.48 Psychosis, Complete Plays 208)

The numerals occupy nearly an entire page and their spacing is at once regular and idiosyncratic, perhaps expressing the speaker's inability quite to seize the arithmetic at hand. The white space of the page may resemble, imply, or represent the "scattering" of the speaker's thoughts (if it is a speech), but the layout provides no real direction for the delivery, theatricalization, incarnation of this text. Unlike the white space of Pinter's plays, which is taken to imply either a temporal and psychological pause (a new intention is brewing) or a more formal break in the interpersonal combat, the semantics of Kane's page bear obscurely on the rhetoric of speech (Graham Saunders, perhaps following the Court productions, says that the characters "do not speak" these lines, but there is no reason to distinguish this page from others in the play ['*Love me or kill me*' 112]). In the performances at the Court – in which an angled mirror above the stage faced the audience throughout, so that the actors were seen simultaneously frontally and from above – the actors wrote the numerals backwards on a table top, so they could be read by the audience.[29]

The second "counting" scene takes a different shape on the page:

100
93
86
79
72
65
58
51
44
37
30
23
16
9
2
　　　　(232)

Does the linearity of this list on the page imply a more orderly delivery in performance? Perhaps. But whether this strategy – ordering verbal fragments in a rationalized sequence, in a visual structure – provides a more adequate strategy for embodying the play should give us pause. The desire to find this point of stillness, to locate the "identity" of the character/speaker or indeed of the author is an understandable, necessary desire for actors; but Kane's list, for all its formality, never quite ends at "one." To stage the play, actors must find a way to place this language, and to do something with it to organize its verbal fragments into an actable order. We might wonder whether this speech – which shapes its bits of language, organizes them conceptually and spatially, and so tracks the words back, almost but not quite, to a single, unified source – is more representative of the play's working than the previous speech, in which the elements of language lie scattered across the page, contesting the assimilation of writing to performance, to speech "originating" in character. Perhaps lyric agency and theatrical agency can't always be resolved into "one."

The two "counting" scenes frame a familiar allegory of poetry in/as performance, at once staging the poem's resistance to theatricalization and showing how performance, with its inevitable assimilation of language to the evocative disciplines of individual acting, at once betrays some of the implications of writing while betraying them into living sense. Tonally, *4.48*

Psychosis couldn't be farther removed from another famous "numbers" play, Gertrude Stein's "small vaudeville," *A Curtain Raiser.*

A CURTAIN RAISER

Six.
Twenty.
Outrageous.

Late.
Weak.
Forty.

More in any wetness.
Sixty three certainly.
Five.
Sixteen.
Seven.
Three.
More in orderly. Seventy-five.

(Stein, Geography and Plays 202)[30]

In the context of Stein's other plays, *A Curtain Raiser* is considerably more challenging than it is here: after all "Six." could easily be a speech prefix. While Kane's experimentation seems not to embrace Stein's play with the accessories of drama, her decision to avoid speech prefixes recalls the challenges that arise in many of Stein's plays, in which it is often difficult to know how many agents are implied (or whether there is a fixed number), or where the "speech" of one speaker begins and that of another ends, a kind of experiment now familiar from more widely performed plays like Peter Handke's *Offending the Audience* and Heiner Müller's *Hamletmachine*, which also resist apportioning the scripted language to individual speakers.

   4.48 Psychosis opens with something approaching conventional drama, stage directions and language in the second person, language that seems, in other words, directed, situational, to pose the subject in ways reminiscent of August Strindberg's *The Stronger*, as the silent site of speechless resistance.

   (A very long silence.)

   But you have friends.

   (A long silence.)

   You have a lot of friends.
   What do you offer your friends to make them so supportive?

   (A long silence.)

   What do you offer your friends to make them so supportive?

(A long silence.)

What do you offer?

(Silence.)

Recalling Hejinian's *Beginning*, as well as Kane's rhetorical emphasis on lineation, we might wonder whether the ambiguous long line "What do you offer your friends to make them so / supportive" is enjambed, or merely in prose. Does the lineation mark a breath, a pause, or has the text merely reached the margin? The relationship between the materiality of the writing and its signaling of speech becomes immediately more problematic, as the minimal stage directions disappear, and the language careens into new psychic, formal, and spatial arenas.

- - - - -

a consolidated consciousness resides in a darkened banqueting
hall near the ceiling of a mind whose floor shifts as ten
thousand cockroaches when a shaft of light enters as all
thoughts unite in an instant of accord body no longer expellent
as the cockroaches comprise a truth which no one ever utters

    I had a night in which everything was revealed to me.
    How can I speak again?

the broken hermaphrodite who trusted hermself alone finds the
room in reality teeming and begs never to wake from the
nightmare

    and they were all there
    every last one of them
    and they knew my name
    as I scuttled like a beetle along the backs of their chairs.

Remember the light and believe the light

An instant of clarity before eternal night

        don't let me forget

- - - - -

I am sad

I feel that the future is hopeless and that things cannot improve

I am bored and dissatisfied with everything

I am a complete failure as a person

I am guilty, I am being punished

I would like to kill myself

(205–206)

Like Suzan-Lori Parks's plays, Kane's have an "architectural look," though it's a very different building (Parks, *Venus* n.p.). Throughout *4.48 Psychosis*, passages are staged lyrically, using the design of the page apparently to encode a formal rhythm, as in the "I am . . ." litany here. The prose (is it prose, or are the lines just long? if it is prose, shouldn't "thousand" be hyphenated, or at least the line be leaded and spaced more evenly to justify the right-hand margin?) seems to demand an alternate sounding, one committed to the rhythms of everyday speech rather than the more distinct emphasis associated with the formal structure of verse-speaking. And then there are passages that seem simply dislocated on the page, so that the rhetoric of space seems significant but mysterious. What is striking here is the range of "sounding" possibilities, the variety of ways Kane's page both implies and resists its incarnation as acting.

Kane's text registers the materiality of language in print through the resources that print uses to convey the impression of sensibility, of a subject. That is, while trading speeches among the actors is perhaps an inevitable strategy for incarnating Kane's range of speech acts, the play also seems to demand a variety of reading (voicing? sounding? acting?) practices, as though to resist assimilation to a single, comfortable "I." Instead, as Charles Altieri suggests of lyric poetry more broadly, if we are to take Kane's writing seriously *as poetry*, we should be prepared to ask how it pushes "the self into an 'open' where thinking and feeling find new directions," in this case an "open" where "thinking and feeling" are terrifyingly elusive ("Some Problems" 190).

I know what I'm doing
all too well

No native speaker

irrational
irreducible
irredeemable
unrecognisable

derailed
deranged
deform
free form

obscure to the point of

> True   Right   Correct
> Anyone or anybody
> Each   every   all

drowning in a sea of logic
>> this monstrous state of palsy
>> still ill (222–23)

Here, despite the claim to be "No native speaker" (of the language of sanity?), the voice moves through a series of adjectives linked by a progressive assonance. The claim of irrationality is at once sustained by the logic of sound rather than sense, and belied by the shrewd progress of adjectives leading from "irrational" to "deform" and then to "free form." The panic of free-form consciousness seems to be enacted on the page by the sharp, formal antithesis between "True Right Correct" – evenly spaced, capitalized, formal, authoritative – and the lines that follow, in which indefinite pronouns (Anyone or anybody) deliquesce into adjectives (Each every all), and the desperate urgency to find the "True Right Correct" is embodied as much by the tight little box of text as by the words themselves, a box that (like the play) appears to contain its subject without making it singular, comprehensible as "one." Even so, this tentative, merely formal resolution almost immediately begins to deform, break down, as the brief phrases – "drowning in a sea of logic / this monstrous state of palsy" – trail off to the final isolated lament: "still ill." As a poem, the page provides evocative information, but it does not provide "direction." Kane's multiplex poetry cannot be readily assimilated to a single protocol of "character."

The page provides only momentary resolutions of "character" that are nonetheless undone, deformed by the progress of the writing. And if some sections seem to call for an alternative "voice,"

> Symptoms: Not eating, not sleeping, not speaking, no sex
> drive, in despair, wants to die
>> (223)

and others witness a mania of self-destruction,

I gassed the Jews, I killed the Kurds, I bombed the
Arabs, I fucked small children while they begged for
mercy, the killing fields are mine, everyone left the
party because of me, I'll suck your fucking eyes out
send them to your mother in a box and when I die
I'm going to be reincarnated as your child only fifty
times worse and mad as all fuck I'm going to make
your life a living fucking hell I REFUSE I REFUSE I
REFUSE LOOK AWAY FROM ME

(227)

many more seem to challenge "speech" itself, even at the moment that
they witness the *animalady* of poetry, incarnating a restless desire to betray
language into sound, into speaking, into action.

flash   flicker   slash   burn   wring   press   dab   slash
flash   flicker   punch   burn   float   flicker dab   flicker
punch   flicker   flash   burn   dab   press   wring press
punch   flicker   float   burn   flash   flicker burn

(231)

At some points, the text seems to enact three positionalities, three sources
of speaking, though the ways this textuality enacts relationship remains
finally opaque:

<blockquote>

                                  to be loved

I'm dying for one who doesn't care
I'm dying for one who doesn't know

                                  you're breaking me
        Speak
        Speak
        Speak

                                  ten yard ring of failure
                                  look away from me
        My final stand

                                  No one speaks   (243)
</blockquote>

In the end, even when the scattered voices seem to resolve themselves into a
single speaker ("watch me vanish / watch me / vanish"), that voice evokes
a scarifying evanescence, an inability finally to inhabit the space of one: "It
is myself I have never met, whose face is pasted on the / underside of my
mind" (245).

Kane's *4.48 Psychosis* uses the design of the page not as a stage direction but as a way to destabilize a conventionally "psychological" approach to acting. *4.48 Psychosis* requires us to read less for "character" than for the shifting, mobile, elusive site of the "lyric agency" of writing. The materiality of the text enforces a repeated encounter with print's various registers of expression, but refuses to direct those resources toward a specific modality of stage performance. In this sense, Kane's work is at once unique and cognate with a range of other experiments that use the mise-en-page to trouble the mise-en-scène. Kane's architecture recalls the "architectural look" of Suzan-Lori Parks's plays, though Kane's emphasis on psychological expression is replaced in Parks's plays by a vivid concern for the use of space, gesture, and embodiment. Parks's plays challenge actors and directors – to say nothing of mere readers – to figure out what, precisely, depends on the material organization of the text. Here is Scene 19 of her play *Venus*, in its entirety (Parks, *Venus* 80).

Scene 19: A Scene of Love (?)

The Venus
The Baron Docteur
The Venus
The Baron Docteur
The Venus
The Baron Docteur
The Venus
The Baron Docteur
The Venus

Parks has numbered the scenes of her play in reverse, and uses a character in the play, The Negro Resurrectionist, to announce each scene as it occurs. In her attention to the ways that documents of the past make their way into the contemporary performance of history, Parks foregrounds the textual process of the play during its performance. So, a director inclined to eliminate this scene will have some serious rewriting to do, and renumbering as well: Parks structures the play as a whole to bring this challenging print object into play.[31] In her notes to *Venus*, Parks reminds her readers that such textual moments should be understood as *spells*:

> An elongated and heightened (*Rest*). Denoted by repetition of figures' names with no dialogue. Has sort of an architectural look:
>
> **The Venus**
> **The Baron Docteur**

The Venus
The Baron Docteur

> This is a place where the figures experience their pure true
> simple state. While no action or stage business is neces-
> sary, directors should fill this moment as they best see fit.
>
> (*Venus* n.p.)

Kane uses punctuation (or the lack of it) rhetorically, to articulate delivery, but the formal design of *4.48 Psychosis* presents a radical formal challenge to any strategy of conventional theatrical realization. Parks's marks here seem both rhetorical and syntactic, to stand outside or beyond an obvious, conventional stage practice, and both directors and actors have to develop ways to theatricalize this text onstage. What does experiencing your "pure true simple state" call on you to experience? And what are you supposed to *do* about it? They will have to begin by reading the page, developing a practice for transforming that column of speech prefixes into something else, though precisely how we might or should engage them remains, I think, an open question. Jennifer Johung suggests, "we can no longer read the spells as solely linguistic determinants of speech, silence or space, but must in fact acquire, in conjunction, a visual articulation that does a different kind of work" ("Figuring"). This materialization strikes me as something more like the challenge first offered to readers of *Waiting for Godot*, or perhaps to readers of "The Love Song of J. Alfred Prufrock," texts that appeared less to direct performance than to claim a space outside contemporary conventions of reading, theatrical or otherwise.

Now, in the "late age of print," the printform of drama provides some evidence for what we might have suspected in other ways, a tension, perhaps even an anxiety not only about the persistence of print, but about a persistent desire to assert print's ongoing, changing cultural meanings relative to embodied regimes of performance. Pinter's *Pauses*, unlike Parks's rests and spells, were immediately assimilated to theatrical production, arguably because the reading habits trained on other kinds of modernist texts enabled them to be read in theatrically useful ways. The material form of Pinter's plays enabled what we take to be one of the most salient dimensions of the performance of his plays; Pinter's *Pauses* and *Silences* very quickly became important conventions of contemporary dramatic writing (like blank verse, or realistic prose in their day). While Grieg's or Kane's prefatory stage directions seem nostalgic, pointing to a sense that print should determine performance that has passed, or is passing, out of view, Kane's final play, like Parks's plays, and like Smith's, point in another direction, to an effort to frame writing as a kind of *animalady*, writing that demands embodiment without being readily assimilable to performance conventions: dramatic writing that demands an experimental experience.[32]

It's fair to say that the landscape, ideological as well as practical, in which theatrical performance takes place has changed dramatically since the premiere of *The Homecoming* in 1965. Western theatre practice has both expanded and diversified in the past forty years (Grotowski, Schechner, Barba, Boal, Suzuki, Bogart, Brook, intercultural performance, deconstructive performance, performance art); directors, designers, and performers have come to exert a kind of authorial presence in the work of theatre (Samuel Beckett, Robert Lepage, Julie Taymor, Anna Deavere Smith); the hegemony of dramatic theatre as the index of performance has been fully and successfully contested by new kinds of performance (in the theatre) and by performance studies (in the academy). In the refined precincts of literary studies, reading strategies have multiplied and diversified and the death of the author and his/her intentions has been accompanied, unsurprisingly enough, by the announcement of the death of print and print culture itself, as digital forms have provided new ways to represent – and possibly supplant – writing, all the while bringing writing (email, the intensive print emulation of the internet) more directly and incessantly into daily living. (In this sense, the long-foretold death of that magnificent, residual invalid, the dramatic theatre, is hardly news.) This is the context in which plays today are published, in which their materiality takes shape. Whether we see a given text as evoking a desire to govern ready-made conventions of performance, or to summon new forms of production, printed drama today arises in the new suspense between print and digital writing, and in the old suspense between writing and performance.

Pauses, ellipses, the appearance and disappearance of commas, the placement (or absence) of speech prefixes – surely such tiny events have only the most trivial bearing on the literary or the theatrical design of the drama. After all, these features often don't even originate with the writer, but are assigned (as stage directions sometimes are) as an after-effect of a given production, or as the design protocol developed by the play's publisher. And, *really*, since actors and directors are sometimes inclined and usually trained to ignore such trifles, what difference can they make to our understanding of modern and postmodern performance? Does the printform of modern drama help to articulate its relation to performance? To modernism?

I think such (very good) questions arise from a surprisingly contradictory impulse: to regard the practice of theatre as the site of the drama's materialization in history, while regarding the practice of the drama's public identity as writing – the printed play – as materially irrelevant to its history, as absorbed into the abstractions of the merely literary. To ignore the consequences of the booking of drama is, though, to ignore one of the crucial dimensions of the drama's cultural identity in the West: the shaping force of print on the interface between literary and performance culture. It has been fashionable to mark the incomplete realization of plays on the page, the ways in which plays have another form of existence, different kinds of meaning, when they are realized in the practice of theatre. Yet the rise of digital culture has not only displaced print as the single dominant form of writing-production, and not only displaced theatre and film/video as the dominant forms of live and recorded performance. It has also provided us with an instrument for the analysis of both print and performance in a non-print medium. One consequence of digital culture (think of the many versions of any extended writing you have done that exist as files on your computer) has been not only the ability to transform and distribute texts online, but a sense of the differential quality of print itself, of the ways in which print's distinctive ways of materializing a work as an event participate in its history (a kind of history that is in most cases obliterated by the present tense of digital writing – do you save *all* your drafts, or simply revise them on the screen?). Both the ideological and the practical properties of print have become more visible as a consequence of new writing technologies, in ways that enable us to open a different kind of perspective on the history of something that has always seemed poorly represented by print: drama. Print bears on the poetics of performance, not only because the material form of printed plays provides the raw material for many theatrical productions, but because print has provided the model, and so the point of resistance, for our understanding of writing, of drama, and of dramatic performance. To the extent that contemporary conceptions of performance, theatre, and drama have arisen in an era in which drama has itself been partly instantiated by print and in print, they remain partly captive to the ideology of print. Reading the signs of that ideological work, even in the accidentals of the printed page, may provide one way to reopen the narrative of the drama's role in modern culture, and to sharpen our understanding of the relation between writing and performance in the modern theatre.

Epilogue: whom the reader will remember

We began with Beckett's staging of the book in *Ohio Impromptu*, a play that enacts the anxious ambivalence of modern drama's dual implication in the printed page and the imprinted stage. In recent years, Beckett's plays have come to epitomize the conflict between literature and theatre in ways that are at once revealing of Beckett's crucial place in the booking of modern drama, and suggestive of the ongoing friction between print and performance. Taken purely on the page, the exiguous lessness of Beckett's efficient theatre machines may seem reciprocal to the flamboyant untheatricality of Stein's drama. Stein absorbs the apparatus of theatre into the "literary" text; her playful experiments with the dramatic genre, and with *play*, resolutely resist imaging the work of the stage. On Beckett's page, the stage directions and other theatrical accessories occupy their conventional place, outside the dialogue, and seem to do their conventional work, directing performance. Yet while Stein's plays engulf the apparatus of the stage, in Beckett's plays these accessories become increasingly prominent, even displacing the dialogue as constitutive of "the play." Some plays (*Play, Come and Go, Not I, That Time, Rockaby*) add a set of "notes," usually in a different font, and often on a different page than the formal "stage directions"; *Quad* is all directions, and the other plays for film and television are usually preceded by diagrams specifying the camera's perspective, a technique used as well for the stage play *Footfalls*, which opens with the diagram of May's nine-step, wheeling journey. For all their differences, though, Stein and Beckett share a motivating sense of the printed mise-en-page as the stage of drama. Stein neglects the work that the accessory text of stage directions might perform in the theatre, absorbing the textual signs of theatre into the scripted drama, *as* the scripted drama. Beckett extends the playwright's authority from the drama to embrace these textual signs – the stage directions – and so to govern the texture of performance.

The "pictorial composition" that "replaces dramatic action, emphasizing frontality and the frame, flatness and absence of perspective" that Bonnie

Marranca sees in Stein's plays is the hallmark of Beckett's theatre, a visual composition that is achieved, again, through an exact reversal of Stein's method (Marranca, "Introduction" xi). The still controversial duality of the play's mise-en-page, the problematic extension of the playwright's proprietary authority to the margins of the printed page inversely enacted by both Stein's and Beckett's plays, has become the defining issue of the recent career of Beckett's plays in the theatre. Beckett's stage is the site of legal struggle, strife that arises from the proprieties of the mise-en-page. The several efforts to prevent all-female or interracial *Godots*, the threatened closing of JoAnne Akalaitis's production of *Endgame* at the American Repertory Theatre in 1984, and the controversy surrounding Deborah Warner's environmental staging of *Footfalls* in London in 1994 all contest the authority that Beckett claimed as a playwright, authority that takes the extension of the playwright's work from the printed dialogue to the stage directions as a trope for extending the playwright's propriety from page to stage. Achieving this pictorial composition creates extraordinary and distinctive demands for Beckett's actors. The physical constraints, the precisely repeated movements, the disconnected speech, the rapid and toneless delivery, the tortuous disembodiment summoned by many of Beckett's plays arise from this "other" text, writing which far from suspending the imagination of performance works fully to determine it. While Stein's writing provides little sense of how to lift the play from the page to the stage, Beckett's scrupulous visual imagination is enacted on the page by claiming the stage directions not as conventional accessories to the drama (that can be conventionally ignored), but as the drama itself. How does this effort to materialize the play on the page, and from the page, reshape the relationship between drama, print, and performance?

Beckett's directions participate in the modern tradition of at once authenticating and displacing this theatrical discourse by giving it an authorial tone, a voice: "*Maximum of simplicity and symmetry,*" *Happy Days* (*Complete Dramatic Works* 138); "*Desert. Dazzling light,*" *Act Without Words I* (203); "*Surprising pair of dirty white boots, size ten at least, very narrow and pointed,*" *Krapp's Last Tape* (215); "*Faces so lost to age and aspect as to seem almost part of urns. But no masks,*" "*Faces impassive throughout. Voices toneless except where an expression is indicated,*" *Play* (307); "The sitting posture results in urns of unacceptable bulk and is not to be considered," *Play* (319); "*Very erect, facing front, hands clasped in laps,*" *Come and Go* (354); "There is just enough pause to contain it as MOUTH recovers from vehement refusal to relinquish third person," *Not I* (375); "Negotiation of E without rupture of rhythm when three or four players cross paths at this point. Or, if ruptures accepted, how best exploit?" *Quad* (453); "*Head bowed. Hands in pockets. Age and physique unimportant*," *Catastrophe* (457); "*Steps: clearly audible rhythmic tread*," *Footfalls* (399). Martin Puchner shrewdly notes that "gestures are Beckett's second, not secondary, language – the counterpart, and often competitor, of dialogue" (*Stage Fright* 164), and describes how the accessory text of Beckett's directions participates in the modernist, antitheatrical "literarization" of dramatic writing: the plays "register the institutionalization of the dramatic text as literature to be read," not by recreating for a reading audience the experience of seeing the play, as Shaw did, but by so controlling the stage from the book that the performance nearly "recreates on the stage the experience of reading a dramatic text and thus demonstrates what it means for a play to address simultaneously a general reader and an audience in the theater" (168). Bernard Shaw's stage directions create a narrative setting for a readerly spectator seated in a virtual proscenium house: the directions fill in the fictional setting of the play from a "theatrical" perspective. While many of Beckett's directions can also be read in this way ("*A country road. A tree. Evening.*"), they often seem, sometimes simultaneously, to speak in both the indicative and the imperative mood, as in the direction for *Play*: "*But no masks.*" Providing a narrative perspective on the action is nothing new. To the degree that Beckett's laconic directions, like Shaw's loquacious ones, provide a description of the stage space or the fictive space, they become a readily dispensable part of that narrative "information" conventionally taken as mere excess in stage practice, as not addressed to performers but merely recoding the drama for the convenience of armchair readers.

Although Beckett's directions speak in the author's *propria persona*, and sometimes seem merely to describe the fictive setting, and sometimes ambiguously to describe and to direct at once, more often they claim to speak directly to a specific set of auditors: the actors, directors, and designers who will put the play into practice. While the narrative directions exemplify the modernist playwright's retreat from theatricality, Beckett's plays reanimate that obsolete nineteenth-century tradition, the use of theatrically oriented stage directions that Shaw rejected precisely to incorporate playwriting as readerly literature. Beckett's plays, in this sense, may address readers and audiences as a secondary effect. By recasting the "acting edition" in the author's voice, Beckett materializes the play's directions not as dispensable narrative, nor as a theatrical discourse specifically distinct from the writer's writing, but as theatrical practice specifically incorporated into the authorized design of the drama. Of course, how the plays are actually used in performance arises from practices that can't be controlled from the page. Much as companies have effectively staged Stein's rebarbative plays (to say nothing of Mary Zimmerman's successful adaptations of nondramatic prose for the stage in *The Notebooks of Leonardo da Vinci*, or Ovid's *Metamorphoses*), so, too, Beckett's directions will be successfully flouted onstage: they must be flouted to some degree, even in "faithful" productions (how toneless is "*toneless*"? how grey are the grey walls of Hamm and Clov's cell?). Beckett's distinctive achievement lies in the claim that performance can be absorbed into the texture of these accessories to the drama. Beckett's mise-en-scène is the side effect of the playwright's strategic mise-en-page.

Given Beckett's extension of the playwright's authorizing voice, it's perhaps not surprising that the battle for the control of the page would find its way to the theatre. At the same time, given the ways that Beckett's texts are seen to enact the playwright's proper authority, it may be startling to discover that the printforms of Beckett's plays are variable, inconsistent, and unstable in ways best described as Shakespearean. Modern Shakespeare editing has energetically confronted the duality of the drama, and the ways that the printed versions of Shakespeare's plays may simultaneously enact (a) "literary" designs ignored by, inassimilable to, and/or intentionally excessive of stage practice; (b) "theatrical" designs stemming from the playwright's savvy immersion in theatre work, from his collaboration with fellows in his company, from performances in which he may have had a hand, from later performances nonetheless associated with his company, or from the conventional practices of the theatre with which he was familiar; (c) other factors ranging across the habits of copyists, the distribution of parts, the ways companies acquired and maintained scripts, the impact of censorship, the habits of printshop work, the distribution and even the shape of type, and so on. Any printed play will necessarily represent "the play" at the interface of performance and writing, and Shakespeare's plays, for all the specificity of their formation and transmission in the intercalated histories of print literature and the stage are hardly unique. The problems enacted by the printforms of Shakespeare's plays are reprised by Beckett's, reprised in ways that extend and specify the trials of drama in modern print culture.

Working as a writer, translator, adviser to productions, and as a director, Beckett played a role in the staging of his plays at least comparable to Shakespeare, and despite the uniform authority typically attributed to Beckett's text, his printed plays evince a similar complexity in their representation of the drama. To speak for the moment simply in terms of Beckett as a "literary dramatist," writing integral, coherent scripts for a literary posterity, we should recall the variety of *Waiting for Godot*, a play Beckett wrote well before his extended involvement with stage production and that most readily conforms to the notion of the nontheatrical integrity of the written drama. Having written *Godot* in French, Beckett made a number of changes of language and action to the subsequent English translation. Since the play's first English-language staging took place in London before the lifting of the censorship, when the play was transferred from the Arts Theatre to the Criterion, the text of the play was altered to appease the Lord Chamberlain's examiner, and it was this censored text that was first published by Faber in 1956 (we might recall the similar effects of censorship on the texts of, say, *King Lear*). As S. E. Gontarski notes, "there are hundreds of variants" between the Grove Press edition published in the U.S. in 1954 and the censored British edition published without comment in 1956 by Faber. While Faber subsequently corrected some of these errors for its 1965 edition, the text of the play published in Faber's 1986 *Samuel Beckett: The Complete Dramatic Works* (timed to coincide with Beckett's eightieth birthday), "inexplicably reprinted the 1956 bowdlerized text of *Waiting for Godot*" ("Editing Beckett" 193).[1] *Come and Go* now appears in none of the popular English-language editions of the play as Beckett may have intended, despite the fact that he read the proofs for at least one edition. Translating the play into French, Beckett added six lines – a sizeable percentage – to his "dramaticule," four new lines to open the play, and two lines to the end of the play. Since the first English edition, *Come and Go: A Dramaticule* (Calder and Boyars, 1967) was set from Beckett's earlier typescript, it did not incorporate this change, which is now standard in French and German texts of the play. The revised opening lines did appear in the first American edition of the play, which appeared in *Cascando and Other Short Dramatic Pieces* (Grove, 1968), but subsequent versions of the play printed in *Collected Shorter Plays of Samuel Beckett* (Grove) and finally in the *Complete Dramatic Works* (Faber) chose to reprint the incomplete 1967 Calder and Boyars text. *Come and Go*, then, exists in several variously authorized printforms, as well as in the "revised text" now published in the fourth volume of *The Theatrical Notebooks of Samuel Beckett*, a version which incorporates these lines, as well as noting other changes to the text – assigning speeches to different speakers – that arose when Beckett directed the play (Gontarski, "Textual Notes" 212–13).

Such instabilities are characteristic of the transmission of all print literature, and are not specific to the drama. But Beckett's printed plays also epitomize problems specific to the printform of plays, problems shared as much by Shakespeare as by printed drama today. Some of Beckett's plays were printed in pre-production versions that were subsequently altered by the author. The Faber edition of *Footfalls* published before the 1976

Royal Court Theatre premiere of the play was set from one of Beckett's working typescript drafts. This text does not contain changes to the dialogue that Beckett made during rehearsals, nor other changes (for example, "*clearly audible rhythmic pad*" to "*clearly audible rhythmic tread*") that, arguably, have more to do with "objectifying" the play for later readers and producers than actually modifying the play's action. And, famously, the 1976 Faber edition has May taking seven steps, which Beckett later changed to nine. Beckett gave Faber a revised text, but the text itself had a number of errors, including the failure to change May's counting of the steps from seven to nine in the dialogue, where she still said "five six seven wheel." This error was corrected, but other inconsistencies were variously reprinted in successive American and English editions.[2] As has been hypothesized for some of Shakespeare's texts, "theatrical" changes – here, authorized changes that arose from Beckett's work in the theatre – have been absorbed inconsistently and rather incoherently to the printed play.

Although Beckett was not a sharer in his own theatrical company like Shakespeare, he did work closely with productions of his plays. He wrote for individual performers (Billie Whitelaw, for example), he chose to work with specific companies, and as a director he frequently changed the language and action of his plays in performance, both in recognition of the specific circumstances of a given production, and as he came to see new, unexpected, or unimagined ways of visualizing his plays onstage. Sometimes Beckett-the-director seems to reject the stagey exuberance of a younger Beckett-the-playwright: no clown shoes for Krapp, no red face for Hamm on Beckett-the-director's stage. We don't have any record of the working-through of Shakespeare's plays at the Globe, other than in the ambiguous signs (if they are signs) traced in the remaining texts of the printed plays. Beckett has left us his notebooks; we have volumes of salient interviews with directors, designers, and actors with whom Beckett worked; many living critics saw the productions in which Beckett had a hand and spoke to Beckett about them; Beckett's productions were widely reviewed; and, of course, we have recordings. Yet this welter of textuality hardly resolves the problems of the plays in print, precisely because the problems of the drama's dual identity in print culture cannot be resolved in or by print. How do we regard Beckett's notebooks and the "text" of his productions? He was certainly an "authorized" director, but was he an authoritative director? Is it possible that other directors might achieve better, even truer results with Beckett's plays for later audiences? If Beckett's plays are to live in the theatre we should hope so.

The effort to retextualize Beckett's plays sustained the signal achievement of Beckett scholarship in the 1990s, and arguably of scholarship on any postwar English-language playwright: the publication of *The Theatrical Notebooks of Samuel Beckett* in four volumes, under the general editorship of James Knowlson. The *Notebooks* do a number of things: they provide an edited text of the plays, often correcting errors found in previous print editions; in many cases, they provide a "revised text," incorporating information from Beckett's manuscripts and the notebooks into a new text of the play; they provide edited facsimile texts of Beckett's meticulous directing notebooks. As the general editor points out, when "Beckett came to direct his own plays for the stage, he introduced numerous changes to the printed texts that consisted of cuts and additions as well as revisions." Some of these changes Beckett resisted incorporating into the published text of the plays, but in working with the editors of *The Theatrical Notebooks* Beckett cooperated on producing a newly definitive text: "Our aim in printing (at last with Beckett's full agreement) revised texts that are based on his productions has been to set down the changes that were made there. The texts are now as close as possible to how Beckett wanted them to be" ("General Editor's Note," in Beckett, *Theatrical Notebooks* IV: vii). Yet as S. E. Gontarski points out, even Beckett's close collaboration with the project could not resolve the dream of incorporating Beckett's dual authorship as writer and as director in the signs on the page. He reports, for example, that Beckett was finally undecided whether Hamm should hold his dog or drop it after Clov smacks him with it in *Endgame*, and while Beckett omitted the Auditor both from the 1978 production of *Not I* he directed with Madeleine Renaud and from the BBC film with Billie Whitelaw, the Auditor continues to appear in all published texts of the play, none of which even "suggests that the elimination of the Auditor is a directorial option" ("Editing Beckett" 198, 203).

Gontarski describes the revised text published in the *Theatrical Notebooks* as "something like a postmodern performance text, with an emphasis on process and transformation, which traces Beckett's post-production creative process," and often records as well the various problems inherent in the published versions of the plays. *The Theatrical Notebooks* not only brings the inconsistencies of Beckett's published plays clearly into view, but also sets the plays in the context of Beckett's other theatrical writing, the elaborate revisions, graphs, diagrams, and drawings he used to bring his fundamentally pictorial sense of the drama to the stage. The dense texture of diacritical marks on the page, as well as the published accessories of Beckett's elaborate directorial *didascalia*, at once enacts Beckett's developing mastery of the drama's dialectical discourses, and the impossibility of dissolving them together in a single text. That is, the *Notebooks* work to stabilize Beckett's writing, but can only do so by recognizing the inherent instability of print's claim to fix the drama, to fix any writing, in a final form. *The Theatrical Notebooks* register Beckett's plays as polymorphous, as composed of writing undertaken at different times and in different places, of writing undertaken at leisure and in the heat of theatrical exigency, and of writing that has already been materialized for the public in a diverse range of printforms and performances. Despite the fact that Beckett's plays now frequently emblematize the conflict between the authority of print and the mutability of the stage, in fact they illustrate a more salient truth: that both the page and the stage provide the material conditions enabling Beckett's plays, and as those conditions change, so will the essentials of Beckett's drama.

Footfalls is one of Beckett's most admired and elegant short plays and in 1994 it was also the subject of the kind of infighting that has become iconic of Beckett's plays in the theatre: a production – directed by Deborah Warner and acted by Fiona Shaw and Susan Engel – that altered the *scenic* design of the play, and so seemed (to some at least, including Beckett's legal representatives) to violate the drama's proper control of the stage. *Footfalls* is typical of Beckett's late, highly visual playwriting. As Billie Whitelaw reported of acting in the premiere of the play under Beckett's watchful eye, the severe demands of the text ("I have made myself ill," she reports, "trying to complete the image he has in his mind's eye and in his ear"), arise from Beckett's essentially visual mode of composition, the "image" of eye and ear: "Perhaps I should be pacing up and down in the Tate Gallery, I don't know, because the way the thing looks and the way he paints with lights is just as important as what comes out of my mouth." As Beckett told the German actress Hildegard Schmahl, "the text, the words were only built up around this picture."[3]

Does Beckett's effort to command the stage picture from the space of the page locate his writing in a different relation to the conventions of modern dramatic writing and of modern stage practice? Does it inscribe the drama differently on the page? Warner's *Footfalls* helps us to explore this question, in part because the production's visual design was at once elegant and tightly prescribed, subjecting the visual element of Beckett's play to a different, nonetheless coherent aesthetic regime. The production played for a week, opening 15 March 1994, at the high-Victorian Garrick Theatre in London's West End; it was the only play on the bill, running for little more than twenty minutes. Although Leah Schmidt, the English agent for the Beckett estate, seemed to threaten Warner with a lifetime ban from the Beckett canon as a result of the production ("'We have not done anything about the fact that she has not followed all the stage directions. Life is too short, but she will not be doing Beckett again'"), in the end Warner was merely prevented from videotaping the production or taking it on a planned tour to Paris. As Edward Beckett explained, "When approached by a theatre or a director for the rights to perform a Beckett play the estate's agents go through the contract and point out the clauses relating to the integrity of the text and stage directions and the fact that they must be adhered to." At the opening night, however, he "was amazed to find that not only had virtually every stage direction been ignored but even the text had been altered" (Warner having reassigned some lines from V to M). "It was decided that faced with this situation the estate had no alternative but to withdraw the rights for the production to tour" (Warner did agree to restore the lines to their proper speakers for the remainder of the brief run).[4]

While it's certainly plausible to think that "virtually every stage direction" had been "ignored," it seems more accurate to describe the production as enacting a systematic reconception of the play's scenic design as a means of theatricalizing – not undoing – Beckett's dramatic action. Shaw's May wore a red (not grey) wrap; she paced in two locations rather than one; her voice seems not to have been "*both low and slow throughout*"; the lighting was not "*dim, strongest at floor level, less on body, least on head*," in part because the house work-lights were left onstage; and, while a proscenium config-uration is perhaps only implied in the stage directions ("*Strip: downstage, parallel with front, length nine steps, width one metre, a little off centre audi-ence right*"), Warner's audience was not situated frontally toward the play.[5] Instead, Warner systematically produced *Footfalls* in the idiom of environ-mental theatre. Warner has an ongoing interest in site-specific performance. Her *St. Pancras Project* (1997) took audiences through a performance of the abandoned railway station, and in *The Angels Project* (2003) she staged the urban geography of New York City. For *Footfalls*, Warner brought the audience into the theatre, which she and designer Hildegard Bechtler transformed into an extension of the play's psychological terrain. As Paul Taylor described it, "The venerably Victorian Garrick had certainly never felt so strange," and was given a "dismantled, desolate look": the house-lights were draped with sheets, lighting provided by a few candles and the theatre's unshaded work-lights – a naked bulb on a stand, which shone on May's desolate treading; the "back of the stalls had been roped off and the plush rows at the front had been annulled as even minimally comfortable seating by a covering of planks"; and a "rostrum, built of planks" was "located just beneath the dress circle." The play opened with Shaw onstage, "first seen shuffling across the vast dark void of the stage," more or less according to Beckett's directions (though the work-lights remained on the stage). "Then, causing those of us who were in the stalls to have to wheel round, she reappeared up on the rostrum where she began talking to the unseen bedridden ninety-year-old mother (whose voice may exist only in May's consciousness) and where she embarked on the compulsive pacing – a superstitiously unvarying routine of nine paces forward and back – that is the play's central image of a life constricted by its own neuroses. Treading this precarious ledge, Shaw had to grab on to the overhanging masonry at each turn." Recalling the March production for his December summary of the season, Taylor found the production to be "the defining moment of my theatrical year," and other critics who were less completely won over nevertheless noted the production's careful effort to extend and concretize the play's literary thematics ("Dead Letter").[6] John Peter remarked, "I sat in the circle a few rows behind Fiona Shaw as she shuffled up and down, taking precisely the number of steps specified by Beckett, a lost, imprisoned creature. [. . .] Her body seemed battered, but also slightly stunted: this was because her head was touching the bottom of the upper circle above her and she had to bend her neck to stay upright. The effect of captivity, physical and spiritual, was complete" ("Many Happy Returns"). Alastair Macaulay noted the sepulchral effect of having Susan Engel's voice as M "emerge from beneath her, so that Shaw, in the very centre of the audience, seems to pace upon her mother's tomb" (Rev. of *Footfalls*), and Taylor also amplified this sense of the production's use of the theatre space: "Does this obliterate the necessary sense of May's constriction? Not if you take the whole of the eerily dislocated Garrick as her psychic prison, a metaphor within which she moves, always in the regulation nine compulsive paces, and palpably gets nowhere" ("Way out of Line"). For the twenty minutes' traffic of the stage, the Garrick was transformed, made to signify in ways that seemed less to place the play before its audience than to absorb the audience into the space of the play: "The production embraced the whole space, making it seem empty even in the presence of a large audience" (Wardle, Rev. of *Footfalls*).

Needless to say, to many, Warner's refusal to understand that "while you direct Shakespeare, you obey Beckett," merely destroyed the play: "The stage directions are laconic, precise; minima which are also maxima" (McCue, "Persisting or Not" 18). When Billie Whitelaw saw the performance, it made her feel "as if Samuel Beckett were burned at the stake; I felt numb, physically ill." Noting the pictorial character of Beckett's direction – "It was like being painted with light. I was a walking, talking Edvard Munch painting" – Whitelaw implies that the inward absorption of Beckett's proscenium staging was precisely challenged by Warner's use of the Garrick: "imitating Beckett's voice, Ms. Whitelaw remembered his advice, 'Inward, Billie, always look inward.' There was, she said, 'nothing inward' about what occurred at the Garrick Theatre" (qtd. Gussow, "Modify Beckett?" 10). Fair enough; subjecting Beckett's play to a different mode of theatricality, Warner provided a distinctly different kind of play for her audiences. In this *Footfalls*, audiences heard "fine text, and saw "a sad life"; they also experienced "a great theatre building" as part of the play, confirming Warner's intent to make the environment of the performance a meaningful part of the life of the play (Coveney, Rev. of *Footfalls*). Warner saw the Garrick as "'an empty house, a devastatingly lonely place,'" in which May is "'crushed between the floor of the dress circle and the roof of the theater, between heaven and hell'" (qtd. Gussow, "Modify Beckett?" 10).

Warner's work here has, I think, been somewhat misunderstood, for it marks less the conflict between the authority of stage and page, or between director and author, than something more ineluctable: the passing of history. Beckett's plays have reshaped modern theatre and modern drama, and they have done so from the proscenium stage. The rigorous, even dehumanizing subjection of actors to the scripted demands of the stage picture enacts the antitheatrical "absorption" characteristic of modernist theatrical experiment, and is oddly enough predicated on maintaining a fixed distance between the artwork and the contaminating presence of its spectators. This aspect of Beckett's theatre – epitomized by the television plays, which dispense with an audience altogether in favor of the camera's controlling eye – is nowhere more visible than in *Play* and *Not I*, which insist on the fiction that the play is underway before it is visible to the audience, and continues on, purgatorially enough, after we have departed. The doubling of the audience's applause in *Catastrophe* – "*Distant storm of applause.* P *raises his head, fixes the audience. The applause falters, dies*" (461) – is perhaps part of this displacement, too, as is the way Bam finally dismisses our attention in *What Where*: "Make sense who may. I switch off" (476).

Warner's *Footfalls* reframes the question of print and performance as a question of historical change. What does it mean to reposition Beckett's modernist strategies for imprinting the stage within an emergent theatrical aesthetic? Much as performances of Sophocles' plays in Greek amphitheatres or Shakespeare's plays at the new Globe theatre in London have shown, efforts to restage or "reconstruct" a play's original circumstances of production invariably speak the play in the accents of the present. Not only are we different from Sophocles' or Shakespeare's original audiences, and not only do we have different means (literary and technological) for representing ourselves in dramatic action and stage spectacle, but both drama and theatre occupy different roles in contemporary culture. Can we see a play at Shakespeare's Globe today without partly experiencing it as an alternative to "theatre," as a bit "theme park" or "touristy," all the while we are also sensing the powerful resonance between Shakespeare's plays and this (mostly) wooden O? Would anyone want to see the Swan Theatre in Stratford destroyed because it is incapable of producing his plays according to any imaginable sense of Shakespeare's actual intentions for the stage?[7] Beckett's scripts struggle to extend the playwright's control over a specific theatrical apparatus, and they successfully transform the proscenium theatre into a vehicle for his strategically antitheatrical drama.[8] Displaced and disembodied, denied the resources of voice and movement, denied even the shreds of "character" that usually enable a transaction with the audience, Beckett's actors are instrumental figures in the cascando of words and image onstage. The proscenium theatre and the relations of visibility it sustains is still very much with us, of course, and we owe much of our understanding of its capacity to Beckett. But Beckett's career is precisely coordinated with an era of theatrical experiment – "poor theatre," happenings, participatory theatre, theatre of images, performance art, environmental and site-specific performance – that often saw in the proscenium theatre's absorbing stasis the signs of an advancing rigor mortis. Beckett's precisely imagined plays took time to get produced, and to get produced with the fidelity to his directions that would enable their real power to emerge, and the moment for doing Beckett "the Beckett way" has certainly not passed. Nevertheless, Warner's systematic effort to produce the play in a different mode of theatricality cannot be dismissed simply as transgression. It is part of the condition of theatre to deploy new ways of performing under the sign of "fidelity": it took time for Ibsen and Chekhov to be legible outside the box-set, and we might well ask how Warner is asking us to rethink Beckett's writing, not from in front of the stage box, but from inside the space we share with the play.

Warner's *Footfalls* participates in the modern theatre's dominant approach to staging the classics: finding a contemporary stage idiom that seems at once surprising and original, and yet to extend the implications of the dramatic text – hip-hop Mercutio, Julie Taymor's Armani Romans, Doctor Faustus joking about his visit with George Bush, and so on.[9] This sense of the work of theatre extends to Beckett's plays as well, surely among the classics of the modern stage: departing from Beckett's directions is not, it turns out, the sure sign of imaginative impoverishment. The striking *Happy Days* directed by Sir Peter Hall and starring Felicity Kendall at the Arts Theatre in November 2003 aroused little irritation from the critics and no apparent ire from the estate, despite completely remapping Beckett's stage geography. In this production, Winnie's defining "*Expanse of scorched grass rising centre to low mound. Gentle slopes down to front and either side of stage*" (*Happy Days* 138) was replaced by an elegant spiral ramp of dirt and grass rising vertically around Winnie. Suspended beneath a blue ribbon-like design representing the sky, Kendall's Winnie might have seemed less the prisoner of a malevolent, grasping earth, than the bright button of a gigantic, if somewhat soiled, daisy. Yet the production maintained the play's visual frontality and, perhaps not incidentally, its traditional use as a star vehicle; while some reviewers complained about the set, most found it at least intriguing, and many noted the production's distinguished lineage (Hall had opened the National Theatre with an acclaimed production of *Happy Days* starring Peggy Ashcroft in 1976, and had directed the English premiere of *Waiting for Godot* at the Arts Theatre in 1955).[10] A distinguished director with full Beckett credentials returning to the scene of Beckett's English invention to reprise a landmark success, this time with one of England's most beloved actresses: despite remaking the stage space, this superb production could hardly have been more canonical.

What is at stake in Warner's production is a more subtle transformation. Beckett's mise-en-page expands the drama from the dialogue to the directions, figuring the space of the page as uniform and homogenously authorial, a page that authoritatively tropes the disposition of the proscenium stage, a space that insists on externalizing the viewer from participation *in* the artwork, and on using the perspective of the auditorium to stage a certain kind of experience – internalized, silent, interior – as *dramatic*, the "inwardness" of the stage reciprocated by the spectator's "inward" engagement. There is no "outside" to Beckett's page other than the space of consumption. Warner's production does not really reject Beckett's authorizing gesture; it adapts it to a different mode of theatricality. Staging *Footfalls* as an environmental rather than a proscenium event, Warner refused to parade May before an invisible, voyeuristic public. Beckett's authoritarian directions direct a spectacle that takes its place *in front of* us; the play is an object complete in itself that displaces the circumstances of theatre as legitimate to our experience, however evocative they are of his characters' plight. Warner's direction places us *in the spectacle*; the apparatus of the theatre, and even the spectators' physical relation to different parts of the performance, is not cancelled as an unfortunate and irrelevant expediency, but is enabled as part of the meaning of the event. We can perhaps feel the passage of history in Warner's disciplined production of Beckett's play, but it would be a mistake to say that this production merely substitutes the director's authority for the author's. Instead, Warner seems to enact the material implications of Beckett's writing through an alternative form of theatrical materialization. Warner's *Footfalls* extends the authority of the drama not merely across the space of the page, and to the space of the stage, but through the space of the theatre as well.

By choosing to stage *Footfalls* as a freestanding play, and not as part of a bill of Beckett shorts, as is typically done in the theatre, Warner's production had the effect of further distinguishing this production from "theatre." Moreover, Warner's production dramatizes the ongoing difficulty of mapping the relations of authority from page to stage. Trying to come to grips with this production, Michael Billington asks, "is a theatrical text simply a blueprint for its interpreters or does it have an integrity of its own that demands respect?" The blueprint is a common metaphor for describing the relationship between writing and performance. It implies on the one hand that the performance will materialize the implications of the text in a very different form, and that the materialization will necessarily specify and particularize the design; on the other hand, it also implies that the final performance is prescribed, that its structures and mechanics have already been laid down, and that the performance is merely following the directions. For Billington, though, Beckett's blueprint is much more the latter case than the former: "What he does is to fuse word, image, light and sound to create something akin to a three-dimensional painting that denies directorial latitude." In this sense, "his later work is too unyielding, too fixed in its theatrical demands, to achieve the malleability of a classic" ("Foot Fault" 4–5).

If Beckett's plays are, as Billington suggests – and he is echoed here by Whitelaw, by Edward Beckett, and others who see Beckett's writing as amenable only to one form of theatricality – so fully dependent on a single mode of theatrical production as to be unrealizable in alternate forms, then the claims for Beckett's ongoing or universal value are surely suspect. And yet, what Warner's production shows is that the rhetoric of authority governing the relationship between writing and performance is always just that, rhetorical. In terms of the environmental aesthetic it deploys, Warner's production makes a credible claim to amplify Beckett's authority over the page, translating that authority into a different mode of theatre that nonetheless captures the thematics of Beckett's play, and elaborates one of the fundamental gestures of Beckett's writing: to enlarge the play-wright's authority from the dramatic dialogue to the drama's accessories, and through them to the shaping of the stage.

Finally, *Footfalls* is an unusually pertinent play for such an engagement with Beckett. For while *Footfalls* is one of Beckett's most poetic plays in the delicacy of its verbal and visual design, it is also a play that exemplifies the volatility of print.[11] For *Footfalls* is not only a play with a vexed history in print – a history in which the text's specification of stage action (the number of May's steps) has been precisely at issue – but a play that dramatizes an elegant suspension between narrative and performance, literature and theatre. May's rhythmic pacing provides the image of her "revolving it all," her need to "hear the feet, however faint they fall" suggesting that it's only the sound of her treading that reinforces May's attenuated sense of her visibly attenuated being. While V, the "WOMAN'S VOICE (V)" of the opening stage directions, tells the story of May's pacing, in the "Sequel," May narrates a story that seems to resume the action of the play itself: a mother and a daughter arguing about whether the daughter "was there," or was merely heard, "distinctly." May's sequel begins *in medias res*, "A little later, when she was quite forgotten, she began to – [*Pause.*] A little later, when as though she had never been, it never been, she began to walk," and goes on to tell the story of a girl slipping out at night and into a little church where she would pace "without pause, up and down, up and down, before vanishing the way she came" (402). This tale of a "tangle of tatters," and her passing "as though never there," is the kind of displaced autobiography that preoccupies Beckett's characters from Hamm onward, but the shape of the story takes a remarkable shift once it joins narration to action, talking to walking. "Soon then after she was gone, as though never there, began to walk, up and down, up and down, that poor arm"; May pauses, paces "*one length*," and then stops, launching suddenly into a *written* story: "Old Mrs Winter, whom the reader will remember." The unnamed daughter asks Mrs Winter whether she is feeling unwell,

Mrs W did not at once reply. But finally, raising her head and fixing Amy – the daughter's given name, as the reader will remember – raising her head and fixing Amy full in the eye she said – [*Pause.*] – she murmured, fixing Amy full in the eye she murmured, Amy did you observe anything . . . strange at Evensong? Amy: No, Mother, I did not. Mrs W: Perhaps it was just my fancy. Amy: Just what exactly, Mother, did you perhaps fancy it was? [*Pause.*] Just what exactly, Mother did you perhaps fancy this . . . strange thing was you observed? [*Pause.*] Mrs W: You yourself observed nothing . . . strange? Amy: No, Mother, I myself did not, to put it mildly. Mrs W: What do you mean, Amy, to put it mildly, what can you possibly mean, Amy, to put it mildly? Amy: I mean, Mother, that to say I observed nothing . . . strange is indeed to put it mildly. For I observed nothing of any kind, strange or otherwise. I saw nothing, heard nothing, of any kind. I was not there. Mrs W: Not there? Amy: Not there.

(Footfalls 402–403)

Unlike *Play*, in which the characters speak in the accents of stage melodrama ("Give him up, she screamed, he's mine" [308]), a theatrical discourse displaced from the audience by its rapid, toneless delivery by three bottled heads, in *Footfalls* May turns emphatically to a writerly discourse, not only addressing the reader twice, but also telling her story, to put it mildly, in an archly archaic diction and syntax. May also tells the story *in dialogue*, usefully providing her "reader" – and Beckett's theatrical auditors – with a series of prefixes to orient the telling of the tale. How are we to understand this little dramaticule-within-the-dramaticule?

In *Footfalls*, word and image, narrative and performance are incommensurable: we see and hear May, but the evidence of the senses is denied, or at the very least challenged, by the two narratives, which seem at once to describe and displace the evidence of the stage. The narratives, too, seem to slip between genres, insisting on a writerly address to a reader ("whom the reader will remember") that belies the dramatic shape of the narrative, and also belies the fact of its performance in the play. And, of course, we might well wonder how much confidence to place in the play's formal organization, since the play's prefixes M and V seem to sort with the Mother's story (of "May" and her "Mother,") but less well with M's story of "Mrs Winter" and "Amy" – the story in which, in however displaced a fashion, she seems finally to find her voice. It is even sometimes difficult to know, on the page or on the stage, who is speaking. The second part of the play opens with "M *discovered facing front at R*," and a speech delivered by the woman's voice, V: "I walk here now. [*Pause.*] Rather I come and stand." It would be easy to be distracted here, to take the voice as May's, but eventually the voice tells its own story, and while the story is not told to a reader, it is again told in the third person, and in dramatic form

Till one night, while still little more than a child, she called her mother and said, Mother, this is not enough. The mother: Not enough? May – the child's given name – May: Not enough. The mother: What do you mean, May, not enough, what can you possibly mean, May, not enough? May: I mean, Mother, that I must hear the feet however faint they fall. The mother: The motion alone is not enough? May: No, Mother, the motion

alone is not enough, I must hear the feet, however faint they fall. [*Pause.*
M *resumes pacing. With pacing.*] Does she still sleep, it may be asked?
(*Footfalls* 401)

The controversy around *Footfalls*, like most controversies surrounding the
fidelity of the stage to the page, involves a reading of the words on the
page and an interpretation of what the words tell the actors to do. But
while our sense of the power of print suggests that the materialities of
the page can govern the practices of the stage, May's dramaticule suggests
something else: what the reader may remember of the printed play during a performance of *Footfalls* is – like May's narrated playlet – always
tangential to performance, however much the book's signs and accessories
may attempt to map it to the stage. For all its insistence on determining
performance, Beckett's text opens a fissure between the materiality of writing, even the materiality of scripted dialogue, and the embodiment of
performance. As *Footfalls* perhaps reminds us, plays are not really frozen
discourse, waiting to be thawed or returned to an original state. Much
as Antin's talk poems represent performance without in fact recording or
prescribing it, the writing that the reader remembers cannot be restored,
re-membered by the stage. Warner's *Footfalls* can be understood as a faithful effort to extend Beckett's characteristic investment in the authority of
the script through an unanticipated order of theatricality. Onstage – at the
Garrick or elsewhere – *Footfalls* necessarily displaces the text, materializing
the printed play as something else, "objectifying" the play in ways that
extend, reify, and so betray the play represented in the accessories of the
page – as any production of any play must do. Even so, Warner's *Footfalls*
also elaborates something *there*, scripted in the breach between the imagination of writing and performing, falling, perhaps, between the softly spoken
words and the just audible rhythmic tread that the spectator will remember.
For even as we consider the transformative power of performance, and the
transformations of writing taking place all around us, *Footfalls* dramatizes –
as much by its failure to imprint the stage as by its effort to do so – the
slippage between print and performance as the condition of a living drama.
As Lyn Hejinian might say,

> Nonetheless, though its punctuation is half hoping for failure,
> the sentence makes an irrevocable address to life.
> (*Happily* 7)

INTRODUCTION: BOOKING THE PLAY

1 Samuel Beckett, *Ohio Impromptu, The Complete Dramatic Works* (London: Faber and Faber, 1990), 443–48. Unless otherwise noted, all references to Beckett's plays are to this edition.

2 Benjamin Bennett, for instance, has recently remarked that "The theatrical process in Beckett could not even begin without the operation of textual meanings" (*All Theater Is Revolutionary Theater* 167); in this fascinating recent book, Bennett argues that dramatic writing always exerts a radical or revolutionary pressure on literature, precisely because it is at once implicated in, and contingent on, the generic categories of literature, and at the same time predicated on the nonliterary materiality of performance. This important study stands alongside my somewhat narrower attention to the consequences of print as the delivery system – well, one delivery system – for modern drama.

3 Both Marshall McLuhan's critique of print in *The Gutenberg Galaxy* and Elizabeth Eisenstein's magisterial history *The Printing Press as an Agent of Change* have been sharply qualified in more recent scholarship; nonetheless, they remain important touchstones for readers unfamiliar with the general contours of this debate. A useful recent collection of essays on this subject is Geoffrey Nunberg, ed., *The Future of the Book*.

4 For a superb history of drama and print, which necessarily treats printed drama's relation to the stage, see Julie Stone Peters, *Theatre of the Book 1480–1880*; Congreve's use of Dutch type is discussed 58. David Kastan discusses Prynne's comments in *Shakespeare after Theory* 68.

5 On the reciprocal relationship between Malone's Enlightenment discourse and the fashioning of Shakespeare as an "author," see de Grazia, *Shakespeare Verbatim* 225–26.

6 The modern theatre's ongoing attraction to automata – Craig's übermarionettes, the "animated hieroglyphs" that Artaud saw in the Balinese dance, even the depersonalized performers of some of Richard Foreman's productions – reflects, in this sense, a desire to replicate the claims of print in a mechanized stage. See W. B. Worthen, "Of Actors and Automata."

7 This understanding of performance is common in Shakespeare criticism, even in criticism that explicitly claims an interest in performance: see Harold Bloom,

Shakespeare: The Invention of the Human, and Harry Berger, Jr., *Imaginary Audition.*
8 See George Bornstein, "Yeats and Textual Reincarnation."
9 See, for example, D. F. McKenzie, *Bibliography and the Sociology of Texts*; Jerome J. McGann, *The Textual Condition*; Jerome J. McGann, *Radiant Textuality*; Roger Chartier, *The Order of Books*; Roger Chartier, *Publishing Drama in Early Modern Europe*; D. C. Greetham, ed., *The Margins of the Text.*

1: PREFIXING THE AUTHOR; OR, AS IT WAS PLAIDE: SHAKESPEARE,
EDITING, AND THE DESIGN OF MODERN DRAMA

1 For a superb reading of Greg's career that is at once clear about the assumptions of the New Bibliography and sensitive to Greg's many and significant hesitations, see Laurie E. Maguire, *Shakespearean Suspect Texts* chapter 2.
2 See Charlton Hinman, *The First Folio of Shakespeare,* and *The Printing and Proof-reading of the First Folio of Shakespeare.* Hinman's facsimile edition was first published by Norton in 1968.
3 Scott McMillin, ed., *The First Quarto of Othello* 49.
4 On Molière, see Chartier, *Publishing Drama* 18–19. Julie Stone Peters sees Congreve's career playing a crucial role in framing a sense of the "dramatic poet" (*Congreve, the Drama, and the Printed Word* 72). Chartier also notes Congreve's standardizing of the appearance of his plays on the page in *Order of Books* 53. And Peters reminds us that Pierre Corneille had adopted Dutch typographic models – "'*ȷ*' as the consonantal form of '*i*,' and '*v*' as the consonantal form of '*u*'" – and was imitated in this regard by Congreve, who accompanied Tonson to Holland to purchase Dutch type, as well as plates and paper, for his 1710 *Works* (*Theatre of the Book* 58).
5 See *William Shakespeare's Romeo and Juliet: The Contemporary Film, The Classic Play*; and Laurie E. Osborne's definitive treatment of "acting editions," *The Trick of Singularity.*
6 This revision is nowhere more visible than in the critique of the relationship between foul papers, fair copies and prompt-copies hypothesized by the New Bibliography, even though, as Paul Werstine has pointed out, editions like the Oxford Shakespeare still have difficulty really separating themselves from these categories; see "McKerrow's 'Suggestion' and Twentieth-Century Shakespeare Textual Criticism" 155. See also Paul Werstine, "Hypertext and Editorial Myth" and Maguire, *Shakespearean Suspect Texts* 23–25, for a summary of the ways contemporary practice has challenged the construction of textual evidence by the New Bibliography.
7 This narrative has been told many times; see Maguire, *Shakespearean Suspect Texts* 4–5 for a useful reading.
8 Greg notes, though, that the "vanishing authority" of the "bad quartos" "approaches, *though I think never quite reaches*, the absolute zero of most derivative editions" (*Editorial Problem* xxxii, my emphasis).

9 Maguire observes, "the evidence suggests that the concept of play reconstruction is not a single sequence of processes with a single objective (reconstruction from memory by actors for the purpose of performance) but a variety of processes involving different kinds of agents (auditors, actors, or other playhouse personnel), different purposes (performance, publication, private transcript), and different combinations of memory and other aids to recall (longhand notes, shorthand notes, reports of narrative outline) often supplemented by new composition" (*Shakespearean Suspect Texts*, 95). The connection between the "bad quartos" and performance is explored by Kathleen O. Irace, *Reforming the "Bad" Quartos*. Tiffany Stern has explored oral transmission as an element of actor training and rehearsal in *Rehearsal from Shakespeare to Sheridan*. On the "residually oral culture" of Shakespeare's theatre, see Robert Weimann, *Author's Pen and Actor's Voice* 43.

10 See Maguire, *Shakespearean Suspect Texts* 135–46.

11 Elizabeth Dyrud Lyman notes "In the spring of 1997, the SSDC (Society of Stage Directors and Choreographers) took legal action against companies which license and publish plays to halt the long-standing practice of incorporating elements from production notebooks (created by stage interpreters) into printed texts (copyrighted by playwrights). The practice is most closely associated with the so-called 'acting' or 'production' editions produced by Samuel French and DPS (Dramatists Play Service), but is not unusual for any publisher. Tom Stoppard, for instance, occasionally incorporates elements of director Peter Wood's staging (with permission, however) into published Faber and Faber texts"; "The Page Refigured" 100 n.8. It should be noted that while Stoppard now acknowledges this practice, this long-standing practice is enshrined in most plays published prior to this lawsuit, and I daresay into many that are published today. See also Philip Gaskell, *From Writer to Reader*.

12 I take this suggestion from William Long, "Perspective on Provenance" 26, who notes, "varying speech-heads are integral parts of the skeleton of the construction of the plays which players found to be useful in creating performances."

13 Lukas Erne develops a critique of the Oxford edition along these lines: since *many* of the surviving texts are too long for performance (both Q2 and F *Hamlet*, for example), "it is simply impossible to know which parts of Shakespeare's overlong plays would not have been performed" (*Shakespeare as Literary Dramatist* 177). To claim, as the Oxford editors do, to be using the more "theatrical" printed text as the basis for their edition tends, Erne suggests, merely to enshrine a fundamentally literary text as having theatrical provenance.

14 Wells, *Re-Editing* 64–65. See also the editorial commentary on *Love's Labour's Lost* and on *Richard II* in Stanley Wells and Gary Taylor, with John Jowett and William Montgomery, *William Shakespeare: A Textual Companion*.

15 On the use of "speech attribution" – a term which doesn't imply that a role must have spoken lines to be important to the acting of a scene – see Lyman, "The Page Refigured" 99 n.3. See also Margaret Jane Kidnie's superb reading of McKerrow in "Text, Performance, and the Editors" 461.

16 See Randall McLeod, "What's the Bastard's Name? Random Cloud." It should be noted that there is a density of typographical play in the setting up of this essay

that makes attribution a bit challenging. "Random Cloud," a name sometimes taken by McLeod, is – unlike authorial names that accompany other articles in this collection – printed in bold face, and followed by a period, making it appear as part of the essay's title. Yet "Random Cloud" is printed as the author's name on the running heads, and at the end of the essay we find it is copyrighted by one "Random Cloud." Yet in the table of contents, "Randall McLeod" is listed as the author of an essay entitled simply "What's the Bastard's Name?" We might think here that Cloud is using the various typographical conventions of this book – authors' names, not titles, appear in running heads; authors' names are not bold-faced, and not followed by punctuation – to enact some of the problematics associated with personhood (the author's, the character's, the actor's) he displays so brilliantly in this article. What's the interface between the author's intention, the character, and the actor's performance?

17 These prefixes are from: Suzan-Lori Parks, *The Death of the Last Black Man in the Whole Entire World* ("The Figures" 100); Adrienne Kennedy, *The Owl Answers* 25; Samuel Beckett, *Play* and *Not I*.

18 In the film, the roles of Kaufman, Belber, Pierotti and other members of Tectonic Theater Project are played by well-known film and television actors; so, too, are the roles of the major townspeople (Catherine Connolly is played by Janeane Garafolo, Doc O'Connor by Steve Buscemi, Moisés Kaufman by Nestor Carbonell). Instead, the TTP actors are given much smaller parts, often of unnamed characters (Stephen Belber plays "Anonymous friend of McKinney") or of characters with very few lines in the film; Clea Duvall plays the central role of "Amanda Gronich," but Amanda Gronich plays "Zackie Salmon." See Moisés Kaufman, dir., *The Laramie Project*, HBO Films and Good Machine Productions, DVD 2002. For details of the trade publication of the play, I refer to Moisés Kaufman and the members of Tectonic Theater Project, *The Laramie Project*: title page and copyright page, Introduction (v), notes on the Denver and New York productions (ix–x), and list of Characters (xi–xiv). Don Shewey notes that the play was the second most produced play by regional theatres of the 2001–2002 season, and was produced over 400 times between January and June of 2003 by high schools, colleges and universities, and amateur groups; see "A Play Has Second Life as a Stage for Discussion."

19 In *Radiant Textuality*, Jerome McGann takes up not only the impact of digital technologies on our research into and representation of written texts, but the important notion that "We no longer have to use books to analyze and study other books or texts. That simple fact carries immense, even catastrophic, significance" (168).

20 Michael Best is well known to Shakespeare scholars as the editor of *The Internet Shakespeare Editions*.

2: ACCESSORY ACTS

1 Shaw had unsuccessfully appealed to Lane to publish his plays on several occasions: see *Collected Letters* 22 November 1892 (370–71) and 16 April 1894 (423–24).

2 On Shaw's publishing habits, on the rise of the "literary" publishing of drama, and of the relationship between Shaw's practices and those of Henry Arthur Jones and Arthur Wing Pinero, see John Russell Stephens, *The Profession of the Playwright* 131–50. See also Joseph Donohue, "Character, Genre, and Ethos in Nineteenth-Century British Drama."

3 Qtd. in Michael Holroyd, *Bernard Shaw* 1:403.

4 Michael Holroyd notes that "Shaw's ideas on book design and elegance of composition derived from William Morris, and he based his page layout and general format on Morris's *Roots of the Mountains*"; "'The only type I like is Caslon's,' he told Holbrook Jackson, 'and my plan is simple: use no leads, but set solid, taking out the space saved by the omission of leads in the bigness of the fount used'" (1: 402–403). Richards also recalled Morris's "persistence that when one opened a book one should see the two printed pages as one whole and not as two, that the inner margins should hardly be greater than was rendered necessary by the requirements of the binder, and that the outer and bottom margins should much exceed those at the top" (*Author Hunting* 30). Katherine E. Kelly concisely treats Shaw's adaptation of Morris's program for a more popular market in "Imprinting" 25–54.

5 I take this sense of the disparities between different versions of "modern" typography from Jerome McGann's excellent account in *Black Riders* 16.

6 Kelly discusses the title page of *Plays: Pleasant and Unpleasant* in very useful detail, and Shaw's various experiments, "Imprinting" 42–45; here and elsewhere I am much indebted to her fine article.

7 Pinero's use of narrative stage directions expanded considerably in later plays; by the time he publishes *The Gay Lord Quex* in 1900, the opening stage directions occupy the first two pages of the play, clearly imitating in detail if not in verve, Shaw's example.

8 My grateful thanks to the late Professor Inga-Stina Ewbank for providing me with information about the publication of Ibsen's plays in Norway during his lifetime; William Heinemann had proofs of this edition sent to him for Archer to translate.

9 The typographic conventions of the third edition, pictured here, are those of the first edition.

10 Qtd. in Bernard Shaw, *Mrs Warren's Profession. A Facsimile of the Holograph Manuscript* ix. Shaw's manuscripts are relatively inconsistent in their way of annotating the theatrical texture of the play: speech prefixes are underlined, but followed by various forms of punctuation (dash, period, or colon); stage directions are frequently added somewhat later, usually for the purpose of printing the play.

11 As Martin Puchner remarks, "not only did Shaw spend an unusual amount of time selecting print, typeset, and format for the publication of his *Plays Pleasant and Unpleasant* but the manner of publication actually altered the dramatic form: Shaw added lengthy prefaces and narrative passages and thus changed the form and function of his stage directions"; *Stage Fright* 21.

12 See Stephens, *The Profession of the Playwright* 111–12.

13 As Craig Dworkin points out in "Reading the Illegible," Howe's poems fore-ground "the so-called 'accidentals' of written language: conventions of capital-ization, abbreviation, spelling, and alphabet. With all of these elements, Howe calls attention to the illusion of the transparency of the printed page, and she thus emphasizes her own works' status as printed artefacts" (47). On modernist experiments with poetics and typography, see also Johanna Drucker, *The Visible Word* and *Figuring the Word*.

14 I cite the poem here with its familiar title, but in its original appearance in Williams's *Spring and All*, and subsequently in *Collected Poems: 1909–1939*, it appears without title, as section XXI.

15 On "The Red Wheelbarrow," Williams's use of white space, and on the devel-opment of the "three-ply line," see Hugh Kenner, *The Pound Era* 541–42.

16 Stein's letter to Mabel Dodge is quoted in Jane Palatini Bowers, *"They Watch Me as They Watch This"* 147 n.45.

17 In this sense, too, Stein's plays evoke Lukas Erne's sense that stage directions are the index of Shakespeare's literary pretensions; see *Shakespeare as Literary Dramatist* 222.

18 On stage productions of this play, see Betsy Alayne Ryan, *Gertrude Stein's Theatre of the Absolute* 137–56. Ryan also has an extensive catalogue of Stein productions, 165–89.

19 See Walter J. Ong, *Orality and Literacy* 37–57.

20 See Bowers, *"They Watch Me as They Watch This"* 132.

21 On the history of production through the 1980s, see Ryan, *Gertrude Stein's Theatre* 165–89, as well as her useful discussion of Stein's "theatrical legacy" in chapter 4. See also Kate Davy, "Richard Foreman's Ontological-Hysteric Theatre" and Randi Koppen, "Formalism and the Return to the Body." In her "Introduction" to *Last Operas and Plays*, Bonnie Marranca also discusses Stein's impact on the Living Theatre, the Judson Poets' Theatre, and Robert Wilson.

22 Comments by Howard, Wellman, and Bernstein here are from "A Play to Be Performed" 13, 17, 25.

23 I am thinking here of J. L. Austin's *How to Do Things with Words*.

24 Unless otherwise noted, I refer to the edition of *The Homecoming* published by Methuen in 1965, with secondary reference to the edition published in Pinter's *Plays Three*, London: Faber and Faber, 1997, from which the following image is taken, reproduced by permission; I here refer to Methuen 6–7, Faber 14–15. The Faber page design is identical to that of the Methuen edition, with the excep-tion of including cast information from the 1978 revival; the comparable 1966 Grove edition and the 1967 Evergreen edition (also Grove) do not include cast information from either the 1965 nor the 1978 productions on the page fac-ing Act One. We might think that the layout of *The Homecoming* is just the Grove house style, but it's not. The 1966 American Grove edition of Genet's *The Balcony* tends to run stage directions into the line of dialogue, and justify the prefixes to the left margin, indenting the dialogue (much as they do in the Grove editions of Brecht, published in the same period, though in a smaller

format; see for example the 1964 Grove Press edition of Bertolt Brecht's *The Threepenny Opera*, English book by Desmond Vesey, English Lyrics by Eric Bentley. The Grove Press editions of Beckett tend to look somewhat more spare, perhaps poetically so. In addition to numbering only recto pages, the 1954 Grove *Waiting for Godot* prints the speech prefixes as a separate column, deeply indenting all the dialogue to a second column. The 1958 Grove *Endgame* prints the characters' names in upper case, beginning dialogue on the line below, slightly indented from the left margin.

25 Shaw not only failed to kill off the acting editions, he failed to remove the-atrical jargon from the reader's page – see stage directions, for example, to Terry Johnson's *Hysteria*: "*1938. Sigmund Freud's study at 20, Maresfield Gardens, Hampstead, London. A large, high-ceilinged room plastered in pastel-blue. The room is furnished richly: dark oaks and mahogany. US French windows lead to a narrow porch and beyond, a well-kept garden. USR the door is a closet. SR a large desk. DSR a wood-burning stove. Along the wall SL, an armless analysis couch covered with a rich Moroccan rug and half a dozen cushions*" (Terry Johnson, *Plays: 2* 90).

26 See Dan Rebellato, *1956 And All That* 121–22.

27 As Joseph Grigely points out, "not only does the surface itself matter (as in Blake's prints and Dickinson's manuscripts), but – to take Cage's reversal seri-ously – so too does the white space between the letters and words, particularly when that white space has a paralinguistic function"; see *Textualterity* 112.

28 Pinter's process of composition is revealing here, too. The manuscript and typescript material on deposit in the manuscript collection at the British Library contains two complete unbound typescripts, a hardbound typescript, and a softbound typescript which is the most like the printed version of the play; there are also several manuscript pages in longhand, some containing very early material (preceding the first TS) and others apparently annotations or additions to TS1 or TS2. In both the longhand manuscript sections and the two unbound typescripts, Pinter's practice is to place a pause (often abbreviated p.) on the next line, deeply but irregularly indented: in the MS, it occurs on the next ruled line, with no extra spacing above or below; in the first TS, which is single-spaced, the *pause* or *p.* occurs on the next line, without an additional space; in the second TS, which is double spaced, it again occurs on the next (double-spaced) line, without additional spacing. Extra spacing occurs for the first time in the bound volumes. It might also be noted that Pinter's manuscripts use a variety of conventions for indicating ellipses, considerably complicating the conventional three dots of the printed texts. Sometimes a single speech – say, Ruth's speech about America in Act 2 – will use several different "sets" of dots, 2-dots, 3-dots, 5-dots, even 9-dots; while the printed text tends to regularize this gap in speech, the manuscripts seem to use the space occupied by punctuation to suggest a different temporal duration.

29 There are several smaller differences between the Grove and Methuen versions of *The Collection*. Methuen occasionally places a *Pause* on the line (*Pause.*), where Grove puts it below the line of dialogue, separated above and below by spacing (see Methuen 9 and Grove 43, for example; the Faber edition, *Plays Two*,

reissued by Faber in 1996 follows the Methuen layout, with some small changes; see 110). Methuen tends to insert articles (a, the) omitted by Grove (compare the Methuen stage direction printed here with Grove), and the opening description of the set is preceded by the word "AUTUMN" in Methuen but not in Grove.

30 It might be thought that, as daughter of the eminent critic of modern poetry Marjorie Perloff, Cary Perloff comes by her sense of the determining force of the poetic text naturally.

31 Marber's text also points to the ways that word-processing at once emulates and refigures print traditions: underlining was (and still is) the way to indicate that words should be *italicized* in print, and printed literature has generally avoided this kind of double-coding of the page. With the rise of digital writing, and its visual enrichment of the "page" of the computer screen, the relationship between these two levels of coding is eroding.

32 Although play is divided into three "Acts," and subdivided into a series of "moments" – a relatively familiar convention both onstage and on the page – Kaufman regards this technique as a distinctive element on the company's work: "It is a method to create and analyze theater from a structuralist (or tectonic) perspective. For this reason, there are no scenes in this play, only moments. A moment does not mean a change of locale or an entrance or exit of actors or characters. It is simply a unit of theatrical time that is then juxtaposed with other units to convey meaning" ("About the Text"), *Laramie Project* xiv. For a useful reading of *The Laramie Project*, see Amy L. Tigner, "*The Laramie Project*."

33 Michael Fellmeth, Publications Director for Dramatists Play Service, notes that DPS generally derives prop lists from the text of the play rather than from the stage manager's book; he also notes that the billing requirements for the play "were not imposed on us for the acting edition but rather were preexisting requirements that we enforce for subsequent productions." I'm very grateful to Mr. Fellmeth for this information, and for his assistance in securing permission to reprint this section of the play.

34 Caryl Churchill's collaboration on *Cloud 9* is well known, and noted in her note to the play, but not otherwise recorded in Caryl Churchill, *Plays: One*. Luis Valdez's collaboration with El Teatro Campesino is partly registered by *Luis Valdez – Early Works: Actos, Bernabé and Pensamiento Serpentino*. The title page does not list an author, incorporating Valdez's name into the title of the book; at the same time, the Library of Congress information on the verso lists the authors as "Luis Valdez and El Teatro Campesino." It might be noted that while the *actos* developed as collaborative works, the full-length *Bernabé* is a conventional single-author play, and that *Pensamiento Serpentino* is a nondramatic meditation, again solely by Valdez. On the problems of attribution, see Yolanda Broyles-González, *El Teatro Campesino*. In a 1980 interview, Beckett remarked that he would not make changes to the printed texts of his plays based on his direction of them; fortunately, he changed his mind and agreed to collaborate on *The Theatrical Notebooks of Samuel Beckett*, gen. ed. James Knowlson, several volumes with different editors. The 1980 interview is reprinted in John Fletcher, *About Beckett* 73.

35 It should be noted that the company has shortened its name to "Complicite" (without accent), and that the copyright is held by the company: "Copyright © 1999, 2001 Complicite."

3: SOMETHING LIKE POETRY

1 Although "performance poetry" would be a logical subject here, most "performance poetry" has relatively little life beyond poetry readings and slam competitions: that is, like the poetry I discuss below, it tends to reject an explicit connection with the dramatic theatre and its means, especially *acting*. One exception would be efforts to theatricalize poetry, as in Ntozake Shange's work (which has had an extensive life in the theatre) and to *Def Poetry Jam* which opened on Broadway in November 2002.

2 I am referring here, of course, to the ways in which J. L. Austin's understanding of "performative" speech – words that *do* something, accomplish an action in the act of being spoken – has been developed into a critical account of the formation of social and individual identity, particularly in Judith Butler's treatment of gender identity and free speech issues. See J. L. Austin, *How to Do Things with Words*, as well as Judith Butler, *Excitable Speech* and *Gender Trouble*.

3 Some of these issues are obliquely charted by Hilary Harris, "Failing 'White Woman.'" On Brecht's sense of empathy and demonstration, see "Appendices to The Short Organum," *Brecht on Theatre* 277. On dramatic performativity, see W. B. Worthen, *Shakespeare and the Force of Modern Performance* chapter 1.

4 While I am not treating this other tradition here, it should be noted that the lineage of performance art stemming from the visual arts rather than from playwriting has its own engagement with the theatre. As Amelia Jones and Andrew Stephenson note in the introduction to their collection *Performing the Body / Performing the Text*, "Since the 1960s, visual art practices, from body art to Minimalism, have opened themselves to the dimension of theatricality in such a way as to suggest that art critics and art historians might reassess our own practices of making meaning through an engagement with the processes of art production and reception as *performative*" (1).

5 *Fires in the Mirror* was nominated for the Pulitzer Prize in 1993, but *Twilight* was dropped from consideration the following year, and does not appear on the list of nominees or finalists for the 1994 prize. In 1993 the prize for drama was given to Tony Kushner, for *Angels in America: Millennium Approaches*; in 1994, to Edward Albee for *Three Tall Women*. It might be noted that Eric Bogosian's *Talk Radio* was nominated in 1988. See the Pulitzer Prize website for information about winners and criteria for the Prize discussed here.

6 It is perhaps notable that *Sunday in the Park* edged out "Nominated Finalist" *The Gospel at Colonus*, which, while nominated, has a somewhat more slippery attribution: "Conceived, adapted and directed by Lee Breuer, music composed, arranged and directed by Bob Tilson" (Pulitzer Prize website). My thanks to members of the 2003–2004 Politics and Performance Mellon Seminar at Stanford University for drawing my attention to the Pulitzer's complex attitude toward musical theatre (or perhaps we should say musical drama).

7 This sense of the performance as "derivative creativity" is, of course, common in drama studies; I take the term from Michael D. Bristol's searching discussion, *Big-Time Shakespeare* 61.

8 See Paul Harris, "House Arrest: First Edition" and Charles Isherwood, "House Arrest." For an extended reading of Smith's experimentation with her own working methods, see Dorinne Kondo, "(Re)Visions of Race."

9 The effort to use the metrical conventions of Shakespearean writing as an index to character psychology is, by now, fully conventional in actor training; like others who regard the early texts of Shakespeare's plays as offering a similar index to character, Smith also regards "Shakespeare's technology" as "A printing press, and accepted poetic rhythms" (*Talk to Me* 41). On some of the problems of Shakespearean authority and actor training, see W. B. Worthen, *Shakespeare and the Authority of Performance* 119–25.

10 Although it is possible to take issue with the schematics of orality and literacy in Ong's influential presentation, the sense that orality is decisively marked by the impact of literacy seems indisputable; on "secondary orality," see Walter J. Ong, *Orality and Literacy* 122.

11 The book also marks its relation to the video production staged by the Public Television Service *American Playhouse* series: "The Crown Heights Conflict: Background Information" pages contain this note: "© WGBH Educational Foundation. Excerpted from educational materials created for AMERICAN PLAYHOUSE's public television production of 'Fires in the Mirror'" (*Fires* xliii).

12 Although this edition was first published in 1993 shortly after the initial celebrity of Smith's performances, it was reprinted in 1997 – implying the possibility of including additional material if that material were desirable.

13 On Olson's place in the modern / postmodern lineage of American poetics, see Charles Altieri's elegant essay, "Some Problems about Agency" 168.

14 See also the notes to Olson, "Projective Verse" 425.

15 Shange notes that when *for colored girls*, first produced as performance poetry at coffee houses and in Womens' Studies Departments, took on a theatrical life, "Those institutions I had shunned as a poet – producers, theaters, actresses, & sets – now were essential to us" (*for colored girls* xx).

16 Though hardly a "school," Language writing is generally located around the journal *L=A=N=G=U=A=G=E* edited by the poets Charles Bernstein and Bruce Andrews in the 1970s and 1980s. Language writing energetically blends poetry and poetics: most of the poets have not only written extensive "theoretical" essays, but have also written "theoretical" poems (Bob Perelman's "An Alphabet of Literary History," the epigraph to this chapter, is one example), and see a close interpenetration of the objectives of aesthetics, performance, and the politics of language.

17 Again, as a riposte to the "incantatory lyricism of the poetry sentence, where writer finds voice and depoliticized universe fitting together without struggle," the "new sentence, on the other hand, is defiantly unpoetic. Its shifts break up attempts at the natural reading of universal, authentic statements," often through "a high degree of syntactic and verbal fracturing" sometimes explicitly

connected with "Marxist critiques" of "commodity and referential fetishism" (Perelman, *Marginalization of Poetry* 64–65).

18 I am thinking, of course, of Galileo's famous reply to Andrea's lament, "Unhappy the land that has no heroes!": "No. Unhappy the land where heroes are needed" (Brecht, *Life of Galileo* 98).

19 See Bruce Andrews and Sally Silvers, "MOVEMENT/WRITING//WRITING /MOVEMENT," in Bruce Andrews, *EX WHY ZEE* 14. Of course, Susan Howe is a painter and, like Johanna Drucker and Lyn Hejinian, a printer; several of the San Francisco area poets are associated with performance poetry. See also Carla Harryman, "Performing Objects in the Sub World (excerpts)" and Leslie Scalapino, "The Hind."

20 Shannon Jackson also notes the impact of Fried's sense of absorption and theatricality in the formation of modern disciplines of performance studies: "A modernist focus on artistic essentials was undone if one of those essentials was the audience relation. Theatricality's pure nature was thus itself an impure essence, corrupted by its fundamental status as a relational encounter" (*Professing Performance* 141).

21 For Rothenberg, who has worked extensively with oral poetics, ritual poetry, and Native American literature, performance is critical to the identity of the poem: "My performance is this sounding of a poem: It is renewal of the poem, the poem's enlivening" ("Poetics" 121). Yet at the same time, Rothenberg insists that, "The basis of the poetry performance is in fact hostile to the presence, the manner, of the professional actor. That the poet is otherwise motivated, otherwise related to the poem, is here a shared assumption: an insistence on a lack of separation between the maker & his work, & of a virtual innocence of any means of performance beyond the ones immediately to hand" so that "as a witness to the *poet's* words, the actor's credibility has yet to be established" (122–23). It's notable that this talk was given as an address to the American Theatre Association in 1975. For a remarkable update on this conversation, see Jessica Smith, "Silent Protest" and Norma Cole, et al., "Remarks on Poets' Theater."

22 When, in the earlier essay "On Theatricality," Bernstein notes that "the only theater I can imagine valuing is one that defeats its theatricality by total immersion in its production of space and time without acknowledging the 'real-time' response of the audience," we can hear the accent not only of Grotowski, but of the entire modernist project of a literary theatre, echoed as much in Rothenberg's "solitary stance" as in Stanislavsky's "public solitude": to constitute an absolute, "absorptive" experience without the overt mediation of the artifice of the stage (Bernstein, "On Theatricality" 206).

23 Janelle Reinelt has described some of the ways the video performance of Smith's *Fires in the Mirror* alters the performative structure of the work – in this case, as in the case of the broadcast of *Twilight* a few years later, using considerably more makeup, costume, and set design to establish the "characters" of Smith's performance than are used onstage; see "Performing Race."

24 To distinguish between the print and VHS forms of *Fires,* I will cite the VHS by its director, George C. Wolfe.

25 As Debby Thompson suggests in a fine reading of *Fires*, "Angela Davis puts 'race' in quotation marks, because it is, in a sense, a trap – a trap constructed by and upholding racism"; yet while the printed text appropriately inserts quotation marks here, we might wonder whether Smith "heard" the scare quotes, or whether they represent an effort to make Davis's remarks more logical and comprehensible on the page. See Debby Thompson, "'Is Race a Trope'?" 137. Smith remarks that "In reality this interview was done on the phone, with myself and Thulani Davis. Thulani and I were calling from an office at the Public Theatre. We do not know exactly what Angela was doing or wearing" (*Fires* 27). The decision to italicize some of Angela Davis's speech ("Now this does not mean that we ignore / *racism*," spoken with a distinct emphasis on each syllable *race-is-em*) as well as to insert the "quotations" she says she uses with the word "race" – are in this sense as imaginary as the decision to play Davis at a chalkboard on television.

26 That the lineation of the page can be made critical to the subject of identity politics is dramatized by Shannon Jackson's superb reading of several passages in *Twilight*; see *Professing Performance* 209–15.

27 Now that the furor over *Blasted* has modulated into a kind of canonical appreciation, Kane's plays are well on the way to a kind of "classic" status, an assimilation already underway in 1995, as Michael Coveney suggested: "At once cool and classical, this atmospheric essay in the end-of-millennium violence of Tarantino and the not-so-new apocalyptic brand in Bond's 'War Plays' (recently acclaimed in Paris) posed a simple question: how do you feel about having the News at Ten made real in the front room? A tense and gripping first hour was followed by horrors, sexual explicitness apart, no worse than in Shakespeare's Titus or Seneca's Thyestes" (Coveney, Rev. of *Blasted*). In 1995, John Peter noted the "half-realistic, half-symbolic" element of *Blasted* (Rev. of *Blasted*), and developed this line in his review of the Royal Court revival in 2001: "It is a visionary play, but its sense of reality is so meticulously and bloodcurdlingly intense that the whole play feels like a symbol: an image in action, as in Strindberg or the early expressionists" (Rev. of *Blasted*).

28 Annabelle Singer argues that this "wider concept of performance" involves a "different way of thinking about theatre" in which Kane moved away from "plays" altogether; to my mind, Kane was, far from resisting writing, moving toward a different articulation between writing and performance. See Annabelle Singer, "Don't Want to Be This" 141.

29 Daniel Evans, one of the actors in the production, reports writing the numbers in this way in Saunders, *'Love me or kill me'* 176.

30 Donald Sutherland describes the play as a "small vaudeville" in *Gertrude Stein* 109.

31 On the relationship between print and history in Parks's plays, and particularly in *Venus*, see W. B. Worthen, "Citing History."

32 Anthony Nielson's comments in his recent volume of plays perhaps suggest how far we have come from Shaw's emphatic booking of the drama; and yet, Nielson's casual regard toward the impact of print seems considerably less provocative – or

potentially productive of either literary or theatrical innovation – than the more print-engaged practices of Kane or Parks.

And that's why, ultimately, I find myself somewhat uncomfortable about this little volume. Publishing plays seems contradictory, reductive. I've a feeling that – like holiday snaps and marriage videos – it all stems from our fear of impermanence, and finally of death. [. . .] I hope, at least, that you're reading this because you want to produce one of these plays. They're not meant to sit on the page. They were not created solely by me, but each by a team of friends and colleagues, and what you really have here is a transcript of our experiences. I would be very happy if you could make them experiences and memories of your own.

To that end, I'd implore you not to be reverent. Change them as you see fit in whatever time and place you are. (*Plays: 1* x)

Nielson's anxiety is in one sense irrelevant: the independence of the sphere of theatrical from textual production ensures that producers must "change them."

EPILOGUE: WHOM THE READER WILL REMEMBER

1 My summary here of the textual problems of Beckett's plays is taken from Gontarski's fine article.

2 See S. E. Gontarski, "Textual Notes" to *Footfalls*; see also Samuel Beckett, *Footfalls* (London: Faber and Faber, 1976).

3 Whitelaw is quoted in Jonathan Kalb, *Beckett in Performance* 235. Beckett's remarks to Schmahl are reported in S. E. Gontarski, *The Intent of Undoing* 164.

4 Leah Schmidt is quoted in Madeleine Bunting and Angella Johnson, "Exit for Life" 1. Edward Beckett's remarks are from his letter to the *Guardian*. I am particularly grateful to the librarians of the Beckett Archive at the University of Reading for bringing this clippings file to my attention.

5 For the convenience of readers, I refer to *Footfalls* as published in *The Complete Dramatic Works*; readers should, however, consult Gontarski's "revised text" in *The Theatrical Notebooks of Samuel Beckett*, IV.

6 Jack Tinker notes that Shaw paused "by the naked bulb" at each end of her pacing (Rev. of *Footfalls*).

7 I have discussed this aspect of Shakespeare's Globe extensively in *Shakespeare and the Force of Modern Performance* 78–116.

8 As Martin Puchner has shown, Beckett's plays are exemplary of the modernist desire to use "diegetic figures [stage directions, for example] to control, confront, and interrupt theatrical representation," as a means of refiguring the stage as a site of the "silent and solitary absorption" in the artwork definitive of modernist experiment (*Stage Fright* 120, 11).

9 I'm thinking here, of course, of the Baz Luhrmann *William Shakespeare's Romeo + Juliet*, Julie Taymor's *Titus*, and an award-winning production of Marlowe's *Doctor Faustus* directed by Michal Dočekal that opened in Prague in 2001 and was still running when I saw it in July 2004; this production made considerable reference to contemporary Czech and global politics, and made it quite clear that both Mephistophilis and Faustus were familiar with the doings of the American president.

10 While Nicholas de Jongh described Kendall's spiral as "a weird garden ornament or a piece of living art in a modish Hoxton Gallery" (Rev. of *Happy Days*), and Ian Shuttleworth complained about the "Expressionist spiral of scorched grass, almost perpendicular to stage, slightly concave towards its centre, with ribbons of blue sky above *and below*" violating Beckett's "notoriously precise" vision of his plays (Rev. of *Happy Days*), many found the "first shock" of finding Winnie "at the centre of a tilting, scrub-coloured spiral" to be overcome by the production, as "the image gradually grows on one, allows the whole audience to see the vertically placed Winnie," and relieving the "visual monotony that can make every Beckett revival seem very much like the last" (Billington, Rev. of *Happy Days*). Georgina Brown, describing Winnie sinking "into the centre of a whorl of earth made out of door-matting, coiled like one of those mosquito repellents one lights on summer nights," nonetheless found this perspective "not simply more interesting and arresting, but all the better for suggesting the way in which Winnie is being sucked in, powerless against the force of nature, of gravity" (Rev. of *Happy Days*). On Hall's career with *Happy Days* and the Arts Theatre, see Paul Taylor, Rev. of *Happy Days*.

11 The troubled history of *Footfalls* in print is extended in S. E. Gontarski's "revised text"; the "publisher's note" alerts us to the fact that "The publisher has taken the opportunity to make a number of minor adjustments to the layout and typographical style adopted for earlier editions of *Footfalls*" – notably laying out the series of questions M asks (on page 400 of the Faber *Complete Dramatic Works*) beginning with "Straighten your pillows?" verse-wise, each question on a separate line and separated by a (*Pause.*), also on a separate line, rather than as a paragraph, as in other editions. See Gontarski, ed., *Theatrical Notebooks* IV: 274, 276.

Works cited

Albery, James. *Two Roses: An Original Comedy in Three Acts. French's Acting Editions*. Vol. 118. London: Samuel French, n.d.

Altieri, Charles. "Some Problems about Agency in the Theories of Radical Poetics." *Postmodernisms Now: Essays on Contemporaneity in the Arts*. University Park PA: Pennsylvania State University Press, 1988. 166–92.

"Taking Lyrics Literally: Teaching Poetry in a Prose Culture." *New Literary History* 32 (2001): 259–81.

Andrews, Bruce. *EX WHY ZEE [Performance texts, Collaborations with Sally Silvers, Word Maps, Bricolage & Improvisations]*. New York: Roof Books, 1995.

Paradise & Method: Poetics & Praxis. Evanston: Northwestern University Press, 1996.

Andrews, Bruce, and Sally Silvers. "MOVEMENT/WRITING// WRITING/MOVEMENT." Andrews *EX WHY ZEE* 14–16.

Antin, David. "is this the right place." *talking at the boundaries* 27–49.

talking at the boundaries. New York: New Directions, 1976.

Antin, David, and Charles Bernstein. *A Conversation with David Antin. Album Notes by David Antin*. New York: Granary Books, 2002.

Austin, J. L. *How to Do Things with Words*. Ed. J. O. Urmson and Marina Sbisà. Cambridge MA: Harvard University Press, 1975.

Bassett, Kate. Rev. of *4.48 Psychosis. Daily Telegraph* 30 June 2000. Rpt. *Theatre Record* 20.13 (2000): 826.

Beckett, Edward. Letter. *Guardian* 24 May 1994.

Beckett, Samuel. *The Complete Dramatic Works*. London: Faber and Faber, 1990.

Endgame: A Play in One Act. Followed by Act Without Words: A Mime for One Player. New York: Grove, 1958.

Footfalls. London: Faber and Faber, 1976.

The Theatrical Notebooks of Samuel Beckett. Vol. I: Waiting for Godot, with a revised text. Ed. Dougald McMillan and James Knowlson. London: Faber and Faber; New York: Grove, 1973.

The Theatrical Notebooks of Samuel Beckett. Vol. II: Endgame, with a revised text. Ed. S. E. Gontarski. London: Faber and Faber; New York: Grove, 1992.

The Theatrical Notebooks of Samuel Beckett. Vol. III: Krapp's Last Tape, with a revised text. Ed. James Knowlson. London: Faber and Faber; New York: Grove, 1992.

The Theatrical Notebooks of Samuel Beckett. Vol. IV: The Shorter Plays, with revised texts for Footfalls, Come and Go and What Where. Ed. S. E. Gontarski. London: Faber and Faber; New York: Grove, 1999.

Waiting for Godot: A Tragicomedy in 2 Acts. New York: Grove, 1954.

Benjamin, Walter. "What Is Epic Theater?" *Illuminations.* Ed. Hannah Arendt. Trans. Harry Zohn. New York: Schocken, 1969. 147–54.

Bennett, Benjamin. *All Theater Is Revolutionary Theater.* Ithaca: Cornell University Press, 2005.

Bentson, Alice N. "Chekhov, Beckett, Pinter: the St(r)ain upon the Silence." *Pinter at Sixty.* Ed. Katherine H. Burkman and John L. Kundert-Gibbs. Bloomington: Indiana University Press, 1993. 111–24.

Berger, Harry, Jr. *Imaginary Audition: Shakespeare on Stage and Page.* Berkeley: University of California Press, 1989.

Bernstein, Charles. "Artifice of Absorption." *A Poetics* 9–89.

Content's Dream: Essays 1975–1984. Los Angeles: Sun & Moon Press, 1986; rpt. Evanston: Northwestern University Press, 2001.

"Introduction." Bernstein, *Close Listening* 3–26.

My Way: Speeches and Poems. University of Chicago Press, 1999.

"On Theatricality." *Content's Dream* 199–207.

A Poetics. Cambridge MA: Harvard University Press, 1992.

"Thelonious Monk and the Performance of Poetry." *My Way* 18–24.

Bernstein, Charles, ed. *Close Listening: Poetry and the Performed Word.* New York: Oxford University Press, 1998.

Billington, Michael. "Foot Fault." *Guardian* 22 March 1994: 4–5.

Billington, Michael. Rev. of *4.48 Psychosis. Guardian* 30 June 2000. Rpt. *Theatre Record* 20.13 (2000): 828.

Billington, Michael. Rev. of *Happy Days. Guardian* 19 November 2003. Rpt. *Theatre Record* 23.23 (2003): 1561.

Bloom, Harold. *Shakespeare: The Invention of the Human.* New York: Riverhead, 1998.

Bornstein, George. "Yeats and Textual Reincarnation: 'When You are Old' and 'September 1913.'" *The Iconic Page in Manuscript, Print, and Digital Culture.* Ann Arbor: University of Michigan Press, 1998. 223–48.

Bornstein, George, and Ralph G. Williams, eds. *Palimpsest: Editorial Theory in the Humanities.* Ann Arbor: University of Michigan Press, 1993.

Bowers, Fredson. *On Editing Shakespeare and the Elizabethan Dramatists.* Philadelphia: University of Pennsylvania Library for the Philip H. and A. S. W. Rosenbach Foundation, 1955.

Bowers, Jane Palatini. *"They Watch Me as They Watch This": Gertrude Stein's Metadrama.* Philadelphia: University of Pennsylvania Press, 1991.

Brecht, Bertolt. *Brecht on Theatre: The Development of an Aesthetic.* Ed. and trans. John Willett. New York: Hill and Wang, 1964.

Life of Galileo. Tr. John Willett. Ed. John Willett and Ralph Mannheim. New York: Arcade, 1994.

The Threepenny Opera. English book by Desmond Vesey. English lyrics by Eric Bentley. New York: Grove, 1964.

Bristol, Michael D. *Big-Time Shakespeare.* London: Routledge, 1996.

Brooks, David. "Ms. Smith Goes to Washington." *New Republic* 11 December 2000: 36.

Brown, Georgina. Rev. of *Happy Days. Mail on Sunday* 23 November 2003. Rpt. *Theatre Record* 23.23 (2003): 1562.

Broyles-González, Yolanda. *El Teatro Campesino: Theater in the Chicano Movement.* Austin: University of Texas Press, 1994.

Bunting, Madeleine, and Angella Johnson. "Exit for Life the Director who Dared Play with Beckett." *Guardian* 19 March 1994: 1.

Butler, Judith. *Excitable Speech: A Politics of the Performative.* New York: Routledge, 1997.

Gender Trouble: Feminism and the Subversion of Identity. New York: Routledge, 1990.

Carlson, Marvin. "After Stein: Traveling the American Theatrical 'Langscape.'" *Land/Scape/Theater.* Ed. Elinor Fuchs and Una Chaudhuri. Ann Arbor: University of Michigan Press, 2002. 145–58.

Chadderton, David. Rev. of *4.48 Psychosis. dlreviews* <http://www.rbcdl.org.uk/article/84.html> 10 June 2004.

Chartier, Roger. *The Order of Books: Readers, Authors, and Libraries in Europe between the Fourteenth and Eighteenth Centuries.* Trans. Lydia G. Cochrane. Stanford University Press, 1994.

Publishing Drama in Early Modern Europe. London: The British Library, 1999.

Churchill, Caryl. *Plays: One.* London: Methuen, 1985.

Cole, Norma, Carla Harryman, Mac McGinnes, Nick Robinson, Leslie Scalapino. "Remarks on Poets' Theater: Poets and Players." *Mantis* 3 (2002): 276–97.

Complicite. *Mnemonic.* London: Methuen Drama, 2001.

Plays: 1. London: Methuen, 2003.

Coveney, Michael. Rev. of *Blasted. Observer* 5 February 1995. Rpt. *Theatre Record* 15:1–2 (1995): 42.

Rev. of *Footfalls. Observer* 20 March 1994. Rpt. *Theatre Record* 14.6 (1994): 317.

Davis, Thulani Nkabinde. "Known Renegades: Recent Black/Brown/Yellow." Vincent and Zweig, *The Poetry Reading* 68–84.

Davy, Kate. "Richard Foreman's Ontological-Hysteric Theatre: the Influence of Gertrude Stein." *Twentieth Century Literature* 24 (1978): 108–26.

de Grazia, Margreta. "The Question of the One and the Many: The Globe Shakespeare, the *Complete King Lear*, and the New Folger Library Shakespeare." *Shakespeare Quarterly* 46 (1995): 245–51.

Shakespeare Verbatim: The Reproduction of Authority and the 1790 Apparatus. Oxford: Clarendon Press, 1991.

de Grazia, Margreta, and Peter Stallybrass. "The Materiality of the Shakespearean Text." *Shakespeare Quarterly* 44 (1993): 255–83.

de Jongh, Nicholas. Rev. of *Happy Days*. *Evening Standard* 19 November 2003. Rpt. *Theatre Record* 23.23 (2003): 1559.

DeLillo, Don. *The Body Artist*. New York: Simon and Schuster, 2001.

Diderot, Denis. *The Paradox of Acting*. Trans. Walter Herries Pollock. London: Chatto and Windus, 1883.

Donohue, Joseph. "Character, Genre, and Ethos in Nineteenth-Century British Drama." *Yearbook of English Studies* 9 (1979): 78–101.

Drucker, Johanna. *Figuring the Word: Essays on Books, Writing, and Visual Poetics*. New York: Granary Books, 1998.

   The Visible Word: Experimental Typography and Modern Art, 1909–1923. University of Chicago Press, 1994.

Dworkin, Craig Douglas. "Reading the Illegible." Ph.D. dissertation, Department of English, University of California, Berkeley, 1998.

Eagleton, Terry. *Criticism and Ideology: A Study in Marxist Literary Theory*. London: Verso, 1978.

Eisenstein, Elizabeth L. *The Printing Press as an Agent of Change: Communications and Cultural Transformations in Early-Modern Europe*. Cambridge University Press, 1979.

Eliot, T. S. *The Waste Land: A Facsimile and Transcript of the Original Drafts Including the Annotations of Ezra Pound*. Ed. Valerie Eliot. New York: Harcourt Brace Jovanovich, 1971.

Erne, Lukas. *Shakespeare as Literary Dramatist*. Cambridge University Press, 2003.

Esslin, Martin. *The Peopled Wound: The Plays of Harold Pinter*. London: Methuen, 1970.

Fellmeth, Michael. Email to the author 12 October 2004.

Fletcher, John. *About Beckett: The Playwright and His Work*. London: Faber and Faber, 2003.

Frank, Robert, and Henry Sayre, eds. *The Line in Postmodern Poetry*. Urbana: University of Illinois Press, 1988.

Gaskell, Philip. *From Writer to Reader: Studies in Editorial Method*. Oxford: Clarendon Press, 1978.

Genet, Jean. *The Balcony*. Trans. Bernard Frechtman. Rev. edn. New York: Grove, 1966.

Goldman, Michael. *On Drama: Boundaries of Genre, Borders of Self*. Ann Arbor: University of Michigan Press, 2000.

Gómez-Peña, Guillermo. *The New World Border*. San Francisco: City Lights, 1996.

   Warrior for Gringostroika: Essays, Performance Texts, and Poetry. St. Paul: Graywolf Press, 1993.

Gontarski, S. E. "Editing Beckett." *Twentieth Century Literature* 41 (1995): 190–207.

   The Intent of Undoing in Samuel Beckett's Dramatic Texts. Bloomington: Indiana University Press, 1985.

   "Textual Notes." *Come and Go. Theatrical Notebooks of Samuel Beckett. Volume IV: The Shorter Plays with revised texts for Footfalls, Come and Go and What Where*. 212–13.

"Textual Notes." *Footfalls. Theatrical Notebooks of Samuel Beckett. Volume IV: The Shorter Plays with revised texts for Footfalls, Come and Go and What Where.* 281–86.

Gontarski, S. E., ed. *Footfalls. Theatrical Notebooks of Samuel Beckett. Volume IV: The Shorter Plays with revised texts for Footfalls, Come and Go and What Where.* 271–93.

The Theatrical Notebooks of Samuel Beckett. Volume IV: The Shorter Plays with revised texts for Footfalls, Come and Go and What Where. London: Faber; New York: Grove, 1999.

Gordon, Lois. "Harold Pinter in New York." *Pinter Review* 3 (1989): 48–52.

Gray, Spalding. *Swimming to Cambodia.* New York: Theatre Communications Group, 1985.

Greetham, D. C., ed. *The Margins of the Text.* Ann Arbor: University of Michigan Press, 1997.

Greg, W. W. *The Editorial Problem in Shakespeare: A Survey of the Foundations of the Text.* 2nd edn. Oxford: Clarendon, 1951.

Greig, David. *Victoria.* London: Methuen, 2000.

Grenier, Robert. "On Speech." Silliman, *In the American Tree* 477–78.

Grigely, Joseph. *Textualterity: Art, Theory, and Textual Criticism.* Ann Arbor: University of Michigan Press, 1995.

Grotowski, Jerzy. *Towards a Poor Theatre.* New York: Simon and Schuster, 1968.

Gussow, Mel. *Conversations with Pinter.* New York: Limelight Press, 1994.

"Modify Beckett? Enter Outrage." *New York Times* 26 March 1994: 9–10.

Handke, Peter. *Die Theaterstucke.* Frankfurt am Main: Suhrkamp, 1992.

Harris, Hilary. "Failing 'White Woman': Interrogating the Performance of Respectability." *Theatre Journal* 52 (2000): 183–209.

Harris, Paul. "House Arrest: First Edition." *Variety* 24 November 1997: 73.

Harryman, Carla. "Performing Objects in the Sub World (excerpts)." *Mantis* 3 (2002): 8–17.

Hejinian, Lyn. *The Beginner.* n.p.: Tuumba Press, 2002.

Happily. Sausalito: Post-Apollo Press, 2000.

"Language and Paradise." *The Language of Inquiry.* Berkeley: University of California Press, 2000. 59–82.

Henderson, Stephen E. "Worrying the Line: Notes on Black American Poetry." Frank and Sayre, *The Line in Postmodern Poetry* 60–82.

Hewison, Robert. Rev. of *4.48 Psychosis. Sunday Times* 2 July 2000. Rpt. *Theatre Record* 20.13 (2000): 827.

Hinman, Charlton. *The First Folio of Shakespeare.* Introd. Peter W. M. Blayney. New York: W. W. Norton, 1996.

The Printing and Proof-reading of the First Folio of Shakespeare. Oxford: Clarendon Press, 1963. 2 vols.

Hoch, Danny. *Jails, Hospitals & Hip-Hop and Some People.* New York: Villard, 1998.

Holroyd, Michael. *Bernard Shaw. Vol. I 1856–1898: The Search for Love.* New York: Random House, 1988.

Bernard Shaw. Vol. III 1918–1950: The Lure of Fantasy. New York: Random House, 1991.

Howard, Richard. "*Operas and Plays* [A Review]." *Gertrude Stein Advanced: An Anthology of Criticism.* Ed. Richard Kostelanetz. Jefferson, NC: McFarland, 1990. 128–31.

Howe, Susan. "Ether Either." Bernstein, *Close Listening* 111–27.

Ibsen, Henrik. *The League of Youth; The Pillars of Society; A Doll's House.* Ed. and trans. William Archer. 3rd edn. London: Walter Scott, 1904.

Samlede Vaerker. Copenhagen: Gyldendal (F. Hegel), 1899.

Irace, Kathleen. *Reforming the "Bad" Quartos: Performance and Provenance of Six Shakespearean First Editions.* Newark: University of Delaware Press; London: Associated University Press, 1994.

Isherwood, Charles. "House Arrest." *Variety* 3 April 2000: 50.

Jackson, Shannon. *Professing Performance: Theatre in the Academy from Philology to Performativity.* Cambridge University Press, 2004.

Jameson, Fredric. *Postmodernism, or, The Cultural Logic of Late Capitalism.* Durham: Duke University Press, 1991.

Johnson, Terry. *Hysteria. Plays: 2.* London: Methuen, 1998.

Johung, Jennifer. "Figuring the 'Spells'/Spelling the Figures: Suzan-Lori Parks's 'Scene of Love(?)'" Unpublished essay.

Jones, Amelia, and Andrew Stephenson, eds. *Performing the Body/Performing the Text.* London: Routledge, 1999.

Joyce, James. *Ulysses.* New York: Vintage, 1986.

Joyce, Michael. *Othermindedness.* Ann Arbor: University of Michigan Press, 2001.

Kalb, Jonathan. *Beckett in Performance.* Cambridge University Press, 1989.

Kane, Sarah. *Complete Plays.* Introd. David Greig. London: Methuen, 2001.

Kastan, David. *Shakespeare after Theory.* New York: Routledge, 1999.

Kaufman, Moisés, dir. *The Laramie Project.* DVD. HBO Films and Good Machines Productions, 2002.

Kaufman, Moisés, dir., and the members of Tectonic Theater Project. *The Laramie Project.* New York: Vintage Books, 2001, sixth printing.

Kaufman, Moisés, dir., and the members of Tectonic Theater Project. *The Laramie Project.* New York: Dramatists Play Service, 2001.

Kelly, Katherine E. "Imprinting the Stage: Shaw and the Publishing Trade." *The Cambridge Companion to George Bernard Shaw.* Ed. Christopher Innes. Cambridge University Press, 1998. 25–54.

Kennedy, Adrienne. *The Owl Answers. In One Act.* Minneapolis: University of Minnesota Press, 1988. 25–45.

Kenner, Hugh. *The Pound Era.* Berkeley: University of California Press, 1971.

Kidnie, Margaret Jane. "Text, Performance, and the Editors: Staging Shakespeare's Drama." *Shakespeare Quarterly* 51 (2000): 456–73.

Kondo, Dorinne. "(Re)Visions of Race: Contemporary Race Theory and the Cultural Politics of Racial Crossover in Documentary Theatre." *Theatre Journal* 52 (2000): 81–107.

Koppen, Randi. "Formalism and the Return to the Body: Stein's and Fornes's Aesthetic of Significant Form." *New Literary History* 28 (1997): 791–809.

Lahr, John, ed. *A Casebook on Harold Pinter's The Homecoming*. New York: Grove, 1971.

The Laramie Project. Dir. Moisés Kaufman. HBO Films and Good Machine Productions, DVD 2002.

Loh, Sandra Tsing. *Aliens in America*. New York: Riverhead, 1997.

Long, William B. "A Perspective on Provenance: the Context of Varying Speech-heads." George Walton Williams, *Shakespeare's Speech-Headings* 21–44.

Lucie, Doug. *Plays: 1*. London: Methuen, 1998.

Lyman, Elizabeth Dyrud. "The Page Refigured: The Verbal and Visual Language of Suzan-Lori Parks." *Performance Research* 7.1 (2002): 90–100.

Macaulay, Alastair. Rev. of *Footfalls*. *Financial Times* 16 March 1994. Rpt. *Theatre Record* 14.6 (1994): 317.

Maguire, Laurie E. *Shakespearean Suspect Texts: The "Bad" Quartos and Their Contexts*. Cambridge University Press, 1996.

Marber, Patrick. *Closer*. New York: Grove, 1999.

Marranca, Bonnie. Introduction. Stein, *Last Operas and Plays* vii–xxvii.

McCaffery, Steve. *North of Intention: Critical Writings 1973–1986*. New York: Roof Books; Toronto: Nightwood Editions, 1986.

McCue, Jim. "Persisting or Not with Life and Beckett." *Times Literary Supplement* 1 April 1994: 18.

McGann, Jerome. *Black Riders: The Visible Language of Modernism*. Princeton University Press, 1993.

Radiant Textuality: Literature after the World Wide Web. Houndmills: Palgrave, 2001.

The Textual Condition. Princeton University Press, 1991.

McKenzie, D. F. *Bibliography and the Sociology of Texts*. Cambridge University Press, 1999.

McKerrow, R. B. *Prolegomena for the Oxford Shakespeare*. Oxford: Clarendon Press, 1939.

"A Suggestion Regarding Shakespeare's Manuscripts." *Review of English Studies* 11 (1935): 459–65. Rpt. George Walton Williams, *Shakespeare's Speech-Headings* 1–9.

McLeod, Randall. "UN *Editing* Shak-speare." *Sub-Stance* 33 (1982): 26–55. Rpt. Orgel and Keilen 60–89.

"What's the Bastard's Name? Random Cloud." George Walton Williams, *Shakespeare's Speech-Headings* 133–209.

McLuhan, Marshall. *The Gutenberg Galaxy: The Making of Typographic Man*. 1962. University of Toronto Press, 1997.

McMillan, Joyce. Rev. of *4.48 Psychosis*. *The Scotsman* 4 July 2000. Rpt. *Theatre Record* 20.13 (2000): 830

McMillin, Scott, ed. *The First Quarto of Othello*. Cambridge University Press, 2001.

Mee, Charles L. *History Plays*. Baltimore: Johns Hopkins University Press, 1998.

Mee, Chuck. *The (Re)Making Project.* <http://charlesmee.org/html/about.html>
19 August 2004.

Mellow, James R. "Foreword: the Word Plays of Gertrude Stein." Stein, *Operas & Plays* 7–9.

Meschonnic, Henri. *Critique du rythme: anthropologie historique du langage.* Paris: Verdier, 1982.

Miller, Tim. *Shirts & Skins.* Los Angeles: Alyson, 1997.

Müller, Heiner. *Hamletmachine. Hamletmachine and Other Texts for the Stage.* Ed. and trans. Carl Weber. New York: Performing Arts Journal Publications, 1984. 49–58.

Nielson, Anthony. Introduction. *Plays: 1.* London: Methuen, 1998.

Nightingale, Benedict. Rev. of *Crave* and *4.48 Psychosis. The Times* 15 May 2001. Rpt. *Theatre Record* 21.10 (2001): 604.

Nunberg, Geoffrey, ed. *The Future of the Book.* Berkeley: University of California Press, 1996.

Olson, Charles. "Projective Verse." *Collected Prose.* Ed. Donald Allen and Benjamin Friedlander. Introd. Robert Creeley. Berkeley: University of California Press, 1997. 239–49.

Ong, Walter J. *Orality and Literacy: The Technologizing of the Word.* London: Routledge, 1982.

Orgel, Stephen. *The Authentic Shakespeare and Other Problems of the Early Modern Stage.* New York: Routledge, 2002.

　"Macbeth and the Antic Round." *The Authentic Shakespeare* 159–72.

　"What Is an Editor?" *Shakespeare Studies* 24 (1996): 23–29. Rpt. Orgel and Keilen 117–23.

Orgel, Stephen, and Sean Keilen, eds. *Shakespeare and the Editorial Tradition.* New York: Garland, 1999.

Osborne, Laurie E. *The Trick of Singularity: 'Twelfth Night' and the Performance Editions.* University of Iowa Press, 1996.

Parks, Suzan-Lori. *The America Play and Other Works.* New York: Theatre Communications Group, 1995.

　The Death of the Last Black Man in the Whole Entire World. The America Play and Other Works 99–131.

　Venus. New York: Theatre Communications Group, 1997.

Perelman, Bob. "An Alphabet of Literary History." Perelman, *Marginalization* 144–55.

Perelman, Bob. *The Marginalization of Poetry: Language Writing and Literary History.* Princeton University Press, 1996.

Perloff, Carey. "Keeping Up the Mask: Some Observations on Directing Pinter." *Pinter Review* 2.1 (1988): 60–65.

Perloff, Marjorie. "After Free Verse: the New Nonlinear Poetics." Bernstein, *Close Listening* 86–110.

　"Talk Poem as Visual Text: David Antin's 'Artist's Books.'" *Review of Contemporary Fiction* 21 (2001): 125–46.

Peter, John. "Many Happy Returns." *Sunday Times* 27 March 1994: 10.26–27.

Rev. of *Blasted*. *Sunday Times* 19 January 1995. Rpt. *Theatre Record* 15:1–2 (1995): 41.

Rev. of *Blasted*. *Sunday Times* 8 April 2001. Rpt. *Theatre Record* 21:7 (2001): 419.

Peters, Julie Stone. *Congreve, the Drama, and the Printed Word*. Stanford University Press, 1990.

Theatre of the Book 1480–1880: Print, Text, and Performance in Europe. Oxford University Press, 2000.

Pinero, Arthur W. *The Gay Lord Quex*. Boston: Walter H. Baker 1900.

The Second Mrs. Tanqueray. London: William Heinemann, 1895.

Pinter, Harold. *The Collection*. *Three Plays: A Slight Ache, The Collection, The Dwarfs*. New York: Grove, n.d. [1962].

The Collection. *The Collection and The Lover*. London: Methuen, 1963.

The Collection: A Play in One Act. London: Samuel French, 1963.

The Collection. *Plays Two*. London: Faber and Faber, 1996.

The Homecoming. London: Methuen, 1965.

The Homecoming. New York: Grove 1966.

The Homecoming. "First Evergreen Edition." New York: Grove, 1967.

The Homecoming. *Plays Three*. London: Faber and Faber, 1997.

"Writing for the Theatre." *Various Voices: Prose, Poetry, Politics 1948–1998*. London: Faber and Faber, 1998. 19–25.

"A Play to Be Performed: Excerpts from the Gertrude Stein Symposium at New York, University. *Theater* 32.2 (2002): 3–25.

Pound, Ezra. *The Cantos of Ezra Pound*. New York: New Directions, 1977.

"A Retrospect." *Literary Essays of Ezra Pound*. Ed. and introd. T. S. Eliot. New York: New Directions, 1968. 3–14.

Puchner, Martin. *Stage Fright: Modernism, Anti-Theatricality, and Drama*. Baltimore: Johns Hopkins University Press, 2002.

Pulitzer Prize website. <http://www.pulitzer.org> 26 August 2003.

Rebellato, Dan. *1956 And All That: The Making of Modern British Drama*. London: Routledge, 1999.

"Rebutting Pulitzer Perception." *New York Times* 22 April 1994: B10.

Reinelt, Janelle. "Performing Race: Anna Deavere Smith's *Fires in the Mirror*." *Modern Drama* 39 (1996): 609–17.

Richards, Grant. *Author Hunting by an Old Literary Sportsman: Memories of Years Spent Mainly in Publishing 1897–1925*. New York: Coward-McCann, 1934.

Rothenberg, Jerome. "The Poetics of Performance." Vincent and Zweig, *The Poetry Reading* 120–29.

Ryan, Betsy Alayne. *Gertrude Stein's Theatre of the Absolute*. Ann Arbor: UMI Research Press, 1984.

Salutin, Rick, and Theatre Passe Muraille. *1837: William Lyon Mackenzie and the Canadian Revolution*. Toronto: Playwrights Canada Press, 1976.

Saunders, Graham. *'Love me or kill me': Sarah Kane and the Theatre of Extremes*. Manchester University Press, 2002.

Sayre, Henry M. *The Visual Text of William Carlos Williams*. Urbana: University of Illinois Press, 1983.

Scalapino, Leslie. "The Hind." *Mantis* 3 (2002): 262–75.

Schechner, Richard. "Collective Reflexivity: Restoration of Behavior." *A Crack in the Mirror: Reflexive Perspectives in Anthropology*. Ed. Jay Ruby. Philadelphia: University of Pennsylvania Press, 1982. 39–81.

Shakespeare, William. *The Norton Shakespeare Based on the Oxford Edition*. Gen. ed. Stephen Greenblatt. New York: W. W. Norton, 1997.

The Riverside Shakespeare. Gen. ed. G. Blakemore Evans. 2nd edn. Boston: Houghton Mifflin, 1997.

Shakespeare's Titus Andronicus: The First Quarto 1594. New York: Charles Scribner's Sons, 1936.

William Shakespeare: The Complete Works. Original-Spelling Edition. Ed. Stanley Wells and Gary Taylor. Oxford: Clarendon Press, 1986.

Shange, Ntozake. *for colored girls who have considered suicide / when the rainbow is enuf. a choreopoem*. 1977; New York: Bantam, 1980.

Shaw, Bernard. *Collected Letters 1874–1897*. Ed. Dan H. Laurence. London: Max Reinhardt, 1965.

Major Barbara. Baltimore: Penguin, 1968.

Mrs Warren's Profession. Plays: Pleasant and Unpleasant. Vol. I.

Mrs Warren's Profession. A Facsimile of the Holograph Manuscript. Introd. Margo Peters. *Bernard Shaw – Early Texts: Play Manuscripts in Facsimile*. Gen. Ed. Dan H. Laurence. New York: Garland, 1981.

Plays: Pleasant and Unpleasant. 2 vols. London: Grant Richards, 1898.

Three Plays for Puritans: The Devil's Disciple, Caesar and Cleopatra, & Captain Brassbound's Conversion. London: Grant Richards, 1901.

Shewey, Don. "A Play Has Second Life as a Stage for Discussion." *New York Times* 1 December 2002: AR 7.

Shillingsburg, Peter L. "Polymorphic, Polysemic, Protean, Reliable, Electronic Texts." Bornstein and Williams, *Palimpsest* 29–43.

Shuttleworth, Ian. Rev. of *Happy Days. Financial Times* 20 November 2003. Rpt. *Theatre Record* 23.23 (2003): 1560.

Silliman, Ron. "Afterword: a Forest For . . . " *In the American Tree* 581–88.

In the American Tree: Language, Realism, Poetry. 1986. Rpt. Orono, ME: National Poetry Foundation, 2002.

"Language, Realism, Poetry." *In the American Tree* xvii–xxiii.

Singer, Annabelle. "Don't Want to Be This: The Elusive Sarah Kane." *TDR: The Drama Review* 48.2 (T182, Summer 2004): 139–71.

Smith, Anna Deavere. *Fires in the Mirror: Crown Heights, Brooklyn and Other Identities*. New York: Anchor, 1993.

"General Production Notes." *House Arrest. House Arrest and Piano*. New York: Anchor, 2004. 5–6.

Fires in the Mirror: Crown Heights, Brooklyn and Other Identities. New York: Dramatists Play Service, 1993, 1997.

Talk to Me: Travels in Media and Politics. New York: Anchor Books, 2001.

Twilight: Los Angeles, 1992. On the Road: A Search for American Character. New York: Anchor Books, 1994.

Smith, Jessica. "Silent Protest: Feminism and Poetry Reading Politics in the 21st Century." *Mantis* 3 (2002): 236–47.

Stein, Gertrude. *Geography and Plays.* 1922. Rpt. Madison: University of Wisconsin Press, 1993.

 Last Operas and Plays. Ed. Carl Van Vechten. Introd. Bonnie Marranca. Baltimore: Johns Hopkins University Press, 1995.

 Operas & Plays. Ed. James R. Mellow. Barrytown NY: Station Hill Press, 1998.

 "Plays." *Last Operas and Plays* xxix–lii.

Stephens, John Russell. *The Profession of the Playwright: British Theatre 1800–1900.* Cambridge University Press, 1992.

Stern, Tiffany. *Rehearsal from Shakespeare to Sheridan.* Oxford: Clarendon Press, 2000.

Sutherland, Donald. *Gertrude Stein: A Biography of Her Work.* New Haven: Yale University Press, 1951.

Taylor, Paul. "The Dead Letter of the Law." *Independent* 21 December 1994: 21.

 Rev. of *Happy Days. Independent* 20 November 2003. Rpt. *Theatre Record* 23.23 (2003): 1559.

 "Way out of Line." *Independent* 18 March 1994: 23.

Theatre Passe Muraille. *The Farm Show: A Collective Creation by Theatre Passe Muraille.* Toronto: Coach House Press, 1976.

Thompson, Debby. "'Is Race a Trope'?: Anna Deavere Smith and the Question of Racial Performativity." *African American Review* 37 (2003): 127–38.

Thompson, Judith. *White Biting Dog.* Toronto: Playwrights Canada Press, 1984.

Tigner, Amy L. "*The Laramie Project*: Western, Pastoral." *Modern Drama* 45 (2002): 138–56.

Tinker, Jack. Rev. of *Footfalls. Daily Mail* 18 March 1994. Rpt. *Theatre Record* 14.6 (1994): 315.

Urkowitz, Steven. *Shakespeare's Revision of 'King Lear'.* Princeton University Press, 1980.

Valdez, Luis, and El Teatro Campesino. *Luis Valdez – Early Works: Actos, Bernabé and Pensamiento, Serpentino.* Houston: Arte Publico Press, 1990.

Verdecchia, Guillermo. *Fronteras Americanas.* Toronto: Coach House, 1993.

Vincent, Stephen, and Ellen Zweig, eds. *The Poetry Reading: A Contemporary Compendium on Language & Performance.* San Francisco: Momo's Press, 1981.

Wardle, Irving. Rev. of *Footfalls. Independent on Sunday* 20 March 1994. Rpt. *Theatre Record* 14.6 (1994): 316–17.

Weimann, Robert. *Author's Pen and Actor's Voice: Playing and Writing in Shakespeare's Theatre.* Ed. Helen Higbee and William West. Cambridge University Press, 2000.

Wells, Stanley. *Re-Editing Shakespeare for the Modern Reader. Based on Lectures Given at the Folger Shakespeare Library Washington, DC.* Oxford: Clarendon Press, 1984.

Wells, Stanley, and Gary Taylor, with John Jowett and William Montgomery. *William Shakespeare: A Textual Companion.* 1987. Rpt. with corrections, New York: W. W. Norton, 1997.

Werstine, Paul. "Hypertext and Editorial Myth." *Early Modern Literary Studies* 33/Special Issue (January 1998). <http:/purl.oclc.org/emls/03-3/wersshak. html> 20 August 2002.

"McKerrow's 'Suggestion' and Twentieth-Century Shakespeare Textual Criticism." *Renaissance Drama* 19 (1986): 149–73. Rpt. Orgel and Keilen 153–77.

"McKerrow's 'Suggestion' and W. W. Greg." George Walton Williams, *Shakespeare's Speech-Headings* 17–16.

Wilde, Oscar. *The Importance of Being Earnest: A Trivial Comedy for Serious People.* By the Author of *Lady Windermere's Fan.* London: Leonard Smithers, 1899.

William Shakespeare's Romeo and Juliet: The Contemporary Film, The Classic Play. Screenplay Craig Pearce and Baz Luhrmann. Play by William Shakespeare. New York: Bantam Doubleday, 1996.

Williams, George Walton, ed. *Shakespeare's Speech-Headings: Speaking the Speech in Shakespeare's Plays.* The Papers of the Seminar in Textual Studies, Shakespeare Association of America, March 29, 1986, Montreal. Newark: University of Delaware Press; London: Associated University Presses, 1997.

Williams, William Carlos. "The Red Wheelbarrow." *Collected Earlier Poems.* New York: New Directions, 1966. 277.

Collected Poems: 1909–1939. New York: New Directions, 1938.

Wolfe, George C., dir. *Fires in the Mirror: Crown Heights, Brooklyn and Other Identities.* VHS. By Anna Deavere Smith. Prod. Cherie Fortis. Hipster Entertainment, 1993.

Worthen, W. B. "Of Actors and Automata: Hieroglyphics of Modernism." *Journal of Dramatic Theory and Criticism* 9.1 (1994): 3–19.

"Border Subjects: Geography, Identity, Performance." *Land/Scape/Theater.* Ed. Una Chaudhuri and Elinor Fuchs. Ann Arbor: University of Michigan Press, 2003. 280–300.

"Citing History: Textuality and Performativity in the Plays of Suzan-Lori Parks." *Essays in Theatre/Etudes théâtrales* 18.1 (November 1999): 3–22.

Shakespeare and the Authority of Performance. Cambridge University Press, 1996.

Shakespeare and the Force of Modern Performance. Cambridge University Press, 2003.

Yeats, W. B. "Certain Noble Plays of Japan." *Essays and Introductions.* New York: Macmillan, 1964. 221–37.

Index

Printed in the United States
127488LV00002B/10/P